Fugitive Slaves and the Underground
Railroad in the Kentucky Borderland

In memory of my grandmother,
Mabel L. Williamson (1885–1986),
granddaughter of an Underground Railroad worker

Fugitive Slaves and the Underground Railroad in the Kentucky Borderland

J. Blaine Hudson

McFarland & Company, Inc., Publishers
Jefferson, North Carolina, and London

Maps courtesy of the University of Louisville Center
for Graphic and Information Systems.

Library of Congress Cataloguing-in-Publication Data

Hudson, J. Blaine.
Fugitive slaves and the Underground Railroad in the Kentucky
borderland / J. Blaine Hudson.
p.   cm.
Includes bibliographical references and index.

ISBN 0-7864-1345-X (illustrated case binding : 50# alkaline paper)

1. Underground railroad — Kentucky.
2. Underground railroad — Tennessee.
3. Underground railroad — Ohio River Valley.
4. Fugitive slaves — Kentucky — History — 19th century.
5. Fugitive slaves — Tennessee — History — 19th Century.
6. Fugitive slaves — Ohio River Valley — History — 19th century.
7. Antislavery movements — Kentucky — History — 19th century.
8. Antislavery movements — Tennessee — History — 19th century.
9. Antislavery movements — Ohio River Valley — History — 19th century.
I. Title.
E450.H86   2002   973.7'115 — dc21   2002007200

British Library cataloguing data are available

*On the cover: "A Ride for Liberty — The Fugitive Slaves," Eastman Johnson,
1863, oil on board 22" × 26¼" (Brooklyn Museum of Art, New York)
©2002 PicturesNow.com*

Manufactured in the United States of America

*McFarland & Company, Inc., Publishers
Box 611, Jefferson, North Carolina 28640
www.mcfarlandpub.com*

Contents

Maps and Tables

Preface

This is the highest wisdom that I own,
The best that mankind ever knew:
Freedom and life are earned by those alone
Who conquer them each day anew ...
At such a throng I fain would stare,
With free men on free ground their freedom share.
— Goethe, *Faust*, Part Two, Act V, 1832.

Several years ago, the city of Louisville, Kentucky, began construction of a "river walk" extending along the banks of the Ohio River from eastern to southwestern Jefferson County. The completed sections of this river walk have become popular with hikers and bikers, at least through the summer months.

Just to the west of downtown Louisville, a canal leads river traffic around the rapids known as the Falls of the Ohio and through the McAlpine lock and dam system. The other entrance from this channel — or exit, depending on one's direction of travel — is near the western limits of the Portland neighborhood; once a separate city, this neighborhood was absorbed by Louisville before the Civil War. Near this western entrance or exit, a ferry once operated between Portland and New Albany, Indiana, in the years before the construction of bridges across the river.

The river walk loops around the locks and returns to the river at this point and stretches through century-old trees and other riverine vegetation. Were it not for the background noise of traffic on Interstate 64, which also runs along the river before crossing into Indiana, someone walking along this path would have no inkling that she or he was in a metropolitan area of roughly one million people.

More than a century and a half ago, the section of Jefferson County west of the canal and the Portland to New Albany ferry was much the same — a forested and

1

marshy spot in the flood plain of what the Native Americans termed the Great River. By the 1840s and 1850s, this was also one of the most important crossing points for fugitive slaves on Kentucky's six hundred mile long Ohio River border. And because Kentucky held, perhaps, some of the most frequently traveled slave escape corridors in the nation, this crossing point was arguably one of the most important in the United States.

The history and deeper meaning of this place are largely unknown. Both the people who crossed the river there and those who sometimes helped them are long forgotten, if not wholly unknown. Consequently, several crucial chapters of state, regional and national history are either incomplete or entirely missing.

The purpose of this book is not "to set the record straight," but rather to present the historical record pertaining to fugitive slaves and the Underground Railroad in Kentucky as fully and as accurately as possible, based on the available evidence. Some of that evidence led to this secluded place along Louisville's river walk, where one can almost hear the voices and feel the presence of hundreds, perhaps thousands, of fugitive slaves. Some of them desperate, all of them brave, they risked their lives for freedom. This book is presented in memory and in honor of those men and women.

CHAPTER I

Introduction

By the 1700s, only persons of African ancestry were subject to the "social death" of slavery in British colonial America. Even for the 5 to 10 percent of the African American population that was not enslaved, color alone was considered prima facie evidence of subordinate status and sufficient justification for their debasement and unequal treatment.[1] In this constrained setting, the journey from slavery to freedom was long, difficult and complex.

This journey began with the struggle to preserve humanity and self-respect, and to enlarge the domain of relative freedom under the physical and emotional depredations of slavery. Frederick Douglass, the most famous fugitive slave of all, observed that finding a "good master," negotiating a less demanding work regimen, and holding one's family together were singular achievements beyond the reach of most enslaved African Americans — and even these great achievements were no more than a first step. Slavery was still slavery, and (again paraphrasing Douglass) if an enslaved African American with a bad master yearned for a "good" one, an enslaved African American with a good master yearned to be free.[2] For this reason, efforts by whites to ameliorate the conditions of slavery invariably failed to lessen the attractions of freedom — even if freedom from bondage marked only the beginning of another long journey toward full equality and empowerment.[3]

There were two paths from slavery to freedom in colonial and antebellum America — one legal and the other illegal. An African American could be born free, but under American law, an enslaved African American was property and could legally become free only by virtue of an emancipatory act initiated by his or her owner or through government action.[4] However, relatively few white Americans were inclined to emancipate their bond-persons, and statewide emancipation occurred only in the northern states between 1777 and roughly 1820. For the vast majority of African Americans, the path to legal freedom was blocked by the determination of white Americans to preserve and profit from the institution of slavery.

The illegal path to freedom forked into two principal branches: flight or revolt. Revolt, while common and significant in the Caribbean and Brazil, was seldom the chosen path in North America. Slave revolts were successful only when Africans had sufficiently large population majorities to offset superior European weaponry and where subsequent formation of and flight to maroon societies in remote areas was feasible. These conditions rarely existed in colonial and antebellum America, where enslaved African Americans were a distinct minority in most regions. Consequently, slave revolt was a spectacular but ultimately suicidal strategy for challenging slavery, and as the regions east of the Mississippi River became more densely settled, maroon societies formed only in backcountry areas such as the Great Dismal Swamp and Florida.[5] On the other hand, the sheer size of the United States and its eventual division into free and slave zones after the American Revolution made escape a viable, although still dangerous, alternative for those African Americans moved to translate their yearning for freedom into concrete action.

The extent to which African Americans employed escape is richly although imperfectly documented in the historical literature. For example, as early as the 1640s, when only a few thousand Africans were resident in British North America, there are records of slaves escaping — often in the company of white indentured servants.[6] This pattern continued as the small African population grew into a massive African American population of over 600,000 by 1770 and the "unsettling effect" of the American Revolution transformed chaos into opportunity — opening a floodgate through which more than 100,000 enslaved African Americans ran from bondage. Georgia lost more than 10,000 and South Carolina more than 25,000 enslaved African Americans during the Revolutionary period, and Virginia may have lost nearly 30,000 in 1778 alone.[7] Between 1810 and 1850, it was estimated that at least another 100,000 African Americans, roughly 2,500 per year, escaped successfully from bondage — a total that excludes recaptured fugitives and temporary runaways who remained in the South.[8]

Slave escapes that received assistance of some sort involved at least one other person who was motivated to render aid in violation of both law and social convention. Such active assistance from free African Americans and a committed white minority was usually subsumed under the rubric of the "Underground Road" before the 1840s or the "Underground Railroad" thereafter as an extension of the American anti-slavery movement.

Although slave escapes are often equated with the Underground Railroad in the public mind, most early escapes and probably the majority of later escapes were largely unaided. In other words, there were fugitive slaves with or without the Underground Railroad, but there could have been no Underground Railroad without fugitive slaves. Consequently, it is not possible to study one fully without studying the other.

As the young nation expanded westward in the early 1800s, slave escapes assumed a new regional configuration that persisted through the antebellum period. Four broad zones of fugitive slave activity emerged, each with its characteristic patterns, challenges, possibilities and limitations:

• the border region east of the Appalachians, with escape routes leading to the mid-Atlantic and New England states or, ultimately, to eastern Canada;
• the border region west of the Appalachians along the Ohio River, with escape routes leading to the midwestern free territories or states or, ultimately, to western Canada (across from Detroit or Cleveland);

- the border west of the Mississippi River, with escape routes leading sometimes into the Ohio River border region or farther west or into Mexico; and
- the southern interior, in which most escapes were temporary acts of resistance, though some escape routes led to the eastern or western border zones — or farther south to Florida or the Caribbean in the early years.

Given the location of the vast majority of enslaved African Americans, the border zones immediately east and west of the Appalachians witnessed the heaviest fugitive slave traffic by far. As slave population and cotton cultivation shifted steadily to the southwest after 1815, escape from Kentucky became more common and escape through Kentucky became the best option available to fugitives from Tennessee, Alabama and other southern states. Thus, Kentucky became central to the history of slave escapes by virtue of its place in the physical and political geography of the young United States. For the same reasons, Kentucky and the states along its northern border became central to the Underground Railroad — and the Ohio River became a veritable River Jordan, the "Dark Line" between slavery and nominal freedom.[9]

Race and Historiography

A review of the most important and influential research creates the impression that the definitive works on both slave escapes and the Underground Railroad have already been written. However, such an impression, on closer inspection and further reflection, is not entirely true. Not only do past and present experts disagree, but fundamental questions and controversies persist as to the number and significance of slave escapes, the characteristics of fugitives and those who aided

them, the role of free persons of color — and whether the Underground Railroad even existed.

Many of these questions are grounded in assumptions derived from the ever-changing meaning of race in American culture since the American Revolution. As Ira Berlin noted, race is an historical rather than a social construct, and how Americans think about race has changed subtly over the course of American history.

In colonial America, there "stood a firm belief that given an opportunity, black people would behave precisely like whites, which was what made African American slaves at once so valuable and so dangerous."[10] From this perspective, enslavement was viewed as a matter of who had sufficient power to deprive others of freedom and who was sufficiently unfortunate to be so deprived. In other words, slavery was a misfortune that could befall anyone under certain circumstances, and while Africans and Europeans were different, such differences were only "skin-deep." Both shared a common humanity and could be expected to react to enslavement in similar ways. Thus, within certain limits, whites could understand and predict the behavior of blacks simply by understanding themselves.

After the American Revolution, the "might makes right" justification of slavery was superseded by a new and fundamentally different racial ideology. In a new nation founded on theories of natural rights and the equality of humankind, slavery was now an institution that required moral and philosophical justification — a practice that now had to be right and good. However, viewed by any objective standard, American slavery was an institution of unusual destructive power and rigor[11] and could be right only if Africans were not people like everyone else — only if the Golden Rule could be applied selectively or abrogated altogether where black people were concerned. Otherwise, if

African Americans were as fully human as white Americans, how could their enslavement be compatible with the principles of American democracy? The ideology that supplied this new justification was rooted in the myth of fixed and profound black inferiority. This ideology assumed, as its first premise, that persons of African descent were different and substandard creatures who did not possess and, more importantly, could not acquire the presumably more advanced traits and abilities of persons of unmixed European ancestry. The new racial ideology shaped American attitudes in both slave and free territory and would survive the end of slavery to grow in virulence after the Civil War.[12]

The reality of slave escapes flatly contradicted this constellation of myths and proved deeply embarrassing to those who defended slavery as a positive good. Each fugitive was, to some extent, a living refutation of stereotypes of racial inferiority, African American dependence on and contentment with slavery, and the ubiquity of kindly and paternalistic masters. That the stereotypes seldom fit the facts created a rather thorny dilemma whose solution necessitated the fabrication of a complex illusion; the illusion in turn required a two-pronged disinformation strategy for its propagation and perpetuation. First, whenever possible, the number of slave escapes was minimized in an effort to deny the existence of the "problem." Second, when the evidence could not be denied, its meaning was interpreted within the limits of prevailing racial myths. As Richard Wade stated, "Negro discontent was early equated with outside agitation in Dixie," and slave escapes were often blamed on "evil" whites who spirited away ignorant slaves, rather than attributed to the initiative of African Americans.[13] However, blaming "Abolitionist shriekers" accounted only for assisted slave escapes. Consequently, pro-slavery

advocates were compelled to invent a new category of mental illness to account for the behavior of fugitives acting clearly on their own. As noted by Thomas and Sillen:

> The black man, it was repeatedly claimed, was uniquely fitted for bondage by his primitive psychological organization. For him, mental health was contentment with his subservient lot, while protest was an infallible symptom of derangement. Thus, a well-known physician of the antebellum South, Dr. Samuel Cartwright of Louisiana, had a psychiatric explanation for runaway slaves. He diagnosed their malady as drapetomania, literally the flight-from-home madness.[14]

Ironically, accounting for slave escapes was often troublesome even to "friends of the fugitives." For example, many who opposed slavery on philosophical grounds had little love for its victims and shared the conviction that enslaved African Americans were incapable of human agency and personal initiative. To them, African Americans were minor players in a drama pitting good white Americans against evil ones—and, hence, the only slave escapes that mattered were those starring noble whites who selflessly assisted helpless and benighted blacks to freedom. To this group, the history of fugitive slaves was actually a story of heroic whites[15], not a history of courageous African Americans.[16]

In other words, this multi-layered illusion popularized and supported several consoling beliefs—that there were only a handful of slave escapes, that fugitive slaves were crazy and that those who assisted them were, depending on the point of view, either evil outsiders or heroes in dramas of their own making. Any alternative construction of the historical evidence offered by African Americans themselves and a few radical whites could be marginalized and ignored quite easily as poor research or special pleading. Thus, the distortions of the nineteenth and early twentieth century, such as the works of Ullrich B. Phillips, became the standard authoritative sources for modern historians—and the received wisdom of modern popular culture.

The dead hand of this received wisdom has held no state more firmly in its grasp than Kentucky. The recycling of familiar myths and anecdotes—including the many persons and events in *Uncle Tom's Cabin*, or the stories of Josiah Henson, Eliza Harris, Delia Webster and Calvin Fairbank, or Margaret Garner—has come to substitute for a comprehensive history of the larger phenomenon of slave escapes.[17] One could argue persuasively that these engrossing anecdotes are often mistaken for such a history and that, based on suspect 1850 and 1860 Census data, there is no other "larger" history to recount. In other words, slavery was "mild" in Kentucky and, with low estimates of only one hundred escapes each year, the fugitive slave issue was "a tempest in a teapot."[18] However, both these low figures and the much higher estimates of 20,000 fugitives per year[19] in earlier studies lack an empirical foundation. Even studies that reject this perspective do so without adding any new information, and their rejection rests on a different point of view or a different argument rather than on better evidence.[20] As one exception, John Hope Franklin and Loren Schweninger added significantly to the field with their study, *Runaway Slaves* (1999), but, unfortunately, their primary focus was the southern interior and Kentucky was not one of the states included in their analysis.[21]

With respect to fugitive slaves and the Underground Railroad in Kentucky, there are many interesting stories and many assumptions, but no historical record within which such stories can be contextualized and against which such assumptions can be tested. There are anecdotes, but there is no history grounded in empirical facts—a few familiary trees, but no credible description of the forest to which they belong.

Purpose of the Study

Interest in fugitive slaves and the Underground Railroad has grown considerably in recent years—stimulated by the publication of old studies, biographies of famous fugitives and Underground Railroad workers, and several collections focusing on sites and escape routes. However, there has been nothing new added to the historical record itself since the WPA interviews of the 1930s and little original research since the publication of Larry Gara's *The Liberty Line* in 1961.

The book began as an examination and interpretation of the available historical evidence pertaining to fugitive slaves and the Underground Railroad in Kentucky. Research in this area must necessarily embrace the southernmost sections of the free states bordering Kentucky along the Ohio River and, to a lesser extent, the slave states to the immediate south.

Research and reflection eventually gave rise to five fundamental and inter-related theses:

1. Slave escapes from and through Kentucky were far more numerous than assumed in previous studies and popular accounts.
2. Most Kentucky fugitive slaves received little or no assistance, direct or indirect.
3. When slave escapes were aided, such aid came primarily from other African Americans—and primarily through free black settlements and communities.
4. Anti-slavery whites were not numerous, but created effective escape networks—often working in concert with free African Americans.
5. While much of the aid rendered to fugitives was random and passive,

an organized Underground Railroad network existed in certain sections of the Kentucky border region, particularly by the 1850s.

The book explores these theses as it paints a true picture of slavery and slave escapes in the Kentucky Borderland.

Research Method and Standards of Evidence

This book relies principally on historical source materials created by those who lived in the period under study. These primary sources, most of which have not been examined systematically before, are supplemented by information and insights accessible in an extensive secondary literature. Each of these sources has important uses and equally important limitations.

The primary source record concerning fugitive slaves and the Underground Railroad in Kentucky can best be described as a few pools of information — deep, but neither wide nor always connected. There was no binding legal requirement that slave escapes be documented; consequently, unlike tax records, wills and court actions, slave escapes did not produce a specific body of records retrievable from some central place. Furthermore, few slaveholders had the education or the leisure to produce collections of personal or family papers in which slave escapes might be mentioned, and those collections that have survived are rare and often silent on the topic of fugitives. Even fewer African Americans had the opportunity to produce documents that captured their perspective as historical actors in or observers of this history.

Among the most useful primary sources are antebellum newspapers. However, these sources have two inescapable limitations. First, most antebellum Kentucky newspapers were not preserved, cer-

tainly not as complete sets. Second, not all slave escapes were reported, and there is no reliable formula for determining what percentage of slave escapes left any record at all. As a result, even a complete newspaper record, if such existed, could not be construed as a comprehensive record of slave escapes. Fortunately, at least the major Louisville, Frankfort and Lexington (and Cincinnati) newspapers have survived — with the Lexington-based *Kentucky Gazette* serving as a statewide organ in early Kentucky history and the major Louisville newspapers serving a comparable purpose after 1830. These publications often carried fugitive slave advertisements and reprinted news items from other regions of the state. While the records of western, southern and eastern Kentucky are either decidedly uneven or nonexistent, these statewide sources, supplemented by fragments of local information, make it possible to construct the historical framework essential to the validity of this book's conclusions.

These sources have much to offer despite their many limitations. Fugitive slave advertisements, news articles and court records can be used to estimate the actual number, frequency and patterns of slave escapes. Beyond purely quantitative data, such sources add fascinating and valuable qualitative information regarding fugitives and their escapes. For example, long before Kentucky was settled, fugitive slave notices developed their characteristic form in the early newspapers of slaveholding colonies east of the Appalachians. Over time, stock engravings of runaway males and females developed to draw the attention of readers.

Typically, the reward offered for the return of the fugitive was highlighted, usually increasing as the fugitive fled farther from his or her place of enslavement. The name and residence of the slaveholder and the date of the escape would be noted next. Then followed the body of the advertisement in which the slaveholder or his or her agent provided information intended to help identify and locate the fugitive.

Such information included the name of the runaway and other names by which he or she might be known, and a physical description usually noting approximate age, color, weight, height, clothing, identifying marks, scars or physical defects. Many advertisements

FIFTY DOLLARS REWARD.— Ran away from the subscriber, living in Spencer county, Ky. on the 11th of this month, a Negro man named SAM, between 35 and 40 years of age, of a dark complexion, about 5 feet 10 inches high, heavy made; his upper front teeth somewhat decayed; had on when he left a brown Jeans roundabout, pantaloons of the same, an old drab overcoat and a white hat a good deal worn.— The above reward will be given for the delivery of said negro, or confined in jail so that I get him again. jan 25   w3°   GEO. K. SLONE.

This fugitive slave notice, like many others, employed a stock engraving of a runaway male. *Louisville Journal,* January 25, 1837.

mentioned character or personality traits or unusual skills or abilities. Some also mentioned the presumed escape motive, possible destinations and whether the fugitive was thought to have received any assistance — and, occasionally, from whom. By the 1850s, similar information could be found in editorials and news articles.

Slave escapes and attempts to assist fugitives often resulted in one or more parties finding themselves in court and in prison. An enslaved African American who successfully escaped represented a substantial property loss to his or her owner — a loss to which a dollar value could be attached. While this loss could not be recovered from the fugitive, slaveowners often sued for compensation from individuals or businesses that might have unintentionally facilitated or consciously abetted the escape. Many of these cases were adjudicated in local courts, but some were appealed to the State Court of Appeals, Kentucky's highest court, through the antebellum period. Such lawsuits left records at various levels of the state and the federal judicial system, and the rulings sometimes reveal much concerning slavery and slave escapes in Kentucky.

Other individuals suspected of aiding fugitives in some way were often arrested and tried in city or county courts. Once

again, these criminal case records — as reported in the press or maintained as court documents — often provide important information concerning the identity and strategies of fugitives and their friends. Of course, court records of this kind, much prison records, involve only the individuals who got caught — who were arrested and possibly convicted of violating a specific law — and, as such, represent only a fraction of the friends of the fugitive in a given region.

Fugitives from Kentucky who left no records in Kentucky often left traces in the records of the states across the Ohio River border or even in Canada. Consequently, the Wilbur H. Siebert Papers, housed at the Ohio Historical Society, were an equally important source of evidence — particularly the materials bearing on Illinois, Indiana and Ohio. Professor Siebert, in researching the Underground Railroad in the 1890s, contacted hundreds of individuals thought to have been involved in or to have some knowledge of the Underground Railroad. Many of these letters and related documents were cited in Siebert's seminal work, *The Underground Railroad from Slavery to Freedom* (1898). However, much original material was not included, and much new material was added to the collection after Siebert became an acknowledged authority in his field — some by graduate students who conducted dissertation research on the Underground Railroad under Siebert's supervision.

Interestingly, while Siebert's book tended to emphasize the role of whites in assisting fugitives, the role of African Americans looms much larger in the Siebert Papers.

A research framework comprised of thousands of small bits of information has obvious strengths but also potential dangers that must be borne clearly in mind. The chief dangers are misrepresentation and misinterpretation. Large bodies of information allow for the conscious or inadvertent selection and elucidation of non-representative anecdotes or episodes. To construct a forest from these thousands of trees, information drawn particularly from newspaper sources has been treated not only as historical evidence, but as empirical data subject to analysis and interpretation using the statistical techniques of the social sciences. Such a multidisciplinary approach, ideally, can identify and illuminate patterns in the data that might otherwise be overlooked or misconstrued. On that basis, a range of examples can be cited in relation to those patterns.

Finally, beyond these traditional sources, what constitutes legitimate evidence in this field of historical research is subject at times to intense and bitter debate. The nature of American slavery created formidable barriers to the creation of primary source records by African Americans themselves. This is not to imply that antebellum African Americans left no paper trail, only that the quantity of such evidence is disproportionately small compared to that produced by white Americans. Not surprisingly, much of this evidence is also considered subjective and unreliable according to standards created by traditional historians that privilege certain types of evidence. However, what was preserved or can be reconstructed is invaluable — for example, oral traditions, family and community legends, the findings of archaeologists, slave narratives, the black and anti-slavery press[22], and post–Civil War interviews with and memoirs of former slaves. This body of evidence will be cited extensively in this study — corroborated insofar as possible by more traditional sources— to permit the men and women of the past, black and white, to describe their world in their own now disembodied voices.

CHAPTER II

The Borderland

What I am bringing to your attention ... is a strip of land between northern and southern states which I call the Borderland. In my particular instance it was between Kentucky and Ohio, with the Ohio River flowing between.... It was through this Borderland that slaves made their way going north to Canada.

—*John Parker*, Ripley, Ohio[1]

Like all small- or large-scale human migrations, the movement of enslaved African Americans fleeing from bondage in the American South was shaped by four primary forces: "push" factors, "pull" factors, the "line of least resistance," and distance.[2] The conditions of slavery were more than sufficient as "push" factors. The prospect of freedom and finding a safe haven in which to enjoy its benefits were powerful forces that "pulled" runaway slaves toward free territory or Canada. The "line of least resistance" was simply the most promising and efficient route for the clandestine journey to either destination. Distance was self-explanatory in the most superficial sense, but, perhaps the most critical factor of all as it enhanced or less-ened the influence of the other factors. In other words, the closer to free territory, the greater the likelihood that an enslaved African American would escape and the greater the likelihood that he or she would succeed.

In this respect, fugitive slaves escaping from or through Kentucky followed routes determined by the human, political and physical geography of the region. This geography was shaped by a multitude of secondary factors: the location of mountains and river systems; the location of natural trails, man-made roads and, eventually, railroads; in the early years, the location of "friendly" Native Americans; the location of free African American settlements or communities; the location of

11

sympathetic white Americans; and the location of effective counter-measures such as patrols. How these factors interacted often determined the timing of an escape attempt, the means of escape and the specific direction chosen by the fugitive.

The purpose of this section of the larger study is simply to sketch, very briefly, the physical, political and human dimensions of the Kentucky borderland — beginning with the great boundary between slave and free territory in the trans–Appalachian west, the Ohio River.

The Great River

The Ohio River that greeted the French explorers in the seventeenth and the British explorers and settlers in the eighteenth centuries drained an area the size of France. Flowing down-hill from the Appalachians to the Mississippi River over the 981 miles between Pittsburgh, Pennsylvania and Cairo, Illinois, the land elevation drops from 710 to 250 feet above sea level, with a drop of more than 200 feet along the extent of Kentucky's more than 600 mile northern border (see Appendix I-1). While this vast river system, with its major tributaries and countless smaller creeks and rivers, is now regulated by an extensive system of dams and locks, the Ohio River of the antebellum years lacked such man-made controls. The Ohio was then a "turbulent, free-flowing and obstructed stream ... littered with snags and strewn with boulders, its flow broken by sand bars, rock ripples, and falls, especially the Falls of the Ohio where it dropped twenty-five feet over a two-mile stretch of limestone."[3] During rainy periods, the river and its tributaries would flood (as they still do), producing strong and dangerous currents. During dry periods, the river would shrink to a shallow rivulet in some areas, making navigation difficult even for the shallow-draft steamboats that

appeared after the War of 1812. During extremely cold periods, the river would freeze and, where shallow, would freeze very rapidly — allowing people to skate on or walk across the ice. The return of warm weather would prompt rapid melting, sweeping massive ice floes down-river on powerful currents.[4]

Depending on a largely untamed river for trade and transportation proved increasingly problematic as population increased in the trans–Appalachian west. Recognizing the importance of the river to the movement of people and commerce, politicians throughout the region pressed consistently for federal legislation to underwrite large-scale engineering projects including the clearance of sandbars and other obstructions, and the construction of canals and dams. The Army Corps of Engineers was assigned this responsibility, but federal support ebbed and flowed, and well over a century would be required to complete this massive project.[5]

Fugitive slaves escaping from or through Kentucky could not reach free territory without crossing the Ohio River and, because no bridges were built until after the Civil War, the river could only be crossed by boat (skiff, ferry or steamboat), on foot (if frozen) or by swimming. For fugitive slaves and those who assisted them, the nature of the "Great River" and its conditions at a given time and place were crucial factors. A flooded river was a problem. A river of low to average depth was not. Extreme cold, despite its other inconveniences, changed the elemental property of the river altogether and made it possible simply to run across. In any case, fugitive African Americans and those who assisted them were quite literally at the mercy of the Ohio River of their time.

The Ohio River, looking west from near Madison, Indiana.

The Human Landscape: Kentucky

Slave escapes from or through Kentucky occurred in an historical setting as fluid and volatile as the Great River. The motives and actions of fugitive slaves and those who assisted them cannot be interpreted, evaluated or understood outside this context. In this respect, the human landscape — the numbers and locations of both enslaved African Americans and free people of color — were as important as the location of mountains, rivers and roads.

The first British explorers to reach the early western frontier found some African Americans — most of whom were, quite fittingly, fugitives from slavery in the eastern seaboard colonies — already living in small numbers among the many Native American societies scattered throughout the region.

One such early arrival was Pompey the "Black Shawnee" who figured prominently at the siege of Boonesborough in the 1770s. Other African Americans entered Kentucky with the earliest European settlers. The monumental tasks of clearing and bringing land under cultivation, building shelter and providing for defense required a large labor force and, with free labor in short supply, the institution of slavery was the predictable, if not inevitable, labor system of choice for pioneers from slave societies east of the Appalachians.[6] By 1800, there were 220,955 people in Kentucky, 41,084 of whom were African American.[7] Patterns of population growth through the remainder of the antebellum period are reflected in Table II-1:

TABLE II-1

African American Population, 1790–1860: Kentucky and the United States[8]

| | Kentucky | | United States | |
	N	% KY	N	% US
1790	11,944	16.3	757,363	19.3
1800	41,084	18.6	1,001,436	18.9
1810	82,274	20.2	1,377,810	19.0
1820	129,491	23.0	1,776,194	18.4
1830	170,130	24.7	2,328,642	18.1
1840	189,575	24.1	2,873,758	16.8
1850	220,992	22.5	3,638,808	15.7
1860	236,167	20.4	4,441,830	14.1

Kentucky developed as a predominantly agricultural state with African Americans concentrated primarily in rural areas. For example, by 1800, African Americans were a comparatively unimportant element in early Kentucky towns—with even Lexington, "the Athens of the West," boasting only 1,795 African Americans, followed by Frankfort (638), Washington (570) and Paris (377) and Louisville (359).[9]

The lives of African Americans in Kentucky were shaped both by the broadly generalizable constraints of American slavery and by conditions unique to the state. For example, the invention of the Cotton Gin (1793) made cotton cultivation immensely profitable and breathed new life into American slavery. However, Kentucky's temperate climate and comparatively short growing season were not conducive to cotton monoculture. While tobacco and hemp cultivation depended heavily on slave labor, neither produced the large plantations and large slave-holdings that became common in the Gulf states after the War of 1812. As a result, fewer Kentucky families owned slave property than did their counterparts in neighboring states. For example, in 1790, an estimated 20 percent of white Kentuckians owned slaves, compared to 41 percent in Maryland, 33 percent in North Carolina and 34 percent in South Carolina.[10] Parallel to the lower percentage of slaveholders in the state population, those who owned slaves did not own large numbers. As another example, in 1790, Kentucky slaveholders owned an average of 4.3 slaves per slaveholding family, compared to 7.5 in Maryland, 6.7 in North Carolina and 12.1 in South Carolina. By 1800, this average remained essentially the same at 4.4 in Kentucky, with roughly 20 percent of Kentucky slaveholders owning only a single enslaved African American.[11]

The conditions of slavery in Kentucky were, to say the least, unappealing from the standpoint of enslaved African Americans. Slave housing was crude, poorly ventilated, and overcrowded. Most enslaved African Americans and most white slaveholders had limited wardrobes made from available materials and suited to the extremes of Kentucky's climate. Even the relatively affluent had few, if any, changes of clothing. Comparatively cold winters made rough fabrics of adequate weight and shoes, at least in season, necessities.[12] As with clothing and shelter, whites and enslaved African Americans ate similar foods. However, less food was available to enslaved African Americans and what they grew or received through rations had less variety and was of lower quality. In some cases, enslaved African Americans had private gardens or shared a common garden where vegetables were grown. Some slaveholders also allowed slaves the opportunity to fish or hunt small game as a means of supplementing their diet, and even to keep small livestock and chickens near their cabins. At best, this diet was "adequate, but repetitious and often unappealing."[13]

As indicated in Table II-1, black population as a percentage of total state population peaked at 24.7 percent (170,130 of 687,917) in 1830 and declined to 20.4 percent by 1860 (236,167 of 1,155,684). While this percentage representation far exceeded that of African Americans in the "free states," where black population was usually well below 5 percent of the state totals, it also fell far short of the percentage representation of African Americans in the mid- to deep southern interior where African Americans— in the cases of Louisiana, Mississippi and South Carolina— even equaled or exceeded whites numerically.[14]

Although annual rainfall amounts were more than adequate to support plantation agriculture, the growing season in most of the state was too short for major tropical or sub-tropical plantation crops such as cotton, sugar cane and rice. Large sections of Kentucky were also mountainous and/or lacked sufficient tillable ground to support productive agriculture. Consequently, the early pioneers and later settlers who ventured through the Cumberland Gap on foot or down the Ohio River in flatboats pushed through the Appalachians to the fertile Bluegrass region. This section of the state stretched from Mason County in the northeast, to Lincoln County in the southeast, to Marion County in the southwest, then north to Jefferson County in the northwest. With

rich, flat or gently undulating farmland, this region was settled first and most heavily in the 1770 to 1800 period — and would become and remain the center of Kentucky's black population. The only exceptions to this general pattern would be the Ohio River counties between Jefferson and Mason Counties where soil and terrain were poorly suited to agricultural uses and the Ohio River counties in western Kentucky and the south central and southwestern counties along the Tennessee border that attracted significant black populations after 1820.

As depicted in Map II-1, by 1850, Kentucky's African American population was concentrated in those regions of the state that had developed and sustained a productive agricultural economy — and was thinly scattered otherwise.[15]

A useful and fascinating account of the human and physical geography of the region was provided by Paul Wilhelm, Duke of Wurttemburg, who toured parts of the early United States between 1822 and 1824, journeying up the Mississippi and then the Ohio Rivers as far as Louisville. His travel commentary offered important insights into the early west and the character of its major rivers. In referring to the meeting of the Mississippi and Ohio, he noted that "no other continent offers a confluence of two similar rivers."[16] Moving eastward, he mentioned the fickle currents, numerous sandbars, the general wilderness on either side of the Ohio. Numerous birds, animals and, of course, the massive expanse of forests and wetland vegetation gave the appearance that much of the borderland had hardly been touched by humans. The former owners had been driven out, but the new masters of the land had only begun to occupy this vast territory — even two generations after the initial settlement of the state.[17] He passed, without much comment, the mouths of the Tennessee, Cumberland and Wabash Rivers, then the village of Hendersonville

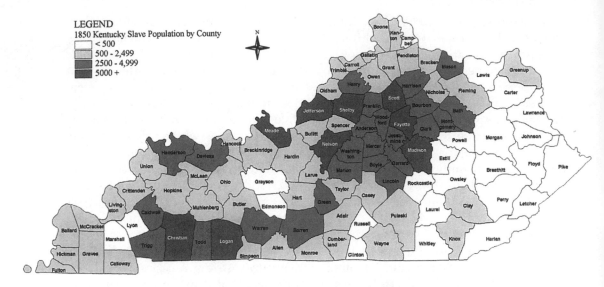

Map II-1. 1850 Kentucky Slave Population by County.

(later Henderson), then "the mouth of a creek called Green River" and eventually, reached Louisville.[18]

Before the completion of the Louisville and Portland Canal (around 1830), "almost all steamboats from western and southern states destined for Louisville" halted at Shippingport, a small hamlet just to the northwest of the larger town, "because during average and low water the rapids extending to the anchorage place of the small town makes further progress very difficult."[19] Louisville, in 1822, had yet to become a major city and displace Lexington as the key urban center in the Commonwealth, but the combined population of the town, surrounding county and small Indiana towns across the river was already considerable. For these reasons, Louisville was clearly the first true center of population encountered by Paul Wilhelm since the beginning of his journey in New Orleans and he offered an illuminating glimpse of "one of the most beautiful and most populous regions of Kentucky ... the beautiful banks of the river, the roaring rapids, the hills covered with luxuriant grass and splendid forests.[20]

Wilhelm was intrigued by Louisville

itself, where "for the first time we were in the vicinity of a U.S. town of size where the area could really be called populated"[21] and by the number of birds attracted by the "billions of insects" that bred in Louisville's comparatively unhealthy valley climate. He also observed that, while "slavery has not been abolished in Kentucky," the economy was not wholly dominated by the planter class (as in Louisiana)—"leaving a place for the manufacturer and the tradesman."[22] Not surprisingly, river conditions prevented him from continuing his journey to the east and, instead, he boarded a westbound steamboat and next visited St. Louis.

In contrast to Louisville, Lexington—Kentucky's earliest true urban area—was land-locked for all practical purposes. Its proximity to the many trails by which the early overland pioneers entered the state contributed to its singular importance in the late 1700s and early 1800s. However, both the expansion of settlement into the regions north of the Ohio River and the expansion of the "cotton kingdom" into the Gulf States to the south made proximity to the Ohio River far more important — and Lexington's location became increasingly disadvantageous relative to that of Louisville. As an outlet for slave-produced agricultural commodities and the center of Kentucky's domestic slave trade, Lexington and its surrounding area were also more deeply rooted in the economy and culture of the Kentucky Bluegrass, which were quite similar to those of central Tennessee. Louisville, on the other hand, was already developing its paradoxical blend of southern culture and northern economic structure.[23]

Enslaved African Americans comprised roughly half of the population of Lexington and Fayette County. In Lexington in the 1850s, "there were blacks everywhere, engaged in a great variety of tasks."[24] Clearly, enslaved African Americans in Louisville and countless other Kentucky towns performed the same tasks. The difference, where Louisville and Lexington were concerned, was one in both degree and kind. In essence, slavery and its traditions were far more central to daily life and life-ways in Lexington. This difference had two consequences of crucial importance with respect to Lexington's role in the history of fugitive slaves and the Underground Railroad. First, the slave system, with the use of police in the city and patrols in the countryside, was somewhat more rigid than in Louisville. Second, free African Americans in Lexington were too small in number, with too many restrictions and too few outlets to evolve into the type of self-conscious and organized community found in Louisville and Cincinnati. In other words, the slave system was stronger and the black community was weaker[25]—and Lexington was roughly sixty-five miles from free territory.

Other travelers also offered their first-hand impressions of the Kentucky borderland during the antebellum period. Venturing down-river by steamboat in 1839, C. B. Ray noted that enslaved African Americans seemed as numerous in the Kentucky Appalachian region as whites were in the Virginia (now West Virginia) mountains. Ray's boat encountered another vessel "aground with a hole in her bottom," whose passengers were rescued and added to Ray's now overcrowded steamboat. From conversations with some of these new passengers, he concluded that "these men ... rank among the biggest of the big among slaveholders." Ray commented that he was annoyed by their presence and their pretensions and, upon finally reaching Cincinnati, "left our boat in short order."[26]

In June 1847, a more colorful and highly textured description of Kentucky slavery was published serially in *The National Era*. Identifying himself as a "practical Anti-Slavery man," the correspondent determined to visit Kentucky and "state my first impressions on passing from the land of freedom to that of slavery." Aware of the familiar notion that, in Kentucky, "slavery is said to be seen in its mildest form," the correspondent recorded two interesting and valuable insights regarding the fully mature slave system that existed in the state by the late 1840s. Writing from Lexington, he noted that, once in Kentucky, he observed "...for the first time in my life, a slave work. The impression will go with me till death. Such a degree of ingenuity to appear to be at work, and yet be as long as possible doing the labor." He then added:

> When you think of the slave in this portion of the country, think not of him as undergoing physical suffering, or being overworked; for most of those that I have seen look "fat and sleek," are decently clad, and on the Sabbath dress as well as the laboring classes of the Northern States. But is there no occasion for pity for the slave? Think, then, of the slave as one from whose mind every ray of light is shut out, whose eye is never lit up by the cheering beam of hope, who does not feel his hands to be his own....[27]

In his second installment, the "Western Man" wondered why, if so many white

Kentuckians "see slavery to be hostile to their true interest ... they not abolish it?" He concluded that slavery had become too "intertwined with all the habits of the people" and that white Kentuckians, "accustomed from childhood to have the attendance of servants ... know not how to make the attempt to do without them." He added, however, that slavery had also crippled many African Americans psychologically and had driven out most free labor — thus rendering any immediate transition to a non-slave society difficult.[28]

When enslaved African Americans acted on their desire for freedom, the factor of distance in relation to the political geography of the United States and the physical geography of Kentucky became critically important. As Lucas noted:

> Though generally poor roads made travel difficult, fewer than a hundred miles separated the state's largest centers of slave population from free soil, with no location more than two hundred miles from the Ohio River. Lexington, the heart of the Bluegrass and the region with the largest slave population, was about sixty-five miles from the Ohio River via either Louisville or Maysville. Covington, on the Ohio River across from Cincinnati, the city with the largest black population in Ohio, lay seventy-nine miles directly north of Lexington. The heavily slave populated counties of western Kentucky were even closer to the Ohio River.[29]

Given these relative distances, the distribution of African Americans in Kentucky and the origins of the majority of fugitives, the broad routes they followed and their most likely sources of aid were anything but random.

Free people of color were one such source of possible assistance. Although a slave state, the number of free people of color living in Kentucky was nearly equal to the total black population of Indiana. In 1850, for example, there were 10,011 free people of color (4.5 percent of the total black population) in Kentucky compared to 11,262 African Americans in all of Indiana. However, as with enslaved African Americans, free people of color were not distributed evenly across the Commonwealth. As depicted in Map II-3, some free people of color were concentrated in or near many of the same centers of slave population in the Bluegrass and western Kentucky. Still, there were fairly significant clusters outside those regions — and counties within those regions that held few, if any, free people of color (see Appendix I-2). In general, free people of color were found more often in small communities in or near Kentucky towns and cities, giving this segment of the African American population a more decidedly urban character — even in Appalachia.[30] This pattern is elaborated in Map II-2.

Finally, enslaved African Americans were property and their economic value was determined as much by regional market forces as by the need, real or perceived, for bound labor in Kentucky. The institutionalization of slavery in Kentucky was accompanied by a significant increase in both the demand for and the average price of enslaved African Americans — first in the state and later in the cotton-growing states to the south.[31] These factors ultimately produced a thriving inter-regional domestic slave trade and gave Kentucky the reputation of being a "slave trading" (if not slave breeding) state.[32]

Still, in the final analysis, Kentucky became a paradox. Despite the importance of slave labor in the process of settling the state, the "institution of slavery in the Bluegrass had outlived its usefulness" by the War of 1812.[33] In Berlin's terms, Kentucky evolved into a "society with slaves" — a state in which slavery was not central to the economy or social structure — as distinct from the "slave societies" found in the rice and later cotton-growing states of the deep southern interior where economic, political and social life were inextricably interwoven with the "peculiar

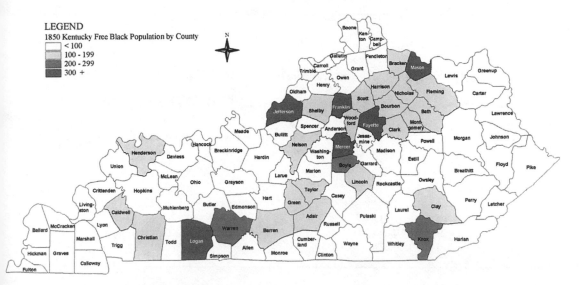

Map II-2. 1850 Kentucky Free Black Population by County.

institution." Only the success of the larger land- and slaveholders in gaining and maintaining control of the political and economic apparatus of state power under the provisions of the 1792 and 1799 Kentucky constitutions—and the economics of domestic slave trade—enabled slavery to survive without serious challenge until the Civil War.[34] The marginality of slavery in Kentucky did not lessen the tenacity with which many white Kentuckians defended it. Few whites in Kentucky could think beyond this paradox. African Americans were trapped by and had ample reason to wish to be free of it.

The Human Landscape: North of Slavery

The borderland north of slave territory was defined not only by geography (see Appendix I-3 and I-4), but by relations between the free and slave border states, and by relations between whites and free African Americans. After the American Revolution, the northern states, where slavery had shallow roots, began the "first emancipation"—the abolition of slavery in New England and the mid-Atlantic states between 1777 and roughly 1820. At the same time, the more southerly states, while contemplating the end of slavery in the 1780s, became its hostage after the invention of the Cotton Gin (1793) revitalized the peculiar institution. Both the enslaved and free African American populations grew dramatically thereafter (see Table II-1, and Table II-2). By 1800, the black American population had grown to slightly more than one million persons, 11 percent of whom were free. By 1830, the black population stood at more than 2,300,000—14 percent of whom were free.[35]

Although an increasing number of African Americans were legally free, their status in American society was ambiguous at best. Because of intense racial antagonism, they were treated as outcasts throughout much of the north and west. However, the strength of this antagonism varied regionally and the implications of such regional variations might best be understood by viewing the antebellum United States—not in terms of "north" and "south," or "free" and "slave" states—but as four political/cultural zones, each distinguishable based on its prevailing

TABLE II-2

Kentucky and United States Free Black Population: 1790–1860

	Kentucky		United States	
	% Ky Black		% US Black	
	Free	Population	Free	Population
1790	114	1.0	59,466	07.9
1800	241	0.6	108,395	10.8
1810	1,713	2.1	186,446	13.5
1820	2,759	2.1	238,156	13.4
1830	4,917	2.9	319,599	13.7
1840	7,317	3.9	386,303	13.4
1850	10,011	4.5	434,495	11.9
1860	10,684	4.5	488,070	11.0

racial attitudes and the degree of its dependence on slavery.

The first was the "southern interior" or "Cotton Kingdom." The states therein were dependent upon and committed uncompromisingly to slavery, with no place for free people of color. The "border and upper south" was the second zone — where slavery existed but climatic conditions did not permit large-scale cotton cultivation. There, free people of color were tolerated, grudgingly, as an alien element. The "lower north" ran through the southern halves of Iowa, Illinois, Indiana, Ohio, Pennsylvania, New York and New Jersey. While slavery did not exist legally in these states and free people of color were numerous, the racial attitudes of whites were quite similar to those just south of the "border." Finally, in the "upper north" or "Greater New England" region, opposition to slavery was strongest and most uncompromising, and free people of color, although few in number and seldom welcomed enthusiastically, were more widely accepted.[36]

Given this framework, as slavery ended in the north, the border-states and the lower north (and the new territories in the "Old Northwest" and the Louisiana Purchase) feared the prospect of becoming havens to the burgeoning free black population. As a result, efforts to prevent the migration of free people of color into the border-states and lower north began as early as 1793 when Virginia barred their entry.[37] In 1806, following the Gabriel (1800) and Sancho (1802) slave conspiracies, Virginia passed additional legislation requiring that emancipated African Americans leave the state within a year of their manumission.[38] These laws were copied widely as the frontier moved westward. Ohio enacted such legislation in 1804 and 1807. Michigan followed suit in 1827, as did Illinois in 1829. After 1831, free African Americans migrating to Indiana were required to register with county authorities and post a bond guaranteeing their good behavior. In the 1851 Indiana Constitution, an absolute prohibition was imposed on the right of free blacks to settle in the state. Thus, while free people of color already resident or born free in these states were not removed, a variety of means were devised to limit their rights and, most importantly, to prevent their numbers from growing larger.[39] Such legislation was seldom enforced uniformly, but its existence reflected strong white antipathy to the presence of free African Americans.

Another pertinent expression of antebellum racism was white mob violence that drove free blacks from many communities and states.[40] Given the prevalence of such violence and repressive legislation, the struggle for equal black citizenship was often complemented by the desperate search for a safe place to live — ideally, a place that promised the possibility of land ownership, work for decent wages or the opportunity to practice a trade. The combined effects of these push and pull factors scattered free African Americans throughout the border-states and the north in towns, cities and rural enclaves where opportunities were greatest and resistance was least. Needless to add, the characteristics that made such communities attractive to free people of color made them attractive as well to fugitive slaves — both as places of sanctuary and sources of aid.

African Americans living north of Kentucky's Ohio River border were not numerous. For example, by 1860, African Americans were only 1.5 percent of the population of Ohio, only 0.85 percent of the population of Indiana and only 0.44 percent of the population of Illinois.[41] However, their presence and, particularly, their geographic distribution, were significant — and require further elaboration.

Illinois

Kentucky's long Ohio River border begins, in the west, at Cairo, Illinois. Like Indiana and Ohio, Illinois was part of the Northwest Territory in which slavery was prohibited under the provisions of the 1787 Northwest Ordinance. The southern section of the territory was bounded by two slave states — Missouri and Kentucky — and was settled earliest and largely by settlers with southern origins who brought their slaveholding proclivities to the western frontier after the War of 1812. Through their influence, although slavery was illegal, long-term indenture arrangements were used as a quasi-legal form of slavery until the 1840s.[42]

In contrast to the populations of Indiana and Ohio, Illinois had relatively few residents in 1850 and, in many respects, was only emerging from its frontier period. Of its 851,470 persons, only 5,436 (0.64 percent) were African Americans who, other than a few concentrations, were scattered very thinly across the state (see Map II-3).[43]

Only a few Illinois counties were home to a sufficient number of free people of color (see Appendix I-5) to constitute small and marginal communities. While extreme southern Illinois would seem a natural escape route for fugitives from the Jackson Purchase region of far western Kentucky and from Tennessee, this section of the state also had a reputation for intense hostility to African Americans and was home to relatively few free people of color. In other words, this region held many dangers and little help. As a consequence, Illinois was not a particularly attractive escape route for Kentucky fugitives. Fugitives from slavery in eastern Missouri had few options — Illinois, Iowa or one of the major rivers. Fugitives from Kentucky, however, could avoid or minimize the duration of their stay in Illinois. The small free black settlements in Pope, Gallatin, White and Lawrence Counties could serve as an escape corridor that passed briefly through Illinois, skirting the Wabash River, then into Indiana. The available records suggest that many Kentucky fugitive slaves chose this option or by-passed Illinois altogether.[44]

Indiana

African Americans were a much more significant presence in Indiana's early history. In the 1700s, enslaved African Americans were found in colonial French settlements such as Vincennes. After the French and Indian War (1754–1763), the British gained ownership of the territory

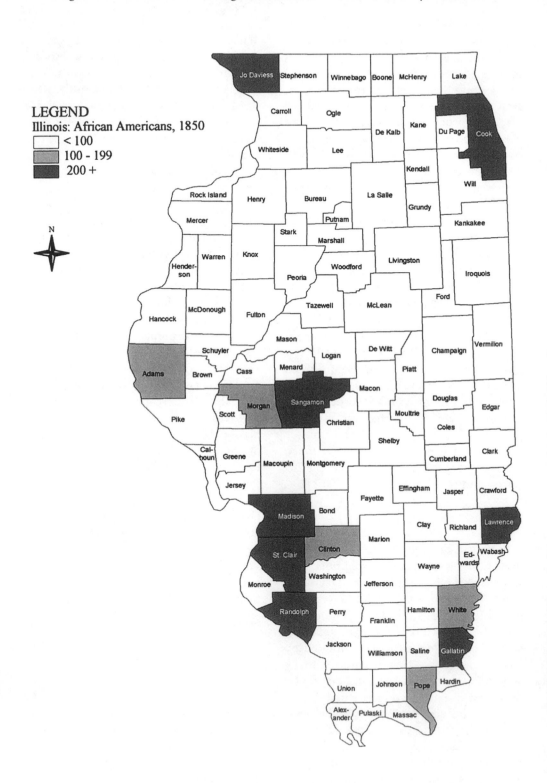

Map II-3. 1850 Illinois Black Population by County.

but did little to dislodge the French settlers therein or to disturb the much larger Native American population. In 1779, when General George Rogers Clark, also the founder of Louisville, captured Vincennes, the entire Northwest Territory — the future states of Indiana, Illinois, Ohio, Michigan and Wisconsin — became first the property of Virginia and, after 1783, the property of the newly fledged United States.[45]

In 1787, the Northwest Ordinance (Article IV) outlawed slavery in this vast region — ensuring that, since slavery had already taken root in Kentucky, the Ohio River would become the boundary between free and slave territory in the early west. Despite this legal prohibition, most African Americans in Indiana remained enslaved through the territorial period. This seeming contradiction was permitted under a rather creative interpretation of Article IV that limited its application to African Americans brought into the territory and exempted those already there.[46] In other words, there was no retroactive effect and enslaved African Americans who were resident in the territory before 1787 were not freed by Article IV.

While Territorial Governor of Indiana, William Henry Harrison was sympathetic to slavery and, during his administration, laws were passed permitting the long-term indenture of African Americans. The first such act was adopted in 1803 and an even stronger law was enacted by the 1805 Territorial Legislature that permitted settlers to bring enslaved African Americans into Indiana, to bind them to indenture agreements (after sixty days) and then to sell or remove them if they refused to accept or abide by the terms of these agreements. These various acts remained in force until the adoption of the state constitution and Indiana's subsequent admission to the Union in 1816 finally ended all forms of legal servitude.[47]

During the territorial and early statehood periods, Indiana was settled primarily along the Ohio and Wabash Rivers. Most early settlements were in the southern section of the state and, not surprisingly, white southerners were most numerous among these early pioneers and, apart from importing servitude of one sort or another, southern racial attitudes also crossed the Ohio River. In later years, the central and more northerly Indiana counties were settled predominantly by northerners or European immigrants—creating, in essence, two "zones" in the state (corresponding to the "lower north" and "upper north") with respect to racial attitudes.[48] One obvious implication of these internal regions was the difficulty enslaved African Americans faced "getting through" southern Indiana even after negotiating a river crossing.

With generally hostile territory on both sides of the river, the location of friends of the fugitive was critically important. One set of potential friends was comprised of southern whites who objected to slavery and moved to Indiana precisely because it was free territory — some emancipating their enslaved African Americans and others even transporting them to Indiana as well. These early antislavery families, of which Quakers represented a prominent sub-set, settled primarily in the eastern section of the state.[49]

Equally, if not more, important were black Americans themselves. However inhospitable, Indiana was still a free state and, as such, was attractive to the hard-pressed free black population. By 1820, 1,420 African Americans, 1.0 percent of Indiana's 146,758 people, claimed residence in the state — increasing to 11,428 in 1860 (0.9 percent of the total state population).[50] Although small in number, the distribution of Indiana's African American population was significant. Map II-4 describes this population distribution, with county figures available in Appendix I-6.

Although African Americans living in

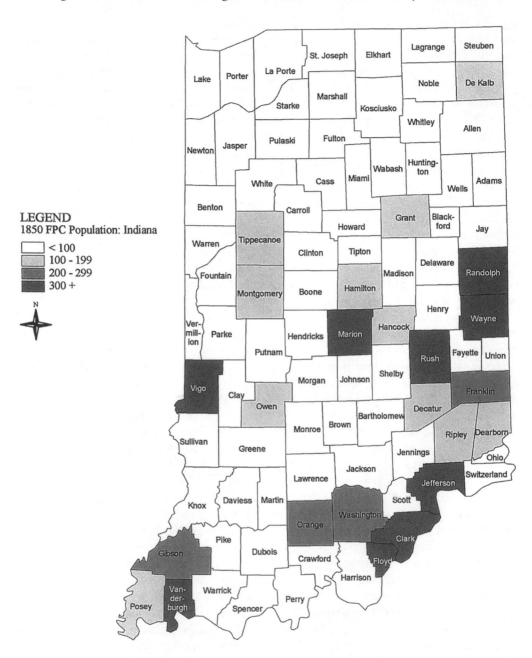

Map II-4. 1850 Indiana Black Population by County.

Indiana were only a small percentage of the state's population, their sheer numbers were far greater than those recorded for Illinois and sufficient to create several small, identifiable communities primarily in the south central and southeastern sections of the state. Each of these small communities had its own unique character and some were major border crossing, harboring and transfer points for fugitive slaves from and through Kentucky.

Several of these small communities deserve mention here and will be discussed in much greater detail in later sections of the study. For example by 1850, African Americans represented 3.9 percent of the total Floyd County population (roughly 5 percent of the population of New Albany) and 3.7 percent of the total population of neighboring Clark County (and roughly 5 percent of Jeffersonville and 6 percent of Charleston). Because these small Indiana communities faced Louisville across the Ohio River — and Louisville, as will be discussed later in the study, became Kentucky's key urban and free black population center — the total free black population in the greater Louisville area (2,698) approached that of greater Cincinnati.[51]

Somewhat to the east, African Americans were 2.4 percent of the population of Jefferson County (Indiana), with a small concentration in Madison. While there was no Kentucky settlement with a significant black population facing Madison, there were sizable clusters of free people of color to the southwest (at Louisville), south (Frankfort) and southeast (Lexington). Furthermore, the Madison area was unique in that, as early as 1839, an active white anti-slavery society existed in nearby Lancaster Township, probably the first in Indiana.[52] To the west, although the numbers for free people of color were negligible on both sides of the river, an Anti-Slavery League was reputed to have played an active role in assisting fugitives from the Bluegrass and from western Kentucky escape northward through Indiana.[53] The involvement of both blacks and whites in visible anti-slavery protests and less visible assistance to fugitive slaves lent these adjacent sections of southern Indiana considerable importance that will be explored in Chapter VI.

After the passage of the 1850 Fugitive Slave Act and the adoption of the 1851 Indiana Constitution, fugitive slaves and free people of color living in Indiana became far more vulnerable to harassment and sometimes kidnapping — particularly those living unprotected along the Ohio River within easy reach of kidnappers and slave-catchers. A veritable "Negro Exodus" commenced as hundreds of black families moved from their small hamlets along the river to points east and north.[54] As the editor of *The National Era* commented, "The Indiana Black Laws have caused the removal of large numbers of colored persons from that State, as the penalties incurred by residence there are quite severe."[55] Thus, as shall be elaborated in the sections that follow, southern Indiana became increasingly inhospitable to fugitives and their friends when the flow of fugitives was heaviest and the need for assistance was most pronounced.

Ohio

The anti-slavery movement was both more visible and more formidable in Ohio than in either Indiana or Illinois. Free black settlements were not necessarily more numerous along the Ohio River border than was the case in Indiana, but were scattered more generally and in greater numbers as one moved through the central section of the state. Organized white anti-slavery activity was also spread more generally from the counties bordering Virginia (now West Virginia) and Kentucky to the major Lake Erie crossings from northern Ohio to Canada West — specifically, Toledo, Sandusky, Cleveland, and Ashtabula.[56]

As a result, Ohio brought together the three elements that attracted fugitive slaves: the presence of free African American communities; the presence of anti-slavery whites; and reasonably direct routes from slave to free territory — eventually to Canada, if necessary. For this reason, much as the majority of fugitive slaves in the trans–Appalachian west escaped from or through Kentucky, the majority of these fugitives probably crossed into and passed through some part of Ohio as they continued their long journey to freedom.

As Map II-5 indicates, African Americans represented only 1.28 percent of the total population of Ohio in 1850. This small population was distributed neither evenly nor randomly. Rather, most Ohio African Americans lived in the southwestern and south central sections of the state, with smaller numbers in a few clusters along the Ohio border with Virginia, Pennsylvania and Lake Erie. Ohio African Americans also tended to live in small rural settlements or urban neighborhoods in those counties in which black population was concentrated (see Appendix I-7). For example, C. B. Ray observed in 1839 that most African Americans in Ohio originated in either Virginia or Kentucky. He noted as well that "the colored population of this State own more land undoubtedly than the same class in all other States besides, and consequently there are more independent farmers among them than of the same class in all of the eastern free States put together."[57]

It is important to note that the attractions of Ohio, from the perspective of both free people of color and fugitive slaves, were not altogether relative. True, Ohio did not welcome African Americans and was only somewhat less hostile to their presence than were neighboring states. Mob violence against African Americans erupted repeatedly during the antebellum period, most notably in Cincinnati in August 1829 and September 1841.[58] Further, in the words of Frederick Douglass, the "wicked and shameful" Ohio Black Laws exemplified this hostility as well.[59]

On the other hand, the Black Laws were seldom enforced and there was a crucial loophole for fugitives created by law and by an 1841 decision of the Ohio Supreme Court. Specifically, " if the owner of a slave brings him into the State or permits him to come, although it should be only for the purpose of visiting, or to pass through the State, the slave, in either case, the moment he touches the soil of Ohio, becomes a free man."[60] This "personal liberty" provision did not exist under the laws of either Illinois or Indiana.

The Human Landscape: Tennessee and Points South

Most fugitives from the southern interior seeking lasting freedom were channeled through Kentucky by land or followed a river that flowed, eventually, into the Ohio or Mississippi Rivers. If they traveled by land or one of the lesser rivers, most had first to reach and traverse Tennessee — then Kentucky. Given Kentucky's irregular shape, runaways from central and western Tennessee had only a slightly lower probability of success than did fugitives from the southern counties of Kentucky since they were nearly as close to free territory. Thus, at least a cursory overview of African Americans in Tennessee, as a "feeder" rather than a border state, is necessary at this point to complete the geographic and demographic "picture" of the overall region.

Table II-3, based on the 1850 Census, reflects the unusual similarity between the aggregate distribution of population by race in Tennessee and Kentucky.[61]

In essence, Tennessee had about 20,000 more residents than did Kentucky. Kentucky's white and free black populations were slightly larger than those of Tennessee, while Tennessee's enslaved black population was somewhat larger than that of Kentucky. Still, with African American populations under 25 percent, both states reflected fairly typical upper south and border state population distributions for states in which large plantation agriculture was not a dominant economic activity.

Neither the enslaved nor the free black populations of Tennessee were distributed

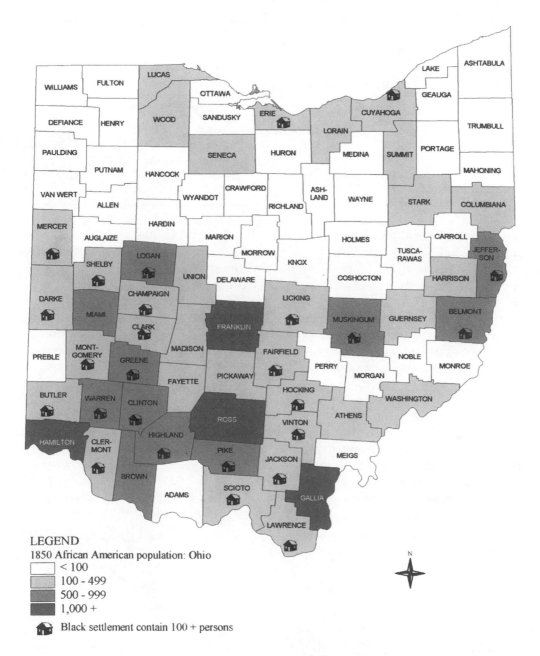

LEGEND
1850 African American population: Ohio
- □ < 100
- 100 - 499
- 500 - 999
- 1,000 +

🏠 Black settlement contain 100 + persons

Map II-5. 1850 Ohio Black Population by County.

evenly throughout the state. Geographically, antebellum Tennessee was divided into three sections, each with its distinctive economic and slave-holding pattern. Eastern Tennessee belonged to the Appalachian upland where large scale farming — and, by extension, slaveholding — did not develop except in the few fertile valleys in which cereal grains could be cultivated. Central Tennessee was fertile and, with its "luxuriant bluegrass," resembled central Kentucky. There, cereal grains and commodity crops such as tobacco could be grown profitably. Finally, the western sec-

TABLE II-3

1850 Population Comparison: Kentucky and Tennessee

	White	Enslaved	Black Free	Total	Total
Kentucky	761,413	210,981	10,011	220,992	982, 405
percent of State	77.5	21.5	1.0	22.5	
Tennessee	756,836	239,459	6,422	245,881	1,002,717
percent of State	75.5	23.9	0.6	24.5	

tion of the state was added in 1818 when Andrew Jackson consummated the "Chickasaw Purchase" and brought the territory between the Tennessee and Mississippi Rivers into the state.[62]

As indicated in Map II-6, African Americans were concentrated in the western and central regions of Tennessee, with some scattered areas of concentration in the eastern valleys. Central Tennessee formed the northern border of Alabama and western Tennessee bore the same relation to northern Mississippi. Consequently, fugitives escaping overland from these cotton-growing states were funneled through central and western Tennessee, then through Kentucky, to free territory.

Nashville and its surrounding Davidson County dominated the central region of the state. As an urban center in the upper south, the African American population of Nashville bore some similarities to those of both Lexington and Louisville — with a number of free people of color and enslaved African Americans hired out in the town. For example, in 1830, there were 1,987 African Americans resident in Nashville, representing 35.7 percent of the town population. Free people of color represented 9.0 percent (i.e., 179 of 1,987) of that number. By 1850, the African American population had increased slightly to 2,539, of whom 20.1 percent (i.e., 511 of 2,539) were free. However, the

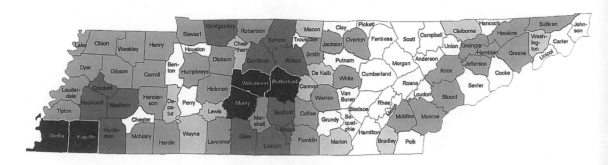

LEGEND
Enlaved African Americans
<500
500 - 999
1,000 - 4,999
5,000 - 9,999
10,000 +

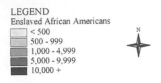

Map II-6. 1850 Tennessee Slave Population by County.

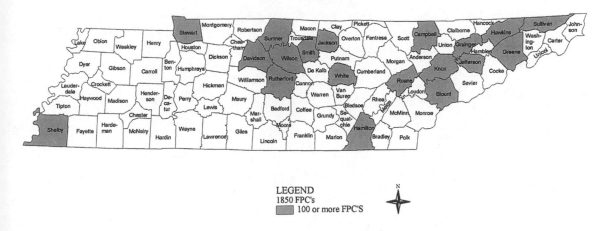

LEGEND
1850 FPC's
100 or more FPC'S

N

Map II-7. 1850 Tennessee Free Black Population by County.

white population had grown disproportionately and the African American percentage of population had dropped to 24.9 percent.[63]

After 1840, the relative status of urban slaves and free people of color deteriorated as European immigrants and non-slaveholding whites pressed for severe restrictions on African Americans to limit competition for jobs and living space. Furthermore, Tennessee became a net exporter of slave property by 1850 and, as a result, "Negro stealing" and "Negro trading" became lucrative businesses. Running away was one response. As Bobby Lovett observed:

> ... the tightening of controls only made Negroes yearn for freedom just that much more. Although no printed record exists that local blacks engaged in any Underground Railroad or an organized rebellion against slavery ... local Negroes continuously resisted slavery in their own ways: running away, disobedience, purchasing their freedom, buying the freedom of relatives, and sometimes through violence.... [I]f there was an "Underground Railroad" out of Nashville, it surely ran through Kentucky and then to Cincinnati.[64]

Tennessee's free black population, although small, was concentrated in pockets in the eastern valleys and in the north central sections of the state — generally along the course of the Cumberland River.

Still, as was the case with Lexington, free people of color in Tennessee and the deep southern interior had far less freedom to assist fugitives and even the potential advantages of their presence in and around Nashville may have been off-set by the sheer distance between northern Tennessee and free territory (by any route).

Finally, by 1850, two major urban population centers had developed in the borderland: Cincinnati in free territory and Louisville in slave territory. Louisville, in particular, was unique — as the only major city in a largely rural state and as the only major city between Baltimore and St. Louis on the "slave side" of the border. Enslaved African Americans (2,406) accounted for 23.3 percent of the Louisville population in 1830, increasing in number to 5,432 in 1850, although declining to 12.6 percent of the city's population due to heavy German and Irish immigration. At the same time, the free black population increased from 232 in 1830 to 1,538 in 1850, and continued to increase. Likewise, in Cincinnati, African Americans increased from 1,090 to 3,237 over the same period, but their percentage representation dropped from 4.4 to 2.8 percent due largely to immigration as well.[65] Each of these population centers would play a pivotal, but different, role in the flow of fugitive slaves through the Kentucky borderland.

Fugitive slaves took advantage of the physical and human geography of the region — and those who wished to assist them worked within those limits.

CHAPTER III

Fugitive Slaves

It was on this soil I first breathed the free air of Heaven, and felt the bitter pangs of slavery — it was here that I first learned to abhor it. It was here I received the first impulse of human rights — it was here that I first entered my protest against the bloody institution of slavery, by running away from it.

Henry Bibb, Fugitive Slave from Kentucky[1]

Enslaved African Americans sometimes escaped across the Appalachians into Kentucky territory before the establishment of early settlements in the 1770s. As the institution of slavery followed the early pioneers and black population increased rapidly in the 1780s, slave escapes from Kentucky became commonplace. As one indication, by far the most frequent references to African Americans in early Kentucky newspapers were advertisements for the return of runaway slaves. For example, 71.2 percent (151 of 212) of the references to African Americans found in the *Kentucky Gazette* between 1788 and 1805, a period not normally associated with a heavy flow of fugitive slaves, fall in this category.[2]

Because slave escapes deprived slaveholders of the monetary value of their slave property, the value of its labor and, if a woman, the value of children she might conceive and bear in the future, slaveholders had good reason to seek the return of runaways. Not surprisingly, antebellum Kentucky newspapers contained thousands of advertisements, articles and other references to fugitive slaves. These advertisements, by their very nature, are mute regarding the eventual fate of the fugitive and cannot in themselves establish the larger context in which slave escapes occurred. However, each fugitive slave notice or article represented a public announcement that an escape had occurred and included information needed to identify and facilitate the recapture of the fugitive. Thus, such notices can be used to describe runaway slaves in varying degrees of detail, the circumstances of their flight and, in the aggregate, can also be used to estimate the number and frequency of slave escapes in purely quantitative terms.

While the selective examination of individual references is illuminating, it is crucial first to describe the total population under study and to identify, if possible, any patterns in the characteristics and/ or behavior of that population. This task requires the use of both historical and social science methods of analysis.

Slave Escapes: The Kentucky Fugitive Slave Data Base

The "Kentucky Fugitive Slave Data Base" is comprised of a total of 801 references to 1,196 fugitive slaves (allowing for escapes involving more than one fugitive). References were selected from Kentucky newspapers published between 1788 and 1863 as follows: complete years between 1788 and 1834; seven "Winter-Spring" and seven "Summer-Fall" half-years between 1835 and 1849; and complete years between 1850 and 1861. The Data Base was analyzed using the SPSS[3], with the .05 level of confidence (i.e., a difference or change with, at best, only a one in twenty probability of occurring by chance) serving as the threshold for determinations of statistical significance.

Beyond the time period reviewed, references were distributed by type as shown in Table III-1, below.

While court reports and articles usually appeared only once, the same fugitive slave advertisement might appear in several newspapers for weeks, even several months. Because of this, fugitive slave notices were entered or counted only once regardless of how often the advertisement was printed — unless the fugitive in question was captured and then escaped a second time.

In the early 1800s, slave escapes were viewed largely as a problem inherent to the nature of slavery itself as a domestic institution. Most references to fugitive slaves in Kentucky and elsewhere appeared in advertisements for their recovery. Over time, slave escapes became a national political issue, a focus of sectional conflict, culminating in the passage of the Fugitive Slave Act of 1850, and the heightened sectional tensions over fugitive slaves in the 1850s. Slave escapes and, particularly, the recapture of fugitives or stories of fugitives who received ill treatment in the northern states or Canada — became news. Advertisements remained commonplace since the flow of fugitives from Kentucky and points south did not diminish. However, news items appeared with far greater

TABLE III-1

Kentucky Fugitive Slave Data Base: Reference Types

Type	N of Cases	% of Total Cases
Fugitive Slave Advertisements	531	66.3
Newspaper Articles	207	25.8
Court Reports	25	3.1
Jail Notices (captured fugitives)	38	4.7
Total	801	

frequency. Another example of the impact of this change is reflected in Table III-2, which charts the references by decade.

Considering reference type and time period together, it becomes apparent that 1850 marked a "dividing line," as noted, in the history of slave escapes that is reflected as clearly in these data (see Table III-3) as in the historical source materials reviewed in the remainder of the study. This dividing line will be retained for comparative purposes throughout this section.

As noted previously, slave escapes in the United States were more often individual rather than group undertakings. This pattern held in Kentucky. However, the number of group escapes— often very large groups by United States standards and sometimes termed "stampedes"— increased significantly in the 1850s, as shown below in Table III-4.

TABLE III-2

Kentucky Fugitive Slave Data Base: References by Decade

Decade	N of Cases	% of Total Cases
Before 1820	44	5.5
1820–1829	106	13.2
1830–1839	113	14.1
1840–1849	112	14.0
1850–1859	340	42.4
1860–1861	86	10.7
Total	801	

TABLE III-3

Kentucky Fugitive Slave Data Base: References by Period

	Before 1850		1850 and After		Total	
	N	%	N	%	N	%
Advertisements	356	94.9	175	41.1	531	66.3
Articles	5	1.3	202	47.4	207	25.8
Court Reports	1	0.3	24	5.6	25	3.1
Jail Notices	13	3.5	25	5.9	38	4.7
Total	375		426		801	

Note: Chi-Square (N=-801, df = 3) = 271.985, p < .001 (see Endnote 2)

TABLE III-4

Kentucky Fugitive Slave Data Base: Group Escapes by Period

	Before 1850		1850 and After		Total	
	N	%	N	%	N	%
Individual Escapes	370	78.4	395	54.6	765	64.0
Group Escapes	102	21.6	329	45.4	431	36.0
Total	472		724		1,196	

Note: Chi-Square (N=1196, df = 1) = 74.40, p < .001.

Considering individual fugitives slaves as the unit of analysis reveals something of the internal structure of this pattern, as reflected in Tables III-5 and III-6, below:

TABLE III-5

Kentucky Fugitive Slave Data Base: Fugitive Slaves by Decade

Type	N of Cases	% of Total Cases
Before 1820	58	4.8
1820–1829	142	11.9
1830–1839	133	11.1
1840–1849	139	11.6
1850–1859	630	52.6
1860–1863	94	7.9
Total	1,196	

Virtually all fugitive slave advertisements and many news articles pertaining to fugitives contained the name and place of residence of the owner of the fugitive in question. Based on this information, as depicted in Map III-1, the geographic distribution of advertised slave escapes within Kentucky can be charted.

Caution should be exercised in interpreting these data in other than a very broad and general sense. To reiterate, not all slave escapes were reported and it is reasonable to assume that more reports of "local" slave escapes were preserved in those regions with major surviving newspapers. For example, there were 411 reported escapes in Jefferson County alone (34.3 percent of the total)—thus skewing the data somewhat. Still, this distribution of slave escapes was generally consistent with the distribution of the enslaved African American population in the state (see Table II-1)—and with the location of free people of color on the Kentucky, Illinois, Indiana and Ohio sides of the Ohio River. Consequently, it is also reasonable to assume that the probability of slave escapes was greater in those counties with larger numbers of enslaved African Americans. The rough correspondence between these patterns cannot be ignored.

Fugitive slaves not only escaped from Kentucky, but those originating in more southerly states passed through Kentucky en route to free territory. Table III-7 lists fugitives' various states of origin.

These data confirm that most (80.3 percent) Kentucky fugitive slaves originated

TABLE III-6

Kentucky Fugitive Slave Data Base: References by Type and by Period

	Before 1850		1850 and After		Total	
	N	%	N	%	N	%
Advertisements	438	92.8	230	31.8	668	55.9
Articles	15	3.2	448	61.9	463	38.7
Court Reports	1	0.2	20	2.8	21	1.8
Jail Notices	18	3.8	26	3.6	44	3.7
Total	472		724		1,196	

Note: Chi-Square (N= 1196, df = 3) = 455.48, p < .001

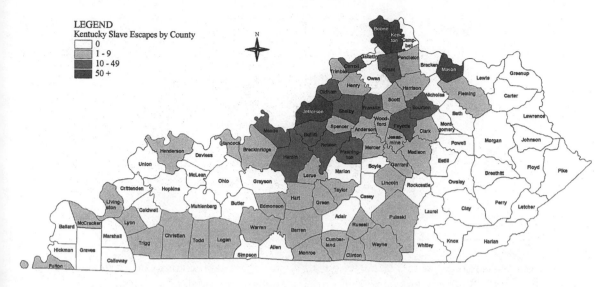

Map III-1. Kentucky Slave Escapes by County.

TABLE III-7

Kentucky Fugitive Slave Data Base: State of Origin

Type	N of Cases	% of Total Cases
Alabama	32	2.7
Arkansas	2	0.2
District of Columbia	2	0.2
Georgia	5	0.4
Kentucky	961	80.3
Louisiana	28	2.4
Mississippi	26	2.2
Missouri	8	0.7
North Carolina	2	0.2
South Carolina	5	0.4
Tennessee	94	7.9
Virginia	7	0.6
No Record	25	2.1
Total	1,196	

in Kentucky. However, Kentucky also served — or, at least, slaveholders certainly thought it served — as an outlet, conduit and/or escape corridor for fugitives fleeing slavery in the deep southern interior. Not surprisingly, the numbers of fugitive slave

notices from Tennessee and even Alabama, Mississippi and Louisiana are considerable, with even an occasional fugitive from east of the Appalachians. It is also important to note that fugitives who escaped through Kentucky, but for whom no or only a local advertisement was placed, would not appear in the Data Base — unless they were caught and became the subjects of a news article, jail notice or court record.

The Kentucky Fugitive Slave Data Base also permitted an examination of some personal characteristics of runaways. As cited by many of the more traditional sources, most fugitive slaves were young adult African American males. As Table III-8 indicates, this pattern certainly held true in Kentucky (gender was not always mentioned in reports of large scale slave escapes or in descriptions of young children).

Clearly, both the frequency of references to fugitives and the proportion of female fugitives increased after 1850. Age remained relatively constant, with the mean dropping only slightly from 25.0 years before 1850 to 24.6 years thereafter. The statistical comparison of means was not significant. However, ages ranged from infancy

TABLE III-8

Kentucky Fugitive Slave Data Base:
Gender by Period

	Before 1850		1850 and After		Total	
	N	%	N	%	N	%
Female	92	20.0	142	27.4	234	23.9
Male	367	80.0	377	72.6	744	76.3
Total	459		519		978	

Note: Chi-Square (N= 978, df = 1) = 7.164, p < .01

to sixty years old — with 57.2 percent of all fugitives falling between twenty and thirty years of age.

Beginning in 1840, the United States Census distinguished between African Americans who were racially mixed, termed "mulattoes," and African Americans of ostensibly pure African ancestry, termed "black" or "Negro." This distinction was not scientific since it ignored the many shadings of complexion found among continental Africans and relied on the different standards of judgment applied by white American Census enumerators. For example, in the "eyes" of one Census enumerator, only an African American who was "nearly white" might qualify as a "mulatto"; in the "eyes" of another, only an African American who was extremely dark complexioned would qualify as "black." The same person might even be classified and coded differently in successive Census enumerations.

Were it not for the mythology of race and the politics of slavery, the issue of color and racial hybridism among African Americans would be of arcane interest at best. However, one of the most disturbing and effective accusations leveled at the South by the Abolitionist Movement after 1830 was the charge of sexual depravity — that the ownership of black women by white men led to forced and illicit interracial sexual contact. The existence of the mulatto population was, so to speak, living proof of sexual depravity and the number of mulattos was a yardstick by which the magnitude of such depravity could be measured. Consequently, the defenders of slavery argued that the mulatto population was an insignificant 10 percent or less of the total African American population, while those opposed to slavery argued that the percentage of African Americans of mixed racial ancestry was much higher.

Because fugitive slave advertisements were intended to facilitate the capture of fugitives, these advertisements represent one of the few — and, perhaps, the only — forms of "southern literature" that offered a physical description of African Americans that African Americans themselves might recognize. Color is often one of the first characteristics mentioned in such descriptions and, thus, the "color" distribution among fugitive slaves can be examined in some detail with relative confidence in the accuracy of the source materials. In Kentucky, this distribution (Table III-9) also shifts significantly after 1850.

As these data indicate, African Americans of mixed racial ancestry were anything but a small minority among Kentucky fugitive slaves. This pattern may be attributable to the presence of a much higher percentage of African Americans of

TABLE III-9

Kentucky Fugitive Slave Data Base:
"Color" by Period

	Before 1850		1850 and After		Total	
	N	*%*	*N*	*%*	*N*	*%*
"Black"	169	45.3	205	53.5	374	49.5
"Mulatto"	204	54.7	178	46.5	382	50.5
Total	373		383		756	

Note: Chi-Square (N= 756, df = 1) = 5.103, p < .02

mixed race in Kentucky than has been supposed or the greater likelihood of mulattoes attempting escape — or both. However, while mulattoes continued to flee in disproportionately large numbers after 1850, the percentage of blacks increased significantly.

As some of the examples cited in later sections of this study suggest, a fair complexion was sometimes an effective disguise. However, few African Americans of mixed race were described as being exceptionally fair. Others suggest that enslaved African Americans with the most freedom or other advantages felt the injustices of slavery more keenly and that mulattoes often enjoyed such relative advantages— and, hence, were more likely to flee. Fugitive slave advertisements confirm the reports from Underground Railroad workers in both the North and Canada that the percentage of fugitives of mixed race was unexpectedly high through the decades preceding the Civil War. Some or all of the factors noted may have contributed to this phenomenon, but precisely why this was so remains a matter of conjecture.

Many fugitive slave advertisements indicate the date and/or day of the week of a given slave escape. Using a perpetual calendar, this information was analyzed to determine whether there were particular times of the week (Table III-10) and/or

times of the year (Table III-11) when slave escapes were most — and least — likely to occur.

As Table III-10 reflects, before 1850, fugitive slaves escaped at random — and opportunistically — throughout the week. In the 1850s, however, escapes became much more common on the weekends. To some extent, this pattern reflects the greater likelihood of group escapes on weekends.

Seasonal escape patterns changed over time as well. After 1850, slave escapes in the autumn months decreased significantly, while those at all other times of year increased somewhat. Underlying this pattern were several large group escapes when the Ohio River froze in the unusually cold winters of the early to mid-1850s.

Finally, these newspaper references often indicated whether (the slave-owner believed) a fugitive slave received any assistance and from whom. As the last series of tables reveals, most fugitive slave references mentioned no knowledge or suspicion of assistance of the type associated with the Underground Railroad.

With more organized and active "friends of the fugitive" in the 1850s, assistance was sought and rendered more often — and far more often than indicated in records created only at the point and time at which an escape began. These patterns will be explored in later sections.

TABLE III-10

Kentucky Fugitive Slave Data Base: Escapes by Weekday

	Before 1850		1850 and After		Total	
	N	%	N	%	N	%
Sunday	51	10.8	138	19.1	189	15.8
Monday	58	12.3	51	7.0	109	9.1
Tuesday	39	8.3	28	3.9	67	5.6
Wednesday	53	11.2	49	6.8	102	8.5
Thursday	36	7.6	33	4.6	69	5.8
Friday	51	10.8	16	2.2	67	5.6
Saturday	49	10.4	80	11.0	129	10.8

Note: Chi-Square (N= 464, df = 7) = 100.81, p < .001

TABLE III-11

Kentucky Fugitive Slave Data Base: Escapes by Season

	Before 1850		1850 and After		Total	
	N	%	N	%	N	%
Winter (December–February)	121	25.6	213	29.4	334	27.9
Spring (March–May)	99	21.0	168	23.2	267	22.3
Summer (June–August)	112	23.7	186	25.7	298	24.9
Autumn (September–November)	140	29.7	157	21.7	297	24.8
Total	472		724		1196	

Note: Chi-Square (N= 1196, df = 4) = 10.46, p < .03

Still, some portion of the perceived increase in aid may be attributable to southern fears of anti-slavery "bogeymen" since, given the proliferation of white slave catchers and even some African American informants, most fugitives feared risking their hope of freedom by trusting others unless absolutely necessary.

Fugitives escaping through the Kentucky borderland could receive three principle types of aid. "Enticing" entailed an exchange of information intended to persuade a fugitive to escape or simply to facilitate his or her escape. "Conducting" entailed more active involvement in an escape such as guiding, accompanying or transporting. "Harboring" entailed concealing a fugitive. Based solely on what was stated in a particular newspaper item or record, slaveholders believed that their

TABLE III-12

Kentucky Fugitive Slave Data Base:
Aided and Unaided Escapes

	Before 1850		1850 and After		Total	
	N	%	N	%	N	%
No Assistance Suspected	382	80.9	486	69.1	868	73.9
Assistance Suspected	90	19.1	217	30.9	307	26.1
Total	472		703		1,175	

Note: Chi-Square (N= 1175, df = 1) = 20.372, p < .001

TABLE III-13

Kentucky Fugitive Slave Data Base:
Type of Aid Received

	Before 1850		1850 and After		Total	
	N	%	N	%	N	%
Enticing	30	33.3	28	13.1	58	19.1
Harboring	44	48.9	60	28.0	104	34.2
Conducting	16	17.8	126	58.9	142	46.7
Total	90		214		304	

Note: Chi-Square (N= 304, df = 2) = 44.580, p < .001

runaways were aided as shown in Table III-13.

As these data suggest, the most common type(s) of aid believed to have been received by Kentucky fugitive slaves—in Kentucky—before 1850 could be categorized as information and sanctuary. After 1850, "friends of the fugitive" played a more active role in actually conducting fugitives, primarily across the Ohio River.

Most of the reported or suspected assistance came from other African Americans. Interestingly, this pattern, as depicted in Table III-14, did not change significantly after 1850.

The form and content of fugitive slave advertisements and related news items did not vary in any meaningful way across different regions of the United States. Con-

sequently, some of the patterns identified in the Kentucky Fugitive Slave Data Base can be compared directly to those examined in Franklin and Schweninger's study of fugitive slaves. Their sample focused principally on the southern interior and included fugitive slave advertisements drawn from newspapers in Virginia, Louisiana, North Carolina, South Carolina and Tennessee—divided into early (1790–1816) and late (1838–1860) periods.[4] The results of this comparison reveal the extent to which the escape patterns and personal characteristics of runaways fleeing from or through Kentucky differed from or resembled those of fugitives in other regions of the United States.

Roughly 80 percent of all fugitives in Franklin and Schweninger's sample were

TABLE III-14

Kentucky Fugitive Slave Data Base:
Race of Suspected "Friends of the Fugitive"

	Before 1850		1850 and After		Total	
	N	%	N	%	N	%
Blacks	49	55.1	105	49.8	154	51.3
Whites	37	41.6	92	43.6	129	43.0
Blacks and Whites	0	0.0	11	5.2	11	3.7
Unknown	3	3.4	3	1.4	6	2.0
Total	89		211		300	

Note: Chi-Square = not significant

male, with the percentage representation of males remaining constant over time. As shown in Table III-8, Kentucky patterns resembled these national patterns quite closely before 1850. However, the representation of females increased in Kentucky after 1850 although they remained a minority of fugitives.[5] Similarly, the average age of fugitives in Franklin and Schweninger's sample was 25 years in the early period and 27 in the later. Once again, Kentucky patterns were quite similar to the larger sample in the early period, with an average age of 25 years, but fugitives were somewhat "younger" in the later period in Kentucky — while "older" elsewhere.[6] Clearly, proximity to free territory made escape a more attractive prospect for women, children and even older African Americans. Still, young men in their teens and twenties were the most likely fugitives, perhaps because

> … many realized that if they did not make an attempt to escape time would run out. Death came early to slaves, and those who reached their twenty-first birthday could expect to live about sixteen or seventeen additional years…. This, coupled with the energy and vitality of youth and the physical stamina it took to go on the run, prompted young men to leave in greatest numbers.[7]

In the larger sample, "most runaways were black" in both the early and late periods, but, as Franklin and Schweninger observe:

> Although a minority of runaways were mulattoes, persons of mixed racial ancestry ran away in greater numbers than their proportion in the slave population would suggest. Except for the virtual elimination of African-born blacks, the increase among mulatto runaways between the early and late periods represented one of the most significant changes that occurred…. The nearly one-third mixed blood among runaways during the early period was … at least three times larger than would be expected…. By the later period, the proportion of advertised mulattoes had risen to 43 percent, more than four times what would be expected … this large percentage was remarkable.[8]

This pattern was even more pronounced in Kentucky, as reflected in Table III-9, where an actual majority of all fugitives were described as mulattoes. Interestingly, the proportion of mulattoes was greatest in the early period in Kentucky, while the reverse was true in the larger sample.

Fugitives in both samples were likely to escape on the weekends and likely to escape alone.[9] Autumn was the least popular season for fugitives in Franklin and Schweninger's sample throughout the antebellum period. However, autumn was the most popular escape season in Kentucky before 1850, but became the least popular thereafter.[10]

Based on the analysis and comparison of these quantitative data, several provisional conclusions may be drawn. Runaways in the aggregate were a diverse group and enslaved African Americans escaping from or through Kentucky were no less diverse than fugitives from the southern interior. Yet, however great the differences within the sample of Kentucky fugitives, the differences between this sample and the fugitives studied by Franklin and Schweninger were even more interesting—even when such differences were slight. In essence, the profile of the typical fugitive slave differed by region much as the conditions of slavery varied by region. More interesting still was the stability in the profiles of fugitives from the southern interior over time in contrast to the changing composition of the Kentucky fugitive slave population. As Franklin and Schweninger note:

> It would probably be difficult to find any group in the United States that changed less over a period of seventy years.... [I]t revealed the nature of slave resistance, those who could best defy the system with even a remote chance of success— young, strong, healthy, intelligent men — continued to do so relentlessly from one generation to another.[11]

With respect to Kentucky, this conclusion holds—but only to a point. As the Tables above describe, Kentucky's fugitive slave population and escape patterns not only differed from those of the southern interior, but the nature and magnitude of the differences changed over time. Undoubtedly, the "fugitive as young warrior" motif remained important. However, proximity to free territory and, as the following

sections will explore at length, to support networks comprised of blacks and whites made flight a more viable option for older African Americans, women and children. In other words, the borderland afforded unique opportunities and posed unique challenges for fugitive slaves.

Fugitive Slaves Before 1850

The patterns revealed in the Kentucky Fugitive Slave Data Base are only the beginning, not the end, of understanding fugitive slaves and those who assisted them. Beyond serving as sources of data, the advertisements and articles of which the Data Base is comprised contain useful qualitative information that conveys much regarding fugitive slaves, slaveholders and the society in which both lived. The nature of slavery was such that, as property under American law, African Americans were usually shrouded in anonymity as individuals. While these snippets of descriptive information are not equivalent to short biographies, they are often the only statements in public records that reveal anything about fugitive slaves as people.

Even the least informative advertisements contained some sort of description of the physical appearance of the fugitive in question. For example, on March 1, 1788, Isaac ran away from John Campbell, who once owned much of western Louisville. Campbell described Isaac as "a small pale coloured fellow, hook nosed, and has lost the toes off one of his feet, very artful and insinuating and impudent...."[12] In 1823, William C. Bullitt of the Oxmoor plantation in Jefferson County advertised for the return of Ben Johnston, "a remarkably stout fellow ... light black color, about 34 or 35 years old. His ears have been bored for ear rings." Bullitt, to whom Johnston may have been hired out, noted that the fugitive was the property of John

Speed of Farmington, another major Jefferson County slaveholder.[13]

Norbon escaped from Bourbon County in June 1836. His owner, James Hughart, described Norbon as "a very bright mulatto; would be taken as a white boy if not closely examined."[14] At the opposite extreme, Ephraim, who ran away from William P. Sale & Co. of Louisville in 1841, was described as "not very black but full blood African"— at a time when probably less than one percent of the African American population was African-born.[15] On August 6, 1848, Harry Straughes and Tom Myers escaped from George W. Grant of Lexington, while an unnamed "mulatto boy" ran away from H. T. Duncan. There was no indication that the "mulatto boy" escaped with the other two. However, all were described cryptically, but interestingly. Straughes, twenty-eight years old, had a "heavy suit of hair, throws his head back, and wears his hat on the side of his head." Myers, about twenty-one years old, "stammers when spoken to." The "mulatto boy" had "gray eyes, fixy hair, genteel appearance" and was "slender made."[16]

Wyatt escaped from David W. Yandell, one of Louisville's most prominent physicians, in June 1852. Yandell offered a $100 reward and described Wyatt as "copper colored, 25 or 26 years old … of large frame, slow and heavy gait … a full head of hair which he combs to the side, quite a pleasing look, and is very likely." Yandell added that Wyatt's "wife is the property of Thos. G. Rowland, Esq., of this city."[17] Along similar lines, Nelson escaped from D. R. Haggard of Burksville in October 1854. Haggard advertised for Nelson's return and noted that the fugitive had a "black complexion," was "rather good looking, quite sensible — has been shot in the wrist with shot. His toes were frosted last winter and are not well yet."[18] On December 20, 1855, Dick ran away from John B. Akin of Danville. Akin described Dick as "about 25 years, of black color, 160 pounds … rather stoop shoul-

dered, has a down look, crooks himself somewhat when walking … and carries his left hand as if he has but little use of it."[19]

While slaveholders stood to benefit from portraying slaves offered for sale or hire in the most attractive "light," slaves who had the temerity to flee or challenge slavery were usually described in rather unflattering terms. This language reflected the standpoint of slaveholders, but, perhaps unwittingly, highlighted traits that could be considered strengths from another point of view. For example, in June 1794, Plato and Easter escaped from Fredericks County, Virginia and were believed bound for the western country. Plato was described as "…30 years of age, thick set and well made, much pitted with the small pox, a forward talkative fellow, and professes to be a kind of Baptist teacher" or, perhaps, a preacher. Easter was "seventeen years old, pretty … and appears to be pregnant." They were believed to have a (forged) pass, probably written by Plato since either a "teacher" or preacher was likely to be at least minimally literate.[20]

Giles, "sometimes called Cudge," ran away from Bennet Barrow of West Feliciana, Louisiana in June 1831. Barrow stated that "he is a good field hand, cook, accustomed to the water, a good house servant…. He is a negro of good sense and much ingenuity: and there are but few better qualified to make their escape than he is."[21] In contrast to the grudging respect betrayed in this testimonial, B. H. Hall of Jefferson County described Isabel, "a Negro Woman" who escaped from his farm in October 1831, in considerably less flattering, but still oddly ambivalent, terms. Hall declared that Isabel fled "without provocation" and that she was "remarkably alert, and exceedingly loquacious, unless observed by those who expect her services." He added that she was "fond of whiskey, and when under its influence talks much about religion" and was "probably the most deceitful of her race."[22]

Few Americans in the antebellum period had more than a few changes of clothing. Enslaved African Americans usually had even fewer and of lesser quality. For this reason, slave holders routinely included clothing in their descriptions of fugitives—assuming that, much as the fugitive could not alter (at least, not easily) his or her physical appearance, the fugitive was equally unlikely to change his or her clothing. For example, Jes, who escaped bondage in Scott County in 1795, was described ungrammatically but dressed memorably and "had on when he went away wooling overalls and a coat which was died a lead color but was worn white, the sleeves was pieced from the elbow down to the wrist, and a striped jacket, the stripes goes round the body."[23] On July 13, 1796, "a mulatto woman, aged about twenty-five years, named Sal" ran away from John Peebel of Bourbon County. Based on two possible outfits, Sal was described as a "...common sized woman, has stones in her ears ... her cloathing was either a calico habit, blue stuff petticoat, shawl handkerchief, or a striped short cotton jacket, striped linsey petticoat, and a spotted silk handkerchief, a high crowned wool hat."[24]

Jorden escaped from John Steele of Lexington on January 27, 1826. Steele described him as wearing "...a black fur hat, a blue cassinet roundabout, a pair of gray cassinet pantaloons, a pair of boots (nearly new), a pair of fine shoes, and other clothing."[25] Harry, owned by John W. Morrision of Oldham County,

Thirty Dollars Reward.

Ran away from the subscriber, living in Oldham county, Ky. on the 27th of March last, a mulatto woman, named LUCY, between 25 and 28 years of age, about 5 feet 5 or 6 inches high, wears her hair long, before, in plaits—clothing not recollected. The above reward will be given, for said negro, if she is taken out of the state and confined so that I get her again—or twenty dollars, if taken in the state, and confined in ike manner—and all reasonable charges paid, if delivered to me.

HENRY CAPLENGER.

may 10—792ds3

$20 REWARD.

Ran away from the subscriber, living in Louisville, on the night of the 18th inst. a negro man, named

MOSES,

About 30 years of age, about 5 feet 9 or 10 inches high, very black, stout and square built, has a scar on the inside of one of his hands, caused by a burnt whether accidental, or for his rascality, is no-known. He has thick lips, speaks freely and pert-ly, and has heavy eyebrows. He is believed to have worn, when he left home, a blue cloth coat, yellow Nankin pantaloons, and a watch in his pock-et. He had, however, other clothing, in a pair of saddlebags, and may change his dress. Moses can read, and I am informed, can write, and it is believed he will attempt to pass as a free man; and that he is endeavoring to make his way to Tennessee. I am also informed, he had from twenty to thirty dollars with him.

☞The above reward will be given, for ap-prehending and securing said negro, in this state or Tennessee, so that I get him again; or forty dol-lars, for apprehending and securing him on the north side of the Ohio river, so that I get him again; and all reasonable expenses will be paid, for bringing him home.

SHAPLEY OWEN.

may 20—795ds3

Fugitive slave notices: "Lucy" and "Moses," *Louisville Public Advertiser*, May 22, 1826. These notices are good examples of descriptions of the clothing and physical characteristics of fugitives.

$75 REWARD.—Ran away, on Saturday, the 15th inst., a copper colored Negro Woman, named MILDRED, about 28 years old, good looking, about middle height, has a wen half as large as a quail's egg on one of her wrists. Wore away a mousseline de laine dress and kid slippers.

I will give the above reward for her apprehension if taken out of this State, or $25 if taken in the State, in either case to be delivered in Louisville, and pay all reasonable expenses.

june 18 d3&w4*   JOSEPH J. DENNY.

Fugitive slave notice: "Mildred," *Louisville Journal,* June 18, 1844.

was hired to the Jones Hotel in Louisville and escaped in February 1854. Morrison offered a $200 reward and added that Harry "has with him several suits of good clothing, among which is a black cloth coat with red lining. Supposed to have had on when he left a green frock coat, black hat and dark pants."[26]

Enslaved African Americans had few personal possessions and the opportunity to accumulate a small wardrobe was highly prized. Such a small wardrobe, acquired or stolen, gave fugitive African Americans the ability to change identity by changing their outward apparel. However, slave-owners and slave catchers were well aware that fugitives often used this stratagem to advantage and, consequently, descriptions of clothing became less detailed and figured far less prominently in notices placed the decade before the Civil War.

Many fugitives were literate, skilled or otherwise accomplished, and their skills and abilities were often used to facilitate escape. For example, Moses, who escaped from Montgomery County, Tennessee in 1819, was described as being "about twenty eight years of age, of the common stature, has a pleasant countenance, very sensible for a Negro." His owner added that Moses would probably "endeavor to get to a free State and commence shoemaking as he has served a little time in that business."[27] In 1822, Ned was sold from Lexington "down the river" to Thomas Fearn of Huntsville, Alabama. Ned escaped in December 1823 and Fearns noted that the fugitive "reads and writes intelligibly."[28] John Todd ran away from W. T. Barry of Lexington in September 1825 and was described as having "...a dark complexion, about 27 years old ... likely, with a lively intelligent countenance and accustomed to waiting in the house, plays the violin and is fond of company."[29] Similarly, Charles escaped from John Speed of Jefferson County in 1826. Betraying considerable respect for Charles' abilities, Speed stated that "he is a very intelligent fellow and remarkably handy; being a shoemaker, working mostly with pegs, preferring to make pegged shoes, and does very good work. He is an excellent gardener—very handy at butchering—can lay brick, etc."[30]

Cynthia, along with being pregnant when she ran away from J. W. Thornberry of Louisville in 1831, had also "learned to read."[31] Frank and Fiatte escaped from John F. Gillespie of Natchez, Mississippi on November 10, 1832. In his advertisement for their return, Gillespie noted that Frank "reads and writes a little, and a blacksmith by trade."[32] Sam Dorsey, who escaped from Mrs. L. M. Bate of Jefferson County in 1836, was described as being "stout made, and very black, fine countenance, large eyes, quick spoken and may be considered intelligent."[33] In May 1841, W. B. Phillips of Jefferson County described Marshall Hawe as "...timid in disposition, polite and mild when spoken to, and very awkwardly to his walk.... He writes indifferently and reads pretty well, and may avail himself of these qualifications to effect his escape."[34] In much the same vein, Martin, who escaped from William Elliot of Meade County in February 1848, was described as a "negro" who "reads and writes tolerably well."[35]

In March 1850, J. H. Owen mentioned that his lost bondsman, Lewis, "loves to play at cards, and is an adept at chuckerluck."[36] Jack, who escaped from Sidney R. Smith in July 1851 "...could play a little on the banjo" and "was fond of playing at night after his work was done."[37] Tom ran away from John Tevis of Shelbyville in December 1852. In advertising for Tom's return, Tevis noted that the fugitive "writes quite a good hand, and will probably provide himself with a pass."[38] Henry Adkins, who ran away from Mrs. Mary Carll in July 1853, was described as "about 28 years old, very dark color ... trimly built, pleasant countenance, talks glibly, of rather genteel appearance, and reads and writes well."[39] Tom ran away from W. G. Hight of Bedford County, Tennessee in December 1855. Hight offered a $100 reward for Tom and noted that Tom "wears his hair plaited" and "...was a good scholar.... He signs his name Tom Wadleigh."[40]

Some fugitives had no intention of leaving slave territory, at least not immediately. While such escapes were far less common in the borderland than in the southern interior, evidence that they were suspected or did occur appears occasionally in antebellum newspapers and other records. For example, Jim and Lewis, who escaped from Lexington in June 1788, "were lately moved from Cumberland county in Virginia" and their owner, B. Wilson, believed that "they may endeavor to pass through the wilderness to the place of their nativity."[41] In 1803, Charles was sold from Jessamine County to Thomas M. Green of the Mississippi Territory. When Charles escaped, it was presumed that he would attempt to return to Jessamine County, "having a wife and children there."[42] John, "a remarkably likely genteel negro man," escaped from W. C. Warfield of Hopkinsville in December 1827. Warfield believed that John "will attempt to go to Lexington, as he was

brought by me from that place; by some means he may have gotten a pass, or attempt to induce others to believe he is a free man."[43] In *Ellis v. Gosney* (April 1829), a suit was brought for the value of Tom, who "fled from the state and took refuge among the Indians."[44] As another example, Horace and Bill escaped together from a hemp factory near Paris, Kentucky. Their owner — Adams, Reynolds and Company — feared they were bound either for Canada, probably via Louisville, or for Georgia, "whence they were brought."[45]

Henry, who escaped from S. Spragens of Jessamine County in 1844, had no immediate plans to leave slave territory, but was thought to be seeking his "wife at Isaac G. Carter's, near Harrodsburg."[46] Family also played a key role in the choice of destinations made by Bob after escaping from the steamboat, Commodore Perry, in 1847. Bob, who was owned by James Rouse of Henderson County had "a mother and brother living in Louisville" and was "probably making his way to them."[47] Similarly for John Morris, who ran away from H. H. Sale of Louisville in July 1847 and who was thought to be seeking his "wife about 14 miles beyond Bardstown, Nelson County, Kentucky."[48]

Notwithstanding occasional exceptions, most fugitives escaping from or through Kentucky aimed at free territory. However, the location of free territory changed as early American history unfolded. In pioneer Kentucky, the Northwest Territory was an attractive, but often uncertain, destination for fugitive slaves as encroaching American settlements provoked widespread hostilities with numerous Native American societies. For example, in April 1794, twenty-five year old Aaron ran away from General George Taylor of Clark County. He was captured two days later and jailed in Lexington, but escaped again and was believed bound for "the north west side of the Ohio."[49] Likewise, the "two likely young Negroe fellows" who escaped from Madison County in March 1799 were "both armed with smooth bored guns and its is expected they are aiming for the north west side of the Ohio, and in all probability will endeavor to pass for free men."[50]

By the early 1800s and definitely after the War of 1812, the Northwest Territory was settled by large numbers of pioneers and the Native Americans were driven out. Thus, crossing the frontier became less attractive to fugitives than crossing the Ohio River boundary between the slave and free states in the west. For example, in June 1821, Charles escaped from Shepherdsville. His owner, Jacob Bowman had reason to believe that Charles was bound for "the state of Indiana or Ohio" through Louisville and that "he may have obtained a free pass, being a very shrewd, cunning fellow." This advertisement appeared for several months with no indication that the fugitive was ever recaptured.[51] In July 1824, rewards were offered for the apprehension of Jack, who escaped from his owner near Harrodsburg, Kentucky, and Bill, who escaped from Columbia, Tennessee, both believed to be moving toward the Ohio River.[52] John, who escaped from Fayetteville, Tennessee in 1822, had "several scars on his back, as if done by a whip." His owner, Henry Roberson, believed that John would "aim (if not conducted by some person) for Illinois, and will try to pass himself for a free person."[53] In 1825, Isaac and Paddy were purchased from Henderson County, Kentucky by Charles Bosley of Nashville. The pair escaped at the first opportunity, were believed to "have money, the amount not known, but believed to be about thirty or forty dollars" and attempting to return to Kentucky and ultimately to reach free territory "west of the Ohio."[54] Frank escaped from Thomas Buckner of Louisville in September 1825, crossed into Indiana, but was captured and jailed in Corydon. Within a few weeks, he escaped again and, presumably, con-

tinued his journey north.[55] Similarly, when George ran away from Elijah Nuttall in 1830, Nuttall stated that "I had him hired at the mouth of the Salt River, from which he crossed over into the state of Indiana with a negro of Henry Ditto's, who has since been taken"[56] The Ditto family, incidentally, will figure prominently in another slave escape in 1850s that will be discussed later in this study.

Irene ran away from George W. Goldman of Jefferson County in December 1838. By September 1839, she remained at large and was "supposed to be in the State of Indiana."[57] Bob and Garrett, two brothers enslaved near Frankfort, escaped from Charles O'Hara in 1842. O'Hara stated that "...they will aim for a free State, and will be inclined to linger about large towns and cities, being active and ingenious jobbers and waiters about such places. They will, perhaps, assume the surname Cox."[58]

Dick, who escaped from John B. Akin of Danville, in December 1855, had "a wife living near Jacksonville, Illinois, who goes by the name of Martha Duncan and he may be making for that direction."[59] Jerry ran away from M. L. Huffman of Robertson County, Tennessee in January 1856. Huffman's advertisement for Jerry's return indicated that the fugitive "was seen in the neighborhood of Middletown, Jefferson county."[60] George escaped from William McGraw of Boyle County in January 1859. McGraw offered a $100 reward and described George as "likely, quick spoken, and polite in his manners," adding "I think he will make for a free State."[61] Similarly, when Frank ran away from Stilwell H. Wekefield of Bullitt County in March 1859, Wekefield noted that "he started towards Louisville, and I think he will make for a free state."[62]

As the Kentucky Fugitive Slave Data Base indicates and as these advertisements confirm, most escapes during this period involved African American men — usually in their late teens through early thirties—

who fled as individuals as opposed to fleeing in groups (a practice more characteristic of African-born fugitives). Still, some group escapes did occur. One that proved a tragic failure took place in October 1849 at West Point, Kentucky and was reported in *The North Star*. Three fugitives ran away, but were overtaken by one of their owners, J. G. Guthrie, and two other men "at the first toll gate on the Salt River road." The article continued:

> When the negroes were surrounded and required to surrender two of them immediately did so. The third — Tom, took the double barrelled shotgun which was in the hands of one of his companions ... swearing at the same time that he would never be taken alive, cocked and commenced raising the gun. At this moment one of the white men discharged a double barrelled fowling piece, loaded with buck-shot at him. One of the shots took effect in the upper jaw.... His recovery is doubtful.[63]

One court case that concluded in the 1850s originated decades before and involved African Americans who were fugitives for more "technical" reasons. In *Anderson, et al. v. Crawford* (January 1855), Milly was a slave whose white father, B. Ray, wished to emancipate but neglected to do so in writing before his death in 1819. As a result, Milly became the property of Ray's daughter, her half-sister, Mrs. Crawford, and remained so until about 1830

> ... when she left with her husband, a free man of color, she being then about 18 years of age.... Crawford made no effort to apprehend her or her children, for a period of nearly 20 years, during a great part of which she was in the adjoining county ... until she left her first husband, and went into a free state, as is supposed with another free man of color.... Milly had four children, all of whom she left behind and of whom three are claiming their freedom.
>
> The Court ruled that the children were free.[64]

By design, few of the documents selected for review and analysis in this section referred directly or indirectly to any sort of assistance received by fugitives— or to any sort of assistance the fugitive expected to receive. Of course, simply because assistance of the type associated with the Underground Railroad was not mentioned does not mean that it was not rendered in many of these cases— only that there is no evidence to that effect. However, these advertisements for individuals or small groups of fugitives who escaped unaided correspond quite closely to the accounts found in many slave narratives and other records left by former slaves.[65]

Fugitive Slaves in the 1850s

By the 1850s, fugitive slave advertisements remained commonplace, but news articles and court reports became particularly numerous and particularly useful sources of historical evidence for reasons related directly to the deepening conflict between North and South. Tensions related to slave escapes were most intense in the border states, as William Freehling notes perceptively:

> Explaining southern motivation for the Fugitive Slave Law requires precision about which Southerners are being analyzed.... On this peculiar occasion, the usually most intransigent South was the least demanding. In the Congress of 1850, Deep South senators emphasized that this "useless" bill measured up dismally against proposed northern gains. Border senators, normally the least insistent Southerners, were the most aggressive on the subject. Kentucky, Maryland, and Virginia ... "have their attention turned closely to the subject...." Not that many slaves had to escape before losses totaled "hundreds of thousands of dollars" annually.... While "very few" Northerners committed "this larceny ... there are enough of them to create serious concern"[66]

In essence, slave escapes were no longer viewed as an unavoidable "cost of doing business" for slave-owners, but were considered volleys in the ideological war between North and South. Successful escapes were attributed to the perfidy of "Abolitionist Shriekers" or "stinking Abolitionists." Failed escape attempts were publicized widely and used to bolster southern confidence that the system of rewards and patrols could deter or frustrate escapes. Slave-owners may have also believed that, since some African Americans could read, articles touting the utter futility of escape attempts and the unfriendly reception awaiting fugitives in the North or Canada might serve to dissuade others contemplating flight.

In particular, enforcing the new Fugitive Slave law in the South and insisting on its enforcement in the North became a socially approved preoccupation in Kentucky and other southern newspapers. In response, the passage of "personal liberty" statutes and the refusal to surrender fugitives became defiant acts of opposition in northern states such as Ohio. Once again, the meaning of slave escapes and aid to fugitives changed as the politics of slavery changed.

As revealed in the Data Base and the many examples cited thus far, the patterns of Kentucky slave escapes and the characteristics of fugitives escaping from or through Kentucky also changed in this decade of crisis. Fugitive slaves became more numerous and more diverse. There were more females, children and older runaways in the 1850s. Runaways were somewhat less likely to be racially mixed. Slave escapes became more structured — by time of week and time of year, with more escapes occurring on weekends and in the winter months. Assistance became more important as police measures became more stringent. The fact that assistance was only available in certain places tended to channel or, more accurately, funnel fugitives as never before along well-defined escape corridors to and through the borderland.

In particular, enslaved African Americans fled more often in groups and one reason for the mounting unease of Kentucky slaveholders in the 1850s was the larger number of fugitives involved in these escapes. For example, in May 1851, the following report was reprinted from the *Maysville Post Boy*:

> During the past week, a leave-taking fever has prevailed among the slaves in this section. On Sunday night, a woman and three children, the property of F. M. Weedon of our city left. On Wednesday night, nineteen in one gang left their owners in Lewis— eight belonging to Mrs. Eliza Shepperd, two to Chas. Wood, and the remainder, owners names not ascertained. From Nicholas several have also departed for freedom during the past few days.[67]

In August 1852, five enslaved African Americans escaped from Mr. C. Q. Armstrong of Louisville. The fugitives "...were taken yesterday morning near Charlestown, Indiana. The four are the woman and her three children. They were found secreted in a negro house, and covered up with a feather bed. The missing woman, it is supposed, has made good her escape."[68] A month later, the remaining fugitive from this unfortunate party, "a girl about 18 years old, was caught...." According to the young woman, she had "concealed herself about the city since she left home."[69] In the next week, "fourteen slaves ran away from Burlington, Ky. They belonged to the following individuals: Ten to Ephraim Porter, two to J. G. Hamilton, one to Dr. J. F. Grubbs, and one to C. L. Sandford."[70] In April 1853, "about twenty slaves belonging to the citizens of Boone county, escaped from their masters." Their plan was well-laid and "at last accounts nothing had been heard of them." The article concluded "they were no doubt aided by Abolitionists of Ohio or Indiana."[71] In June 1854, a mass escape occurred in northern Kentucky, when "twenty-three negroes owned in Grant and adjoining counties, left their masters' roofs, and escaped to the Licking river." There, "they lashed together several canoes ... rowed down the Licking river to the Ohio and crossed." The article stated that the party "disembarked and made a circuitous route to the northern part of Cincinnati."[72]

On October 25, 1854, "another stampede in the slave population of Bourbon took place.... About 15 slaves decamped." One fugitive was soon captured and two others were "seen in the vicinity of Mayslick." The other fugitives remained at large.[73] The small-scale exodus from Bourbon County continued when, only a month later, another news report appeared, this time reprinted from the *Cincinnati Gazette*:

> We learn that during Sunday evening eight negroes, five men and three women, belonging to Jas. Hatfield, of Bourbon county, Ky., made their escape, and it is thought that they crossed the Ohio river a few miles below this city, from the fact that two skiffs fastened on the Kentucky side were found the following morning drifted a short distance down the river on the Ohio side. Mr. H. was in the city on Tuesday and left again in the evening in pursuit of the fugitives, who, he was informed ... were en route for Canada.[74]

To the east, "fourteen slaves decamped from Maysville" in December 1854. The article added that "the negro population of Mason is rapidly becoming decimated by the system of fleeing to freedom."[75] In May 1855, "five slaves belonging to Mr. M. Giltner of Hunter's Bottom, Ky., left for the North," after using a stolen skiff to cross the Ohio River near Carrollton. As reported in a reprint of an article from the *Carrollton Times*, "suspicion soon fastened on a free negro named Edmund Prince" who "was seen on the opposite side of the

river during the preceding evening"—and who had "long been suspected of being connected with the under-ground railway...." Prince was eventually arrested and jailed in Carrollton, although General William Butler, Kentucky hero of the Mexican War and member of the family that formerly owned Prince, interceded on his behalf.[76]

In June 1855, "three negroes, belonging to a Mr. Byrne, of Orange Grove, Bourbon county, Ky., made their escape Thursday, and crossed the river about ten miles below Cincinnati."[77] Charles W. Levering offered a $200 reward for the return of "my negro woman, Matilda, about 24 years old," who "also took with her, her two female children, one about 2 years and the other about eight months old"—when they escaped from Louisville in September 1855.[78] In October 1855, "Ben, a likely colored man, the property of Capt. Wm. C. Hite, escaped from the jail together with a another negro from Spencer county."[79] Ben crossed the river "at the saw mills, and immediately took the line of the Jeffersonville railroad." He was captured in Vienna, Indiana, then escaped on a stolen horse. He was then set upon by dogs and captured again and escaped yet again. Eventually, he was captured and returned to Louisville.[80]

A week after Ben's initial escape, "two negro men escaped form Mr. Garrison's pen, one of whom was caught soon after, but the other succeeded in eluding pursuit and is still at large."[81] In December 1855, "some ten or twelve slaves have, within the last week, made their escape from Maysville and its vicinity. Several have also escaped from Covington."[82] In February 1856, as reported in the *Cincinnati Commercial*, "six slaves, three men, two women and a child, belonging to Mr. Winburne, of Kenton county, Ky., made their escape from bondage night before last." The Ohio River was frozen as Kentucky was in the grips of one of its coldest winters on

$300 REWARD—NEGRO WOMAN AND THREE CHILDREN RANAWAY.

Ranaway from the subscriber, in Jefferson county, Ky., on Tuesday night, October 5th, a NEGRO WOMAN about 26 years old, of bright yellow color and straight hair. She speaks very fluently, has an erect walk, and a scar on her face below the eye, made by a finger nail. Her name is Betsy. She took along with her THREE CHILDREN—Emma, 5 years old, with a wen over one of her eyes; Munson, a boy about 4 years old; and Laura, a girl about two years old. The children are all of a bright yellow color. The woman, Betsy, was far advanced in pregnancy, probably about eight months.

The above reward will be paid if they are caught and put in jail out of the State, so I get them; or $150 if they are caught in Kentucky and put in jail at Louisville.

o7 d&w if   HENRY BANTON.

Fugitive slave notice: "Betsy and children," *Louisville Courier*, October 4, 1858. Example of an escape of a pregnant woman and three children.

record and the fugitives "crossed the ice into this State a short distance below the Fifth Street ferry" and reached safety in Cincinnati.[83]

An 1855 Louisville news article reflected the mounting sense of both bewilderment and anxiety as slave escapes seemed impossible to control despite the power of the law and the ubiquity of the patrols: "There appears to be a regular and constant stampede going on among the slave population in the city and county, not a night scarcely passing without one or more running away…"[84] Matters did not improve over the next few years. The sheer volume of these escapes and the consternation caused thereby were conveyed in an 1858 *Louisville Courier* editorial that applied to many other sections of the state—"Negroes are daily and nightly escaping from their owners in startling numbers. They go off one, two, three, or a dozen at a time."[85]

Fugitive Slaves During the Civil War

Both the volume and significance of slave escapes escalated dramatically with the coming of Civil War. As with the American Revolution, the turmoil of war multiplied the opportunities for flight and the progressive shift in federal policy in favor of general emancipation, for all practical purposes, nullified the Fugitive Slave Act by mid-1862. The boundary between slavery and freedom became "fluid" as the Union army moved into and through Confederate territory. Under these conditions, enslaved African Americans emancipated themselves in massive numbers (probably more than 500,000 by War's end)—and, in the crucible of Civil War, the flight of African Americans from slavery became a social revolution that unfolded against the backdrop of military conflict.[86] Although long ignored by historians, the determination of African Americans to free themselves was both a cause and an effect of making emancipation a war aim, a change that transformed African American runaways from fugitives into refugees.[87]

The War itself and the floodtide of fugitives posed unique problems for Kentucky. When the War began, Kentucky attempted to declare and maintain its neutrality. However, the possibility of neutrality faded by September 1861 when the Confederacy "invaded" the state. Kentucky remained nominally loyal to the Union thereafter, but wanted "Union with slavery"—a political posture that, like the hope of neutrality, became increasingly untenable as the War progressed. Although the 1863 Emancipation Proclamation did not apply to the Commonwealth or the other "Union slave states" (Missouri, Maryland, Delaware, West Virginia), Kentucky could not isolate itself from the broader sweep of national history and slavery began to collapse in the state despite bitter opposition from slaveholders.[88] African Americans who had no intention on waiting for a government edict contributed significantly to this collapse — not by adopting a new strategy to undermine slavery, but by expanding, opportunistically, the use of the old one.

As one example, more fugitives crossed the Ohio River near Owensboro in four months in late 1861 than had done so in the previous fifty years.[89] As another, Louisville became critically important to the War effort in the "west," with more than 80,000 Union troops stationed in or near the city. Pontoon bridges moved war materiel across the Ohio River to the Louisville and Nashville Railroad (L&N) that supplied the "western" theatre of the War. A steady stream of fugitive slaves converged on Louisville. The city's free black community embraced and supported them and the Union army assisted, protected and, eventually, enlisted many of them.[90] As an equally graphic example, in the January 20, 1863 issue of the *Louisville Journal*, there were notices of twenty-seven fugitives being held in the Warren County jail alone and thirty-eight fugitive slave advertisements referencing fugitives from throughout the state and points south.[91]

Even after the Civil War, attempts to recover damages for lost slave property (and to oppose the concept, if not the fact, of emancipation) continued. For example, at issue in *Commonwealth v. Palmer* (October 1866) was a felony-indictment against General John Palmer, Commander of the Department of Kentucky (stationed at Louisville), for "...aiding Ellen, a slave of Womack, to escape from her owner in Kentucky to the State of Indiana.... [T]he slave went to Jeffersonville, Indiana, under cover of a passport issued for that purpose." The Court found Palmer guilty and added, in a statement that reflects Kentucky attitudes following the Civil War:

> President Lincoln's proclamation of emancipation, whatever else might be said of it, excepted Kentucky from its operation, and applied exclusively to the seceding States. That portentous document, therefore, afforded no semblance of pretext for a claim to freedom by the slaves of Kentucky. The unlawful intermeddling of General Palmer inciting a spirit of servile insurrection, and encouraging escapes from servitude, by assuring military protection, invited slaves to crowd Camp Nelson and other encampments of his army ... until but few were left at home, and farmers generally, and many residents of cities and towns, were suddenly left without their accustomed and necessary help, the long-established system of labor terribly disturbed, and citizens excited almost to revolution.[92]

Thus, by the time slavery ended officially in December 1865 (with the ratification of the Thirteenth Amendment), only a shadow of the former institution remained. In this most significant respect, the enslaved African Americans who acted courageously to secure their freedom exemplified the power of human agency and belong at the center of this history — as its true heroes and heroines. It is only fitting that self-emancipation through flight played so prominent a role in the final victory over the "peculiar institution."

From the Perspective of African Americans

Former slaves remembered escapes as important, but atypical events, as rare victories in a long struggle against a massive and formidable institution. Most enslaved African Americans did not risk escape, given the ubiquity of patrols by the 1850s, and the virtual certainty of terrible punishment and subsequent sale for those apprehended and returned. As James Campbell recalled, the fate of one unlucky fugitive, who was whipped nearly to death, "took any such notion out of my head." However, when another fellow slave, Henry

Jones, escaped and was never caught, Campbell added that all those left behind were "powerful glad."[93]

Dr. Henry H. Farmer was a slave-owner and physician in Henderson County who provided at least for the basic education of his bondspersons. Robert Cheatham belonged to a neighboring family and married a woman owned by Farmer. After the Civil War, Cheatham moved to Evansville, Indiana and, in 1937, was interviewed by Laura Creel of the Federal Writers' Project. Cheatham recalled that many of Farmer's enslaved African Americans were so well educated that they could easily escape — or help others escape — by forging entirely credible passes for travel across the Ohio River.[94] In a memorable case, Jim — Farmer's trusted overseer, escaped in the 1850s:

> Jim was smart too, no other Negro youth in that part of the country could read the Bible, the storybooks and letters like Jim could.... Jim had made out his own pass and was on his way to Canada. For many days and nights a posse of armed men both whites and blacks scoured the country in search of Jim Farmer but it was only after the Negroes were emancipated that any news of his whereabouts could be had.

After the Civil War, Jim returned to Kentucky, married and eventually moved to Evansville. There, his friends "often gathered at his cottage while he was a resident and enjoyed hearing him relate how he wrote his own pass into a land of freedom."[95]

During his many years in slavery, Harry Smith became familiar with most of the major slaveholders in the Louisville and Jefferson county area through his wagon-driving and his contacts with other enslaved African Americans— who, according to Smith, had a rather lively social life and a very complex social network largely unknown to whites. One of his more interesting experiences with fugitive slaves concerned "Bill Bullett" (probably William C. Bullitt of Oxmoor) in the 1830s and, perhaps, 1840s—one of the major slaveholders in Kentucky.[96] Smith recalled that "Bullett ... was a very good man, but his overseer was hard on the colored people.... Sometimes there would be several who would run away in the woods and remain several weeks at a time."[97] On one memorable occasion, thirteen fugitives from Tennessee hid in the forests of eastern Jefferson County. In his own words:

> Bullett had some in the woods at the same time. The Tennessee darkies and Bullett's came together and planned how they could get across the Ohio River successfully. They finally wove a lot of hemp together in strips of different lengths. The night was set, which was Saturday. They all met about nine miles above Louisville ... and made rafts.... Smith, with a number of others, assisted in getting them across. They were fed in the woods by Bullett's slaves, Smith, with the rest, doing all they could to assist them. Not learning any more of the fugitives, it was supposed that they reached Canada all safe.[98]

No mention was ever made of assistance from whites or anyone, black or white, on the Indiana side of the river.

As noted previously, many fugitives "never left the cotton kingdom" and others "preferred Mexico as their destination." However, "to the great majority of footloose slaves, the region above the Ohio River had one irresistible attraction Mexico lacked — a substantial black population like themselves in language and outlook."[99] Still, fugitive slaves could find freedom north of the Ohio River, but never security. Only by reaching foreign soil could a fugitive pass beyond the reach of fugitive slave laws, slave catchers and northern prejudice.

Given its northerly location and climate, the slave population of Canada was never large. Emancipatory efforts began in 1793 with the passage of a law that prohibited the further importation of en-slaved Africans and began the gradual emancipation of those already resident in Upper Canada. An 1803 court decision held that slavery in Lower Canada was inconsistent with British law. Consequently, slavery was all but dead long before the British Emancipation Act of 1833. Not surprisingly, Canada assumed almost mythical stature in the worldview of enslaved African Americans as a land of freedom. For this reason, more than 40,000 African Americans settled in Canada between 1830 and 1860.[100]

By the 1850s, the African American community extended into lower Canada. In essence, Canada had become the ultimate destination of fugitive slaves and the northern terminus of the Underground Railroad.

After the passage of the Fugitive Slave Act of 1850, conditions deteriorated for free blacks in the border states and the lower north. For this reason, many free African Americans began migrating from the border region to the more northerly states or to Canada. As an example of growing hostility toward free blacks, in Kentucky, a bill was "introduced that, if passed, would have bound out all free Negro children until they were of age." The system of local patrols was strengthened during the 1850s. These patrollers had great latitude "to visit the houses of free families at midnight,

search their houses, uncover females in their beds, and ask for runaway slaves."[101] William Gibson describes the panic that spread through Louisville's free black community, noting that "an exodus took place" and "families left this city to look for other quarters of freer soil. Some went to northern Ohio, Michigan, Canada, and others left in groups, prospecting for a place to settle."[102]

Finally, while fugitive slave notices, articles, and court and other records open intriguing windows into the lives of individual African Americans, it is important not to overlook the sheer quantity of such documents and the implications thereof. It is clear — based on this evidence — that the frequency of slave escapes from and through Kentucky was far greater than earlier studies and conventional wisdom have suggested. How much greater will be explored in some detail in Chapter VIII.

At this point in the study, it is sufficient simply to state the conclusion that Kentucky slave escapes were never a floodtide. If that were so, the institution of slavery would have melted away like summer snow. However, slave escapes were not rare and exceptional events — and runaway slaves were far more than a minor and manageable annoyance. Perhaps, this illegal out-migration pattern might best be characterized as a steady trickle before 1840, rising to a small stream by the 1850s.

CHAPTER IV

The Anatomy of Slave Escapes

I left because they were about selling my wife and children to the South. I would rather have followed them to the grave, than to see them go down....[1]
   Henry Morehead, 1856, formerly of Louisville, Kentucky

Each slave escape was an event with its own history, much as each fugitive or Underground Railroad worker was a protagonist with a unique and very personal role in that history. There were, however, common challenges confronting all fugitives that can be generalized broadly across the statistical universe of slave escapes in Kentucky (and elsewhere). Many of these challenges and the many strategies for meeting them can be gleaned from the Kentucky Fugitive Slave Data Base and the examples cited previously. However, viewed from a somewhat different perspective, these challenges— along with the human and physical geography of the trans–Appalachian west — lent pattern and structure to slave escapes. Understanding this structure, this anatomy as it were, is indispensable to understanding the formidable task(s) confronting fugitives and how, why and where the Underground Railroad evolved.

Motivations

Slave escapes were motivated by factors intrinsic to the lives and circumstances of fugitives themselves. In some cases, escapes were prompted by some discernible "trigger event." For example, the motives cited most frequently by fugitive slaves were physical or sexual mistreatment or the threat thereof, sale or the threat thereof, or broken promises (for example, if a slave-holder reneged on a promise to permit self-purchase). The threat of sale, with its impact on families, was particularly powerful in a "slave-trading" state such as Kentucky. In other cases, escapes seem to have been motivated only by the simple desire for freedom and, at times, pure opportunism.[2]

Runaway slaves would jeopardize their freedom to be near or seek to free loved ones. For example, in October 1788, James Wilkinson of Lexington offered "Eight Dollars Reward ... for Negro Ben." What is interesting in this otherwise routine fugitive slave notice is the statement that Ben "has a wife at Capt. Flowers, and probably lurks about that neighborhood...."[3] Although enslaved African Americans could not marry, legally, they were often permitted to marry in plantation ceremonies that included rituals such as "jumping the broom" or even in church ceremonies as Christianity became more common among African Americans.[4] Still, such references to wives or husbands appeared fairly often during this early period — for example, to "...a runaway slave, Tom, who has a wife at Stephen Rozel's,"[5]

to "...a runaway slave named Arthur whose wife belongs to Capt. Peter Poindexter of Jessamine County...,[6] and to "...a runaway, Randal, who has a wife at Gen. Levi Todd's."[7]

Fear for the fate of one's children, even those unborn, seems to have prompted many escapes involving enslaved African American women. However, even with considerable assistance, slave escapes were dangerous and physically demanding for African American men. Thus, given the risks of flight, escapes by pregnant women or women with children seemed particularly desperate and suggested either the operation of some powerful triggering event — or, perhaps, the expectation of significant assistance along the escape route that off-set the impracticalities of flight.

Such family considerations were central to the escape of Daphne in May 1821. As indicated in the advertisement placed by Temple Gwathmey of Louisville, "said woman took with her, her child about 4 months old, also a trunk of clothing. She has probably gone into the state of Indiana, as her husband lives in Jeffersonville."[8] Cynthia was pregnant when she "ran away from J. W. Thornberry of Louisville in 1831,"[9] as was Fanny when she escaped from W. H. Pope of Jefferson County in 1836. In seeking her return, Pope stated that she "will no doubt attempt to go to Canada, but may lurk a short time in the neighborhood of Mr. John Edwards, where she has a husband."[10] One can only wonder what prompted the escape of Comford, a twenty year-old woman owned by J. G. Guthrie of Westpoint. Guthrie noted that, in July 1848, Comford "left a child 10 months old and not weaned" and implied that, since "she once lived in Louisville" and "her mother now lives in Cincinnati," she might be

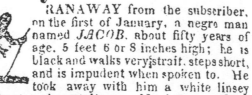

Twenty Dollars Reward.

RANAWAY from the subscriber, on the first of January, a negro man named JACOB, about fifty years of age, 5 feet 6 or 8 inches high; he is black and walks very strait, steps short, and is impudent when spoken to. He took away with him a white linsey roundabout and pantaloons. He has a wife at James Earickson's, in the Pond Settlement — He has been seen in Louisville and Shippingport.

I will give the above reward if taken out of the state, or ten dollars if taken in the state, and delivered to me or secured in the Louisville Jail.

ABIJAH SWEARINGEN.

Jefferson Co. Ky. Feb. 26.   458—6ds

Fugitive slave notice: "Jacob," *Louisville Public Advertiser,* February 26, 1823. Example of an older fugitive and the role of family relations in escapes; also of Louisville as an early harboring place.

bound toward one (or both) of those cities.[11]

In one of the most poignant accounts, a fugitive slave family, determined not to risk betrayal by asking for any assistance, made a courageous dash for freedom in 1854 and was rescued, ultimately, by friends of the fugitive. The husband, Henry Morehead, was interviewed in Canada in 1856, indicating that he had been "born and bred a slave" in Louisville, but that:

> I left slavery a little more than a year ago. I brought my wife and three children with me, and had not enough to bring us through…. I left because they were about selling my wife and children to the South. I would rather have followed them to the grave, than to see them go down … so I took them and started for Canada. I was pursued — my owners watched for me in a free State, but, to their sad disappointment, I took another road. A hundred miles further on, I saw my advertisements again offering $500 for me and my family…. I was longer on the road than I should have been without my burden: one child was nine months old, one two years old and one four. The weather was cold and my feet were frostbitten, as I gave my wife my socks to pull on over her shoes. With all the sufferings of the frost and the fatigues of travel, it was not so bad as the effects of slavery.[12]

Thus, although Morehead eventually "took the Underground Railroad" to complete his journey to Canada, his escape was unaided until its final phases — a testament to his courage and that of his family.

The fact or prospect of brutal physical punishment was often the proximate cause of an escape — the one indignity too many for an enslaved African American to endure. For example, John escaped from John Hogan in Franklin County Alabama on October 11, 1822. In advertising for John's return, Hogan stated that "he has made the attempt before" and that "his back is considerably scarred by a whipping he received the day previous to his going off."[13] In an especially graphic account,

Henry Bibb, a fugitive himself from Kentucky (whose exploits will be described in Chapter VII), introduced Lewis Richardson, another fugitive from Kentucky, on March 13, 1846 in Amherstburg, Canada West. Richardson, whose flight was prompted by a severe beating, proceeded to deliver a simple, but stirring, anti-slavery address. Concerning his illustrious former master, Richardson stated:

> I am free from American slavery, after wearing the galling chains on my limbs 53 years, 9 of which it has been my unhappy lot to be the slave of Henry Clay. It has been said by some, that Clay's slaves had rather live with him than be free, but I had rather this day, have a millstone tied to my neck, and be sunk to the bottom of Detroit River, than go back to Ashland and be his slave for life.[14]

Joseph Sanford was also a "trusted slave" in Campbell County, Kentucky. In the early 1850s, after being mistreated by an overseer, Sanford, his wife and four children, and eight others from the immediate vicinity resolved "to break and run away, hit or miss, live or die." One went to Covington and "made the arrangements." The party crossed the Ohio to Cincinnati in a skiff. They were nearly captured in Michigan, but were released by a judge and finally crossed the border into Canada.[15]

As an example of the impact of broken promises, George Williams was born enslaved in Virginia in 1802 and sold to a slaveholder in Maysville, Kentucky in 1816. After his owner reneged on a self-purchase agreement, Williams escaped in the 1830s, worked on an Ohio farm for six years and then migrated to Upper Canada. He moved to Canada West in 1841 and became active in anti-slavery politics in the 1850s.[16] In a similar vein, Kitty Ann ran away from A. Bodine in May 1858. Bodine offered a $100 reward for her return and described her has "about 23 years old, dark copper color … quick spoken and impertinent when spoken to; sets up a false claim to her freedom by the will of her mistress."[17] An even more famous fugitive, Josiah Henson was born enslaved in Maryland in 1789. An upright man, he became a respected plantation manager and minister. Henson had an opportunity to escape slavery in 1825 when he conveyed eighteen other enslaved African Americans to Kentucky, but followed his owner's instructions and returned. However, in 1830, after his owner reneged on a self-purchase agreement, Henson escaped to Upper Canada with his wife and four children.

Henson's personal history crosses into the stream of Kentucky history on two other occasions. According to his autobiography, he ventured secretly into the state twice to lead other enslaved African Americans to freedom and even as an aging man, he was an occasional conductor on the Underground Railroad. However, he became far better known as the model for the character, Uncle Tom, in Harriett Beecher Stowe's *Uncle Tom's Cabin*—incidentally, with its Kentucky setting. Before he died in 1883, he visited England, was presented to Queen Victoria and spoke to large crowds anxious to hear "the original Uncle Tom.[18]

Escape Strategies

A successful escape required information, planning, timing, resources (if possible), courage and good fortune. At one extreme, an enslaved African American could act on impulse or out of desperation — with little preparation and little knowledge beyond a vague sense of where "north" or some temporary haven might be found. Such escapes were likely to fail unless fugitives had a very steep "learning curve" and were very lucky. At the other extreme, an escape could be planned carefully over time.

Accurate information was critically important to planning a successful escape and, since information usually had a source, few successful slave escapes in Kentucky were completely unaided even if the aid was rendered passively or inadvertently. Nevertheless, with good information and preparation, the fugitive would then proceed on his or her own, usually having obtained some food and/or clothing, sometimes some money, perhaps a weapon of some kind — and hope to elude capture en route to or in a free state. If successful, the fugitive would ultimately cross the U.S.-Canadian border or live "passing for free" in some northern or western community. The historical literature attests to the presence of many Kentucky fugitives in Canada West and northern free black communities who reached freedom in this way.[19]

After 1830, the anti-slavery movement entered a more militant phase that was typified, on one hand, by the uncompromising commitment to abolition of white leaders such as William Lloyd Garrison and, on the other hand, by the complementary development of organized opposition to slavery and support of black civil rights among free people of color.[20] Growing dependence on cotton and slavery strengthened the determination of the slaveholding states to defend the peculiar institution and their way of life. At the same time, the hysteria occasioned by the 1831 Nat Turner Revolt made southern whites evermore fearful of the enslaved African Americans who made that way of life possible and resentful of the northerners who seemed both to countenance rebellion and advocate the violation of southern rights to property in human beings.[21] As sectional divisions deepened, the slave system became more unyielding and escape from slave territory became more difficult. At the same time, the likelihood that fugitives could find assistance in the borderland and in the North increased, as did the likelihood that this assistance was an outgrowth, philosophically if not organizationally, of the anti-slavery movement. These developments did not supplant the old pattern of slave escapes with a new one, but merely added an important new political dimension

Several escape strategies evolved through trial and error over time under these fluid conditions, some of which have been noted in the Data Base and other documents cited thus far. For example, because not all African Americans were enslaved, a fugitive slave could not be identified by color alone and pretending to be free or abroad on legitimate business were often effective ruses. Among the more commonly used stratagems were the use forged passes or certificates of emancipation (free papers) that enabled fugitive slaves to pose as free men. Deceptions and disguises that enabled very fair complexioned African Americans to pass as white Americans were sometimes employed. In general, the simplest and most straightforward strategies were the most effective and there was virtually no limit to the inventiveness — and often the desperation — of the fugitives who conceived and executed such strategies.

For example, John Lewis, who ran away from George Mansel of Lexington in 1799, "had passed for a free man for six years," had served with the army and was believed to have "a discharge of that kind with him."[22] Joshua fled Missouri Territory in 1819, was captured and jailed, and subsequently escaped. The advertisement placed by Hugh Gordon, his owner, stated that Joshua "probably may pass for a free

Fifty Dollars Reward.

RANAWAY from the subscriber, on Saturday night the 6th inst. a bright mulatto man named

PHILL,

About thirty years of age, slender made, and about 6 feet high; has rather the appearance of an Indian. He was formerly owned by Alfred Roberts. It is believed he has a scar on some part of his face.—Any person who will deliver said negro to me in Shepherdsville, or confine him in any jail in this state, so that I get him, shall receive the above reward, with all reasonable expenses.

NATHAN MILES.

Oct. 13, 1821.   3t5—ow

Fugitive slave notice: "Phill," *Louisville Public Advertiser*, March 2, 1822. Escape from the Shepherdsville area (near Louisville).

man, and no doubt but he will make for Canada."[23] Phill, who ran away from William Cummings near Westport in 1820, was described in extensive detail, including his attire and his escape strategy. Cummings noted that Phill escaped in "leg irons, a band around each ankle, and chain of the log chain size attached to each," but that "he took with him a ... skiff and caulking chisel, perhaps with a view to disengage himself of his irons."[24]

Charles escaped from Bullitt County in June 1821. In advertising for his recovery, Jacob Bowman stated the "It is supposed that he has made for the state of Indiana or Ohio. Possibly he may have obtained a free pass, being a very shrewd, cunning fellow."[25] Daniel and Frank escaped together from Limestone County, Alabama in 1822. Their owner, Hardy Robinson, noted that Daniel "in all probably ... will try to pass for a free man, and change his name as he has done before."[26] John S. Hanna stated that George Casey escaped from Shelby County in 1823 by driving Hanna's team to Louisville and vanishing after "leaving the waggon and team standing in the streets."[27] When Frank escaped from Pulaski County in 1825, his owner, Obediah Denham, stated that "...he will make for a free state, as he has once before made an attempt of that kind, relying on his remarkably bright color, for a Negro."[28] Frazier, who "was quite intelligent," escaped from John Speed of Jefferson County, in 1826 using a forged pass. Frazier ran south to Shepherdsville, where he was caught and jailed. He escaped again and Speed stated that should Frazier "attempt to go into Illinois, Indiana or Ohio, it is more than probable he will procure, again, some forged paper."[29]

In November 1829, "a likely mulatto boy, copper colored, 21 years of age" (otherwise unnamed) escaped from William Hickman. Interestingly, the "boy" was owned by David Small of Mason County, but had been hired out to Hickman who lived "two miles back of New Albany, Indiana."[30] On December 14, 1829, James "...left the steamboat '76 on her passage down the River." His owner, A. H. Buckner of Winchester, stated that James "was raised in Virginia and purchased by me in Richmond" and apparently escaped after having been hired out to work on the river.[31] A month later, an unnamed fourteen year old "Negro Girl" escaped from Shepherd Whitman of Louisville who had hired her from Daniel Thornbury of Bullitt County.[32] Yet another illuminating advertisement concerned Amos, a twenty-five year old mulatto man, who escaped "from the Farm of J. Reed, of Shelby County, Ky" where he had been hired out by his owner, Lewis K. Grigsby. Grigsby stated that Amos "...is a pretty shrewd fellow, but looks like he had about half sense; it is unnecessary to describe his clothes, for he has plenty of money and can very easily change them. He may make for New Orleans, as I purchased him there about two months ago.[33]

On November 19, 1830, Andrew Jones, his wife, Maria, and their four children escaped from their various Louisville slave owners. The advertisement for their recovery stated that "previous to their departure, a pass was given to the woman, with leave of absence for 12 days, under the impression that they were going to Frankfort... There can be little doubt that they have forged free papers in their possession."[34] Frank and Fiatte escaped from John F. Gillespie of Natchez, Mississippi on November 10, 1832. In his advertisement for their return, Gillespie noted that Frank "...took off a large bay horse, eight or nine years old, a natural pacer," adding that Fiatte "has a horse also" and that "Frank may attempt to pass Fiatte as his servant."[35] When Allin escaped from Z. R. Craddock of Jefferson County in 1839, he too stole a "heavy, well-quartered SORREL HORSE."[36] Similarly, when Robin fled Louisville in 1839, his owner stated that he was "a shrewd, smart fellow, and no doubt will endeavor to get in with some white man to assist him along. I think it probable that he will make for Ohio or Indiana."[37]

Allowing enslaved African Americans some relative freedom of movement often allowed them the opportunity to escape. For example, the case of *Ewing v. Gist* (June 1842) involved a slave for hire who "...was permitted to go off and make his escape; and from the evidence it is probable that he has gone to Ohio or Canada, and that any attempt to retake him, if not utterly hopeless, must be attended by great expense and trouble."[38] Sixteen-year-old Kitty's strategy was simple and, when she escaped in 1844, James B. Huie stated that "she will probably attempt to cross the river, as she has before attempted it."[39] Soon afterward, Anthony ran away from J. P. Davidson of Louisville in 1844. Davidson declared that Anthony "...rode away a small sorrel mare" and that he "had a letter directed to Mr. James W. Simmons, at Mr. Summers's, Bullitt county, Ky., and on the corner of the letter, by boy Anthony."[40]

In 1845, when Charles escaped from David N. Maxwell of Edmonton County, he, too, "rode off on a sorrel mare."[41]

In July 1853, an article reprinted from the *Maysville Eagle* stated that "a negro man belonging to Dr. McDowell, of Flemingsburg, and a girl belonging to Mr. Ed Pearce," escaped the previous Saturday night. The notice added that "they stole a horse and about $20 in silver from Mr. Samuel Feemster and crossed the river at Cabin Creek."[42] The horse was a means of crossing the river and the money could help finance their flight. Whether planned or not, these fugitives joined with others escaping from the same region or others being assisted along the same Underground Railroad route. Unfortunately, they were overtaken near Rainsboro, Ohio by a posse from Kentucky. The news account continued:

> The negroes, in the charge of a white man named Sumner, fired on their pursuers, and a bloody fight ensued, in which the negro man of Mr. McDowell and a girl of Ed. Pearce were shot and badly wounded, but succeeded in escaping. Sumner was shot and badly beaten. A negro man, belong to Mr. Dobyns, near Lewisburg, had joined them, and after being severely cut, was taken prisoner...[43]

The one fugitive apprehended was jailed in Maysville; the fates of Sumner and the others were never reported.

When Charles ran away from Joseph W. Aikin of Louisville, "he left with the avowed intention of going to Bardstown, Ky. ... since which time he has not been heard of."[44] Miles escaped from John W. Lynn of Louisville in November 1852. Lynn noted that Miles had "a pass from Louisville to Owenton, Owen county, Ky., and back" and used this pass to facilitate his escape.[45] Although not reported in the local press, Isaac Throgmorton escaped from bondage in Louisville in 1853 and was interviewed years later by the American Freedmen's Inquiry Commission.

Throgmorton's account of his escape suggested how subterfuge could be employed effectively by fugitives who were both bold and cool-headed. One day, Throgmorton went to the Ohio River ferry with a free person of color. His companion produced a certificate of emancipation for the ferryman and vouched that, although Throgmorton had forgotten his "free papers," he was in fact free. The two men were allowed to board the ferry, crossed the river and returned that evening. The next day, Throgmorton returned to the ferry alone, was recognized by the boatman and conveyed across the river again without question. Of course, this time, Throgmorton did not return and eventually reached Canada.[46]

Another ruse was employed with equal effectiveness by Clarinda, "a large sized, well formed, good looking, yellow woman ... aged about 35 years," in escaping from S. W. Stone of Louisville. Stone stated in the advertisement for her return that "she was first missed on Saturday last, not returning as she agreed to do from a temporary visit to her mother, whom she said resided at Portland." Stone continued, "I have since learned that her mother does not reside at Portland, hence conclude that she has run away, although no possible cause existed."[47]

Obtaining money or goods that could be exchanged for money to finance an escape was a recurrent theme before the Civil War. For example, in May 1855, George, an enslaved African American, was tried in the Louisville Police Court and sentenced to receive ten lashes for "stealing a coat and a lot of jewelry, and selling the same to raise funds to pay his fare on the underground railroad through Cincinnati to Canada West." The court report added that "the boy has been hiding about town for two weeks, and his master represents him as a bad fellow, and has determined to sell him out of the State."[48]

Sometimes, simple opportunism was sufficient. For example, in June 1856, Mr.

McClelland, a hack driver, was sued by Smith for the value of "a slave girl" who escaped while being transported by McClelland from Portland to Louisville. According to testimony in Jefferson Circuit Court, McClelland delivered the young woman to the wrong place and, when left unattended, "she made good her escape and was never recovered." The Court ruled in McClelland's favor, accepting his claim that he did not know the young woman was enslaved.[49] A case that described another common escape strategy that employed public transportation was heard in a Louisville courtroom in early January 1857. William Hosea, "a resident of New Albany, the driver of the New Albany omnibus that plies regularly to this city, was arrested by Officer Seay ... on the suspicion of running off negroes." Hosea was noticed "for about two hours, dodging about, evidently looking for someone." He was also noticed "in communication with Ralph, a slave of Bishop Spaulding" who was also suspected of "assisting slaves to run away." Several witnesses vouched for Hosea's good character and, in the absence of any discernible offense, he was discharged. However, the court report added the following comments:

> The slave question has excited much feeling of late.... It has also been pretty well ascertained that the slaves who so mysteriously disappear every now and then, have been smuggled off in wagons or carriages. A special, detective police will have to be organized in the city whose duty it will be to examine and inspect all vehicles as they cross the river."[50]

In 1857, an article entitled, "Kentucky Slaves in London," indicated that some fugitives did not follow the more common escape routes and reached destinations far beyond the northern states or Canada. Specifically, two young women "who alleged they were fugitive slaves from Kentucky, were recently arrested in the streets of London for begging." They testified that "they escaped from Kentucky to Philadelphia, and there embarked for England."[51]

The perils and insecurities of owning slaves near the Ohio River border were captured in *McClain V. Esham* (June 1856). In this case, a slave belonging to Mrs. Esham "embarked upon the boat at Vanceburg, in Lewis county, in this state, on the 4th of September, 1855, in company with Thomas and William Stricklett, proceeded with them to Portsmouth, Ohio, and had not returned or been heard of since." The Court added that "it was hazardous to keep slaves near the Ohio, and especially to permit them to go at large."[52] In *Meekin v. Thomas* (January 1857), a suit was brought against "Meekin ... who was captain of the steamboat, Empire, to recover the value of a negro boy, Lewis, hired to Meekin as a fireman, who made his escape from the steamer into the state of Ohio, whilst she was lying at the wharf at Cincinnati." The Court held that Meekin was not liable, noting that "it is more hazardous to land with slaves at Cincinnati, than at other points in free territory on the Ohio river."[53]

In April 1853, an article reprinted from the *Cincinnati Gazette* described a desperate and, apparently successful, escape across the Ohio River:

> A negro was seen to run down to the river on the Kentucky side, near Jamestown on Sunday morning, and jumping into the river, swim over to the Ohio side landing near Pendleton. After resting himself (for he was very much fatigued) he started off over the hills. Shortly after two white men were seen to ride down to the edge of the river and cross over. They were in pursuit of the negro, who was a runaway slave.... They had chased him from near Alexandria, the county seat of Campbell county.[54]

In an unusually effective deception, Levi was reported as having escaped from Joseph Metcalfe in June 1857. However, as Metcalfe's advertisement stated, Levi probably escaped some time before and that "on the 27th day of December, 1856, my boy Levi, as I was informed, hired himself on board of the steamer 'Fashion.' Today I was credibly informed he has not been on the boat for two trips."[55]

Mailing oneself to freedom was yet another daring strategy and one made famous by Henry "Box" Brown, a rather diminutive fugitive, who escaped from bondage by having himself shipped in a crate to William Still in Philadelphia.[56] This method was also employed occasionally in the trans–Appalachian west. One example is described in the following article published in Louisville in 1858:

$50 REWARD.

RANAWAY from the subscriber, living in the town of Shelbyville, Ky. on the night of the 19th of November last; a mulatto woman, (not very bright,) named HARRIET. between eighteen and twenty years of age, 4 feet 8 or 10 inches high, one of her upper teeth out before; pleasant countenance, large breasts, slender built and curly hair. In all probability, she will endeavour to get on board some steam boat, or make her way to Indiana, as her father lives at or near Madison, in that State. I will give the above reward, if taken out of the State; $25, if taken in the State, and $15 if taken in the county of Shelby,   (dec 10—1481dn3)   Z. BELL.

Fugitive slave notice: "Harriet," *Louisville Public Advertiser*, December 11, 1830. Early example of a suspected escape by steamboat; also the early role of Madison, Indiana.

On Thursday, the steamer Portsmouth, at this port from Nashville, was boarded by a police officer, who handed the Captain a telegraphic despatch announcing that a negro slave aged thirty-five years, belonging to Mrs. Susan Pugh, of Stewart county, Tennessee, had fled from his mistress, in company of a poor white woman named Lucinda Leggett, and it was believed they boarded the steamer... The steamer was immediately ransacked from stem to stern, and Mrs. Leggett, with three children and a dog, beside a small quantity of household furniture, with a pine box, were found, but no nigger. On the trip to Cincinnati the nigger was discovered in the pine box aforesaid. The officers placed him in the Covington (Ky.) jail, while Mrs. Leggett, the three children and the dog ... vamoosed.[57]

A kindred strategy was attempted by "a slave of Mr. Miller" of Louisville in the same month. The fugitive hid in a water wheel box "while the steamer Telegraph was at the wharf." His escape failed when he nearly drowned while attempting "to reach the stern guards" from his hiding place. He was discovered and "sent back to Louisville."[58] Likewise, George Washington, "owned by Simpson, Peters & Co., of New Orleans ... secreted himself on board of a steamer leaving that port, and rode to some place below Louisville, where he stepped ashore and walked to this city." He then attempted to reach Cincinnati on a mail boat by hiding "amongst some furniture and wood." Unfortunately, the mail boat stopped at Covington, on the Kentucky side of the river, and he was captured and jailed.[59]

Timing was a critical factor as well. Slave escapes usually occurred at night and fugitives usually traveled by night unless in disguise or when using roads, railroad or rivers by subterfuge. However, some nights were far more promising than others. For example, enslaved African Americans were often allowed to tend their own gardens or the slave provision grounds on Saturdays and Sundays (which lowered the cost to slaveholders). As a result, enslaved African Americans were seldom supervised closely between Saturday evenings and Monday mornings and, as confirmed by the Kentucky Fugitive Slave Data Base (Table III-10), fugitives took advantage of this work routine and often fled on Saturday or Sunday nights—giving themselves a "head-start" of a day or more.[60]

Beyond time of the day and week,

time of year was another crucial variable related both to the vagaries of Kentucky's temperate climate and to changes in the local politics of slavery. Interestingly, before 1815, slave escapes from or through Kentucky were far more likely to occur during the warm months.[61] However, as slaveholders and local authorities mobilized to prevent slave escapes in the late antebellum period, slave escapes were more likely to occur in the cooler months and, as indicated in the Kentucky Fugitive Slave Data Base (Table III-11), were most likely to occur in the winter months after 1850. Although it is possible only to speculate, a plausible explanation for this change was that work hours were sometimes extended, and fields and roads were often more crowded during harvest season — adding to the likelihood of detection and hence to the difficulty of escape. In addition, while travel was more difficult for fugitives in colder weather, pursuit was also more difficult for patrols and posses.[62]

Timing was important in other respects. Oddly enough, because no slave escape from Kentucky could succeed without crossing the Ohio River at some point, winter — particularly when the Ohio River was frozen — was an exceptionally opportune time for flight. Former President Rutherford B. Hayes, who defended fugitives in Cincinnati early in his career, noted that "when the Ohio River was frozen over there was terror among the slaveholders of Kentucky. During the winters of 1850-51, 1852-53 and 1855-56, the river was frozen and numerous crossings were made, especially at Ripley, Ohio and at Cincinnati."[63] Otherwise, crossings were made more readily when the river level was very low or when river depths were moderate.

As an illustration of the necessarily opportunistic nature of many slave escapes, the editor of the *Louisville Courier* estimated that, in the extreme cold of January and February 1856, more than 250 enslaved African Americans escaped from or through Kentucky. This number included the family of Margaret Garner, the young African American woman who killed her own daughter rather than permit the child's return to slavery (whose case will be discussed in Chapter VII).[64]

Once again, given hostile surroundings and meager resources, most successful slave escapes employed very simple, straightforward and flexible strategies, and relied on the assistance of as few people as possible. As revealed in these documents, fugitives used disguises (including passing for white or the opposite gender), followed or shadowed established roads, used upland trails, hid on board steamboats and trains. In regions with well established free African American communities and Underground networks, rudimentary systems of signals and passwords developed by which fugitives and friends of the fugitive could recognize one another. The list is long indeed: bird calls; a certain sequence of knocks on a door or window; lamps or candles in windows; coded messages sent by regular mail (in which fugitives were referred to as "packages" being sent from one place to another); Masonic signs and cabalistic symbols; coins emblazoned with anti-slavery sentiments (such as "Am I Not a Man and a Brother" or "Am I Not a Woman and a Sister"); ribbons tied to trees; broken branches; hitching posts and many others.[65] All of these devices were undoubtedly used in some way, but the available evidence suggests that their use was local, situationally specific and limited. Indeed, the only essential requirement of any signaling system was that the signals were understandable to all parties to an escape and not easily recognizable by others.

Even more sophisticated signaling systems are cited in the secondary literature. For example, some have contended that quilts using certain African-derived symbols were employed in the Carolinas to help fugitives choose the time, route and destination of their escape.[66] Such systems may have been used in Kentucky, but, as yet, neither corroborative documentary evidence nor surviving quilts have been found.

By Road, River and Rail

On foot, fugitive slaves could seldom travel more than ten to fifteen miles per night and the longer they were on the road, the more vulnerable they were to hunger, the vagaries of the climate, and the snares of patrols and slave-catchers.[67] Consequently, transportation was yet another critical factor. While most escapes in the 1700s and early 1800s involved relatively young men, the increasing proportion of fugitive slave women and children after 1830 made the use of horses and carriages, drays and wagons more common. Somewhat later, access to the actual "steel" railroad in the 1850s became an important factor in free territory.[68] Furthermore, while fugitives could cross land by foot, only on those rare occasions when the Ohio was frozen could the river be crossed without a boat — a skiff, or ferry or steamboat. For most fugitives, transportation across the river was a necessity rather than a luxury since, given the number of fugitives who drowned after boat accidents, many enslaved African Americans never learned or were never taught to swim.

Large numbers of both free and enslaved African Americans worked on the many steamboats moving along the Ohio and Mississippi Rivers. These vessels were important means of inter-regional communication and sometimes offered convenient and rapid means of escape. The importance of traveling swiftly, particularly from the southern interior, should not be underestimated as it greatly enhanced the probability of reaching free territory. The problem was how to travel fast and, at the same time, avoid detection. Despite the risks, such escapes occurred frequently. To illustrate, in July 1821, "Silvie, Diana, Diana's son and George" escaped together from the vicinity of New Orleans. As advertisement placed by C. & T. Bullitt, a local concern, stated, "...they are supposed to have gone in the Steam Boat Feliciana."[69] Charles escaped from New Orleans in 1822 and was described as "an old boatman and a very artful villain." There was strong suspicion Charles "pass as a free man, and will probably attempt to get on board a steamboat, and perhaps may also change his name."[70]

In 1822, when Spencer fled Wilkinson County, Mississippi, his owner, James Cage, stated in his advertisement that Spencer escaped with four other fugitives. Cage suspected that the runaway "no doubt has changed his name, and may have brought with him, or obtained free papers ... it is expected he will either attempt to go through to Nashville, or get on board of some steamboat and go up to Kentucky, or into some of the states north of the Ohio river.[71] An advertisement that revealed, inadvertently, some of the inner-workings of the slave system appeared in 1829. Andrew Barnett of Greensburg, Kentucky, offered a $100.00 reward for the capture of Frank who "reads very well," adding that:

> His transgressions impelled me, some years since to take him to Orleans and sell him, where he became the property of a Spaniard, who branded him on each cheek ... which is plain to see when said negro is newly shaved. I went to New Orleans again last May, where, having my feelings excited by the tale Frank told me, I purchased him again.... [I]f the person who may apprehend and deliver him in Louisville should prefer it, he shall be sold at public sale.... Frank is about thirty years of age, and probably aimed to get on board a steam boat, as he endeavored to do so about the first of October last.[72]

Jorden escaped from John Steele of Lexington on January 27, 1826. In the advertisement for Jorden's return, Steele stated "it is likely that he will make for

A RUNAWAY NEGRO CAUGHT.—Just previous to the arrival of the mail boat, Jacob Strader, at Cincinnati, on a recent trip, a negro who gave his name as George Washington, was found secreted amongst some furniture and wood. All that was seen of him was his boots, which happened to protrude a little too far, and on pulling *them* from their hiding place, they were followed by a negro. According to his story, he is owned by Simpson, Peters & Co., of New Orleans, and secreted himself on board of a steamer leaving that port, and rode to some place below Louisville. where he stepped ashore and walked to this city. Going on board the Strader unobserved, he secreted himself and was rapidly making his way to Ohio when his well-laid scheme was entirely frustrated by the steamer stopping upon the Kentucky side of the river, and the confinement of the negro in the jail at Covington, to await orders from his owners.

News article: "A Runaway Negro Caught," *Louisville Courier*, May 11, 1858. A failed escape from New Orleans by steamboat.

Canada, or endeavor to get on board of steam boat."[73] Gilbert ran away from William Henry Sparks of Assumption, Louisiana, in July 1830. Sparks believed that Gilbert would probably attempt to escape by steamboat and stated that he "is well known on several boats, having been, for some time, a fireman on them" and that sold "from the neighborhood of Louisville, some two years since." Gilbert was described as "very smart, and should he be detected, will doubtless disown me as his master, and represent himself as the slave of some other person."[74] Similarly, Ben, "property of Major Hooks of Tuscumbia, Alabama," escaped from the steamer Mohican in May 1835. Forsyth & Co., to which he was hired, stated he was "a bright mulatto man, about 26 years of age, employed as a fireman on board said boat; he is a smart, shrewd fellow, and will no doubt attempt to get into a free State and pass for a free man."[75] Further, on

September 15, 1836, Sabra, "a trusted servant of James Brown" of Jefferson County, was dispatched to Louisville on an errand. Sabra had money, a written pass and, unbeknownst to her owner, a plan of her own. She disappeared and was "assumed to have used the money to board a steamboat for free territory."[76]

In a rather bizarre case, *Parks v. Richardson* (October 1843), a Louisiana planter killed a man and ran away to Texas. His flight and consequent absence from his plantation created an escape opportunity for some of his slaves and one of them, "the slave Tom, under the name of Henry, was taken from the steamboat and put into the work house in Louisville as a runaway, in June 1837" from which he subsequently escaped.[77] In *Case v. Woolley* (October 1837), William Gorden was "taken ... on board the steam boat, Lancaster, from Louisville in Kentucky, the place of his residence, to New Orleans, whence he had fled to some place unknown."[78] Loss through negligence could be alleged, as in *Waltham v. Oldham* (October 1839) in which the Court issued a decree for damages against the owners of a ferry-boat between Louisville and Jeffersonville "on the ground that the ferryman had permitted a slave of the appellees to pass on the boat ... from the Kentucky to the Indiana shore, whence he had fled to Canada.[79]

In December 1840, John A. Holton, "Master of the Steam Boat Ambassador" advertised for the return of Bill Cole. Cole belonged to James Elliot of Frankfort, Kenucky, and had escaped from the steamboat to which he had been hired.[80]

Similarly, in *Strader v. Fore* (October 1841), damages were awarded for the unauthorized transportation "and consequential escape of a slave on the steamboat Pike."[81] *Gordon v. Longest* (January 1842) was a suit to recover the value of a certain slave who "the commander of the steamboat, Guyandotte, then proceeding from Louisville ... was alleged to have taken on board as a passenger to Cincinnati."[82] Likewise, Jeff fled from William Chipley of Columbus, Georgia in 1843. In the ensuing fugitive slave advertisement, Chipley stated that Jeff "has been engaged as a cook on a steamboat" and suspected that "he was assisted off by some white man" and "that he is probably on a boat on the Western waters, and may be found in some of the Western cities."[83] Fountaine escaped from E. T. Dustin of Louisville, boarded the "steamer Blue Wing, on or about the 28th of June" 1848 and was last seen leaving the boat at Madison, Indiana." Fountaine was twenty years old, had lived for sometime near Frankfort, had been hired on the river for several years as a cook and also used his familiarity with the river to make his escape.[84] Jacob Greene escaped slavery in Kentucky twice only to be captured and returned, ultimately, to bondage in Louisville. He escaped a third time by stowing away aboard a steamboat and, by this means, reached Cincinnati. There, he made contact with the Underground Railroad and, with the help of its operatives, was disguised as a woman and moved by railroad to Cleveland and then, by ship, to Toronto.[85]

As early as 1840, escapes by steamboat became so common that the editor of the *St. Louis Gazette* recommended "the disuse, on board steamboats navigating the western waters, of all free negroes ... as they cause excitement and discontent among slaves of the states through which they pass, many of whom they induce to run away." The editor of *The Colored American* responded that, if free people of color

were banned, "what would they then have to do—take slaves? How glad they (the slaves) would be to get to Cincinnati, to Steubenville, to Wellsville, and to Pittsburgh. The boats would certainly have to get new help to go back with."[86]

Both the use of steamboats as means of escape and the propensity of African Americans with familiarity with the river to become fugitives remained common in the 1850s. The opportunity to hide, travel in disguise, pass for white or as a free person of color—with a bit of money—was often sufficient for a successful escape by river. For example, Lewis escaped from J. H. Owen of Louisville in December 1849 and remained at large well into 1850. Owen offered $200 for the return of Lewis and noted that he "...has been hired as fireman or second cook on many of the principal steamboats running from Louisville, Ky., to New Orleans, and is well known by a large majority of steamboatmen on the Ohio and Mississippi rivers."[87]

In another incident, the Captain of the steamboat Indiana "lodged a negro man in jail" in February 1852. The fugitive "had hidden himself in the hold, and it is thought he belongs to Mr. Bobs, of Algiers, opposite New Orleans."[88] When Charles ran away from J. M. Pendleton on December 22, 1852, Pendleton stated in the advertisement for Charles' return that "he was employed as a fireman on the Mary Hunt. I will give a handsome reward for the arrest of said negro if I can get him."[89] Sam ran away from H. J. Craycroft of Louisville on September 1, 1853. Craycroft offered $150 for Sam's return and noted that "he has been about the city within the last few days. He has been running on the river and may be on some boat."[90] On February 23, 1855, "a Negro boy belonging to L. Taylor, Esq., of Henderson" escaped from the steamboat R. J. Ward "while lying at Portland."[91] In August 1856, Charles Crossgrove of Louisville offered a $200 reward for the return of Monroe and stated, in the advertisement for the return of this fugitive, that "on the 7th day of August, I purchased from W. H. Richardson, residing near Brandenburg, a slave named Monroe, aged about 28 years." However, "on the night of the 20th of the same month, about 15 miles below Brandenburg, said boy jumped into the Ohio river from the steamer Ella and swam on shore."[92]

By the 1850s, the steel railroad enabled fugitives to travel with unparalleled speed. Although there were no bridges across the Ohio River, escape by rail to a river town and, even more so, escape northward by railroad through Indiana, Illinois or Ohio became an often used means of escape for Kentucky fugitives. As with steamboats, the advantages of rapid flight often outweighed the heightened risk of capture and enslaved African Americans attempted escapes by rail quite often. For example, in April 1854, a white Louisville seamstress, Mary Affleck, was arrested and "charged with enticing away and running off a negro woman belonging to Prof. Gross." The article continued, "Mrs. A. went to the Jeffersonville railroad office and bought a ticket purporting to be for her own use. She gave the ticket to the negro woman, who was to go over in the omnibus on the following morning."[93] According to a subsequent police report, Affleck bought three tickets. One ticket was given to the black woman referenced above. However, testimony in Louisville Police Court indicated that another ticket was given to Joe, also a slave of Dr. Samuel D. Gross. Joe was arrested on the ferry to Jeffersonville. The fate of the "negro woman" remained unknown. The recipient of the third ticket also remained unknown.[94]

In December 1854, the *Cleveland Herald* published the following report of Kentucky fugitives passing through Ohio en route to Canada:

...on the Wednesday afternoon train from Pittsburgh ... there were six runaway slaves, two women and four men, from Lexington, Kentucky. They probably got upon the train at Wellsville. Their owner was in the city soon after their arrival, but they succeeded in eluding him and went upon the night train to Buffalo, and are probably ere this, safe in Canada.[95]

The *Vincennes Gazette* reported that, in September 1855, a conductor on the Evansville and Crawfordsville Railroad, "having previously been supplied with a description of a gang of runaway negroes recognized eight of them, who came aboard his train at a colored settlement on the road, known as Africa." Unfortunately for the fugitives, they were all in one car and the conductor "turned the key on them and took them to Terre Haute for safe keeping."[96]

Frederick Douglass painted a revealing picture of the Kentucky-Indiana section of the borderland in 1854 and commented on the impact of this new means of flight. Douglass, who often visited the "west" on speaking tours and for anti-slavery meetings, noted that "Indiana is nominally a free State, that she is free in fact is by no means certain. This is border country, on the Ohio River. Jeffersonville is its largest town...." Douglass then explained that the Cincinnati and St. Louis Railroad had been completed as far as Seymour, "where it crosses the Jeffersonville and Indianapolis road," and added that "Louisville slaves have heard of and traveled over this road" in escaping from bondage, but "...the Jeffersonville road plays slave-catcher for its Louisville friends, and will carry no colored man, unless he can show that he is a free man." He concluded by labeling the practice "infamous."[97]

Risks

Although some aid was often crucial, there were serious risks associated with seeking and accepting such assistance. Sizable rewards for fugitive slaves made slave-catching a dirty but profitable business—and at times even other African Americans would facilitate the capture of fugitives for this reason. Even otherwise innocent free people of color were vulnerable to kidnappers who would sell them into slavery or slave-catchers who would claim them (falsely) as fugitives.[98]

For example, in 1837, four white men from Kentucky "came armed to the house of Gabriel Johnson, a colored man in the neighborhood of Ripley, Ohio." Johnson was absent, but the men "seized his wife, whipped her severely to make her submit, forced her on a horse ... and dragged her to Kentucky" on the pretext of her being a fugitive slave. No evidence was produced to support that claim and two of her abductors were arrested and jailed in Ohio. However, the unfortunate woman, instead of being returned to her family, was confined in the "Washington jail, as a runaway slave."[99]

In 1844, John White escaped from Kentucky and settled in Indiana. In 1849, White resolved to return to Kentucky and "undertake the rescue of his beloved wife and five endeared children." He located his family and was able to bring them across the Ohio River, but the group was overtaken by slave catchers in Dearborn County, Indiana—"White alone escaping." After wandering "about in the woods for two weeks," White was "betrayed by a monster in the shape of a colored man, and fell victim to his pursuers," and was lodged in the Bedford jail in Trimble County. At this point, matters took an interesting turn and White

> ... told the kidnapper that he thought he could raise ... three hundred and fifty dollars by writing to a friend of his in Michigan, on condition that he would be released from slavery. The offer was accepted by the kidnapper and White caused a letter to be written to his friend, who

borrowed the money from a Dr. Judkins of Cincinnati.

Once free, White enlisted the help of Frederick Douglass to raise funds with which to repay his benefactor and ransom his family.[100]

In June 1854, nine fugitives, including women and children, escaped from William Walton of Boone County and were "captured ... on their way to Canada, about one mile from the Lunatic Asylum after being betrayed by a free person of color posing as their benefactor."[101] The runaways were jailed in Cincinnati and a trial ensued "with a large crowd of white and colored people" in and around the courtroom. According to testimony given:

> ... the escape was made on Sunday night last; the Ohio was crossed at Lawrenceburg, where they fell in with a colored man named John Gyser, alias Jones, who promised to conduct them on the way to Canada; he brought them to the stable of Weedon Humes, some two miles from ... this city, where he left them on Wednesday morning promising to come back at night with money and provisions. Instead of doing this, however, he went over to Covington, found that a reward of $1,000 had been offered for the runaways, and he immediately gave information, so that they were surrounded and taken.

John Joliffe, who would later represent Margaret Garner in 1856, was legal counsel for the fugitives.[102]

What emerges most clearly from the source materials examined thus far is an anatomy of slave escapes stripped down to the barest essentials. The simpler the strategy, the less likely it would unravel with the first delay or unforeseen event. The fewer people aware, the lower the probability of inadvertent or intentional betrayal. The better one's directions, the more rapidly and efficiently one could travel. The better provisioned, the longer one could hide or journey without risking exposure through hunting, asking for or stealing food. If one had money and/or guile, the more likely one could travel faster and in greater comfort, if not greater safety, aboard a steamboat, stage-coach or train.

Fugitives and friends of the fugitive agreed that, if there was an Underground Railroad network in slave territory, it existed only in the extended borderland. By the 1830s and 1840s, once fugitives reached the vicinity of the Ohio River, assistance became more readily available as will be documented in subsequent sections of this study. However, this was essentially a "passive network" through which assistance was rendered, if sought. Most fugitives, until they reached the borderland, were largely on their own and devised and executed their escape strategies accordingly.

CHAPTER V

Friends of the Fugitive in the Kentucky Borderland

To a Negro abolitionist, few things could be so satisfying as helping a runaway.[1]

Most white Americans in Kentucky and elsewhere learned to expect flights from slavery as inevitable and, hence, predictable acts of resistance — realizing that some enslaved African Americans behaved more like captives than slaves and worked to undermine the institution simply by striving to maintain their humanity or to achieve freedom. Such resistance could not be extinguished entirely despite the best efforts of slaveholders and other defenders of slavery. However, its effects could, as noted previously, be limited and controlled through the use of deterrents, careful policing and disinformation.

While some resistance from black

Americans was conceded, whites who opposed slavery posed a special and profoundly irksome problem. This problem became particularly acute after the 1831 Nat Turner Revolt. Stated simply, for a generation or more after the American Revolution, anti-slavery sentiment in the United States was conservative, gradualistic and often linked to "colonizationist" schemes to send (free) blacks to Africa. Northern politicians did not challenge slavery in the southern states and remained largely silent and non-judgmental when Virginia was threatened by the Gabriel and Sancho conspiracies of 1800 and 1802, respectively — and, for that matter, when there were insurrection scares in Lexington in 1811 and Louisville in 1812.[2]

By the time of the Denmark Vesey conspiracy in 1822 (Charleston, South Carolina), growing sectional divisions over the extension of slavery into the Louisiana Territory had already prompted the 1820 Missouri Compromise. Still, Northerners sympathized, in general, with the Southerners traumatized by Vesey's massive conspiracy.[3] However, by the time Nat Turner's revolt swept through Southampton County Virginia in late August 1831, North and South had drifted farther apart and a more militant anti-slavery movement extended no sympathy to the South — provoking a fateful reaction. As Stephen Oates observed insightfully:

> Desperately needing to blame somebody for Nat Turner besides themselves, Southern whites inevitably linked the revolt to a sinister Northern abolitionist plot to destroy their cherished way of life.... What followed was the Great Southern Reaction of the 1830s and 1840s, a time when the Old South, menaced it seemed by internal slave disaffection and outside abolitionist agitation, became a closed, martial society... By the 1840s, with its repressive slave controls, police measures and toughened military forces, the Old South had devised a slave system oppressive enough to make organized rebellion all but impossible.[4]

By the 1840s, active sympathy for and assistance rendered to fugitive slaves came to be associated with the term, "Underground" or "Underground Road." Ironically appropriate, given the focus of this study on Kentucky, legend holds that the term originated in Kentucky in roughly 1831 when Tice Davids escaped across the Ohio River at Maysville — and his owner was said to have exclaimed that Davids "must have gone off on an underground road."[5]

Whatever its derivation, the Underground Road — or Underground Railroad after the invention of the actual steel railroad — can be defined minimally as "a form of combined defiance of law ... and the unconstitutional but logical refusal of several thousand people to acknowledge that they owed any regard to slavery."[6] This willingness to break the law implied not only commitment but the conviction, which many white abolitionists did not share, that the United States could and should become a multiracial democracy.

The Underground Road: Assisting Fugitive Slaves Before 1850

The Underground Railroad was more than slave escapes, more than the totality of thousands of random or planned acts of kindness — more than an attitude of sympathy toward fugitive slaves. At the same time, the Underground Railroad was less than or merely different from an organization in any conventional sense. In other words, assisted slave escapes in and of themselves did not connote the existence of an Underground Railroad — but the predisposition to aid fugitives was a necessary precondition for its evolution.

By the time of the Missouri Compromise (1820), Kentucky had already gained a reputation for being helpful to and as a haven for fugitive slaves. As Paul Wilhelm, Duke of Wurttemburg, was informed on his travels through sections of the Mississippi and Ohio valleys between 1822 and 1824:

> Negroes are often helped by Kentuckians in their flight to neighboring states. This is sometimes the cause of unpleasantness arising between them and their neighbors for Negroes frequently seek Kentucky as a haven of rescue where they are concealed and protected. The Kentuckians take most of their products ... to Louisiana, and on these occasions, many a Negro slave obtains his freedom. The law, to be sure, forbids hiding runaway slaves and permits the search of homes, boats

and property in which one suspects a hidden Negro. But ... many fugitives make their lucky escape.[7]

Under Kentucky law, such humane acts were proscribed. Termed "assisting" or "enticing slaves to escape" or "harboring," these were the criminal offenses typically committed by persons who assisted fugitive slaves in violation of Kentucky and American law. As noted briefly in Chapter III, "assisting slaves to escape" encompassed the full range of acts by which free people might help fugitives through and from slave territory. The use of "enticing" in the wording of the law implied that, apart from enslaved African Americans whose escapes were presumably a manifestation of mental illness, others— who were supposedly content with bondage— could nonetheless be led astray by nefarious outsiders. In other words, had there been no enticement, there would have been no escapes. The available records suggest, however, that enslaved African Americans required little or no enticement, but did seek, value and use information and other forms of assistance in planning and executing escapes. Those who provided such information, often termed "field agents," did so at great risk and were directly involved in the initial and often the later phases of many escapes.

In early Kentucky, enslaved African Americans were sometimes assisted in their flight toward freedom by other African Americans and sometimes by whites. Nothing yet existed that was analogous to the Underground Railroad, but the anti-slavery sentiments of the Revolutionary era persisted in the thinking of a minority of whites. For example, *The Kentucky Gazette* reported occasionally the type of "aided" escape normally associated with the later antebellum period. To illustrate, Robert Clarke, of Clarke County, advertised for "...a Negro Boy, about seventeen or eighteen years old ... his name Britain, but originally called Ned ... the said boy was some weeks past taken up by a gentleman on the North side of the Ohio River, and made his escape."[8]

Along with whites who sometimes aided fugitive slaves, there were whites who fled with them — whites who were not benefactors motivated by anti-slavery ideals, but rather whites who were fellow fugitives and co-conspirators. Typically, whites willing to make common cause with African Americans, such as bound apprentices and criminals, were those who had little or no stake in the system of wealth and privilege evolving in early Kentucky. Thus, much as strong bonds existed between African Americans and Native Americans under certain conditions, inter-racial class alliances often existed between African Americans and poor whites— under certain conditions. These alliances were rare and were usually short-lived, but the fugitive slave advertisements referring to whites and blacks escaping together substantiate that they were forged occasionally.[9]

Numerous other references to actual or suspected enticement can be found in Kentucky newspapers and court records from the generations before the Civil War. In July 1821, "Silvie, Diana, Diana's son and George" escaped together from the vicinity of New Orleans. The advertisement for their return stated that the fugitives had fled "in the Steam Boat Feliciana" and that they had "been enticed away by two American white men, who worked for the Plantation" by the names of "Coleman and William Nash."[10] After Ned escaped from Thomas Fearn of Huntsville, Alabama in December 1823, Fearn noted that the fugitive had also stolen a "Sorrel Horse" from his neighbor. Fearn's fugitive slave notice contained an unusually detailed description of Ned's escape route and strategy. Specifically,

Ned was seen at several places on his way to Nashville, Tenn. a few days after his elopement, in company with a white man, sometimes the one and sometimes the other, riding a horse of the above description. Ned was stopped at the bridge in Nashville, on this horse, but, shewing a free pass, was permitted to proceed on. Since that time he has been seen near Lexington, Ky and afterwards in the state of Indiana, well dressed, on horseback, with gun and pistols; says he is a free man, and has by some means, procured the county seal to papers attesting his freedom.[11]

One of the more interesting advertisements concerned the following incident. On September 14, 1829, Henly escaped from Abraham Hite of Louisville. Four horses and two saddles also disappeared on the same night. The advertisement continued, stating that "there were two white men on foot, seen on Monday, at different times, in company with the negro ... who, it is presumed, stole the horses and enticed the negro away."[12] In September 1830, Thornton ran away from Thomas O. Drane of Logan County. Thornton was 24 or 25 years old and described variously as a skilled blacksmith, carpenter and flutist. Drane added that "he has probably fled to the eastward, as he has been heard to say that he has friends in Cincinnati, and relations in Baltimore.... He had some money when he went off, and ... it is supposed he is in company with some white villain as his servant." Drane observed that Thornton "may have a free pass and endeavor to pass as a freeman, as he will no doubt rely much on his knowledge of reading and writing."[13]

Assistance from other African Americans was often reported. For example, in 1796, "a Negro Wench, named Alice, with her two children, a boy and girl," Tom and Olive, ran away from Daniel Stringer of Pendleton County. Stringer believed that Alice and her children had been "stolen" by Sam, another enslaved African American owned by Elijah Tucker — also of Pendleton County. Sam was described as "artful and active ... a good fiddler and delights

in company to play for dancers...."[14] On May 22, 1831, an unnamed "likely negro woman ... far advanced in pregnancy" ran away from Robert Nicholson in Louisville to whom she had been hired-out by her owner, J. W. Thornberry. The advertisement expressed the strong suspicion that "she has been conveyed away by some free negro, with whom she may attempt to pass as his wife" and that "she may have free papers with her, as I understand she learned to read and write in Louisville."[15] Needless to add, the circumstances of her pregnancy, the fact that she was moved to flee late in her pregnancy, that she already had connections in Louisville and had become literate make this a case that leaves many tantalizingly suggestive questions unanswered and probably unanswerable.

On December 14, 1833, Cage, Killis and Harry escaped from P. O. Williams of Clinton, Mississippi. Williams offered $300 for their return and added that "said Negroes have been seduced from their owner by some white man, and probably taken to a free State."[16] Stephan Sanders feared that the same sinister forces were at work when Jacob escaped in September 1839 and stated that Jacob may have been "decoyed off by some designing person."[17] Such suspicions were rather common. Martha, who ran away from Samuel Yenawine of Jefferson County in December 1843, was "supposed to have been enticed away, and has probably left the city by the Flat Lick road."[18] When John escaped from L. Powell of Louisville in 1844, he was thought "to have absconded or been seduced away" and "is in all probability skulking about the city."[19] In 1844, Ben D. Harris of Madison County, Alabama advertised for the return of Mary, who escaped from him a few days after he had hired her. Harris believed that Mary would traverse Kentucky en route to free territory as she had been "decoyed off by some villain."[20] In late November 1848, "about forty negroes had made arrangements to leave their masters

FIFTY DOLLARS REWARD.

RAN AWAY from the subscriber, living in Louisville, on the 30th of September last, a negro man, named JACOB, about twenty-five years old; had on, when he went away, linen pantaloons and rounda-bout; said negro is near six feet high, straight and heavy built, moderately black, and has a fine countenance; he wears a shoe No. 14; he has a scar on the back of his right hand, occasioned by a splinter; his hand was much swollen from having caught cold in it; he is pleasing in his man-ners and excessively fond of liquor; and I have no doubt that he is yet in the neighborhood of the Pond settle-ments, if not decoyed off by some designing person. Any persons finding said negro and confining him in any jail, and giving information so that I can get him again, shall be entitled to the above reward, if taken out of the State; twenty dollars if taken out of the county, or ten dollars if taken in the county.

nov 8-swtf   STEPHEN SANDERS.

Fugitive slave notice: "Jacob," *Louisville Public Advertiser*, November 14, 1839. Example of an escape in which assistance was suspected.

in Woodford county." The plot was betrayed "by a negro ... who was requested to join in it." Once questioned, "the negroes stated that two or three white men who had been in the neighborhood some days, furnished them free passes."[21] Similarly, Stewart, who escaped from Worden Masden of Bullitt County in 1849, was thought to "have been persuaded off by some white men or some person who may have forged a pass for him."[22]

On August 8, 1852, twenty-five year old Mary, along with her three children, escaped from Charles Q. Armstrong of Louisville. Armstrong offered a $500 reward for the return of the fugitive family and added that "two white men were seen with them just before they left, and I suppose they have stolen the negroes."[23] Later in 1852, Reuben Johnson, a free African American, was suspected of and charged with "aiding and abetting in the escape of several negroes, the property of C. Q. Armstrong." Johnson was tried and acquitted in Jefferson Circuit Court.[24] The record is mute regarding who—if anyone—actually assisted the fugitives. The circumstances surrounding their capture will be discussed later in this section of the study.

In August 1854, an unnamed "free man of color" operating "in and about Carrollton, mouth of the Kentucky river" attempted to "run off a couple of slaves." The article continued that "he started with them in a skiff, and took his course down stream, when he was overhauled by parties in pursuit, and the slaves recaptured, but the free fellow escaped."[25]

News of Kentucky fugitives often arrived through unconventional channels. In April 1855, the editor of the *Louisville Courier* received, in his words, "a dirty and greasy looking sheet called the *Voice of Liberty and Canadian Independent*, published at Windsor, Canada West," one of the newspapers that featured articles on fugitive slaves in Canada. This edition contained several items of particular interest to Kentucky slaveholders in a "Report from the Under-Ground Railroad — Fugitives in Canada." For example,

> Milly Banks, father, mother and two children arrived in safety just last week from Kentucky; after their best wishes to Mr. Beal and family, they would inform him that they are much pleased with the country.... One of the Conductors of the road arrived safe with a full train, fifteen in all.... Arrived at Windsor, C. W., from the Galt House, Louisville, Polly Jackson, Aug. 17th. She wishes to be kindly remembered to Mrs. Ellen Jarvis, the widow who claimed the right to her person.... The first impressions of a free country have fully met her former anticipation.[26]

In September 1857, "four negro men suddenly disappeared and it was soon ascertained that they had runaway" from their owners in Louisville and Bardstown. A few days later, they were captured "over in Indiana, between Hanover and Madison" and returned to Louisville. The article continued, noting that "a couple of white men, it was ascertained, had taken them across the river below the falls to New Albany, where they were received by a third white man, who planned their escape.... They all had money when they started...."[27] One of the several ramifications of this case was played out a few days later when "Wash, a slave of Dr. Gaither" was arrested "for stealing ... a gold watch and a carpet sack, the property of Mr. Ellis." According to testimony in the trial, Tom, the fugitive who escaped from Mr. Ballard, had actually stolen the watch and bag, but had given them to Wash "to hold." Wash had hidden these purloined articles "under a pile of straw." When Tom was prepared to "travel," the two white men "informed him that he couldn't take any baggage," leaving Wash holding the proverbial bag. Since Tom was soon captured, "the case against Wash was dismissed and the watch returned to Mr. Ellis."[28]

In an intriguing advertisement, David L Stover of Carter County, Tennessee, advertised for the return of twenty-four year old Nias, "a bright Mulatto" who escaped in August 1858. Stover stated much and implied more:

> It is supposed that said boy left in company with a white girl, of medium size, dark skin, blue eyes and light hair, rather full featured. She had with her a yellow calico dress, black figured stripe, and bonnet of the sam.... It is supposed they are making their way to a free State, and will probably pass through Kentucky. The girl has relations living in Lee county, who it is thought have agreed to assist them in getting to Ohio. The girl's uncle, a dark-skinned man, with a large roman nose, will probably be found in their company.[29]

These instances of enticing or assisting runaways were, for the most part, individual acts of kindness—violations of law based on moral values or political ideals. The deepening crisis of the 1850s forced friends of the fugitive in the borderland and farther north both to intensify and organize these efforts. The few Underground Railroad agents daring to venture into the southern interior could not operate openly, but often disguised themselves as innocuous peddlers, itinerant preachers, geologists and the like. For example, Thomas Brown and his family moved from Cincinnati to Henderson County in 1850. Brown's wife operated a "millinery shop" and Brown peddled his wares in the country-side from a small horse-drawn wagon. The wagon was "heavily curtained," ostensibly "to protect his goods from the weather." However, Brown used his peddling to canvass the area and identify enslaved African Americans interested in reaching free territory, dispensing information to prospective fugitives and often transporting them in his wagon. Unfortunately, after slave escapes escalated steeply in Daviess, Union and Hancock counties in 1854, Brown was arrested and sentenced to the penitentiary in April 1855.[30]

At times, information alone was the most crucial type of assistance, enabling a fugitive to formulate a sound escape plan. As an illustration, Alexander Ross, the young Abolitionist from Canada, ventured into Kentucky in the 1850s. Upon reaching the Bardstown area, he met Peter, an enslaved African American whose wife, Polly, had been sold to someone in Covington. Ross informed the distraught husband that, if he could reach Cincinnati and find the house of a certain free person of color, arrangements would then be made for the rest of the northward journey — including the rescue of and reunion with his wife. How the fugitive reached Cincinnati is not stated, but he did in fact arrive. Documents suggest that one or both were hidden for some period of time in the famous Carneal House station in Covington and were conveyed to the river using its tunnel. The fugitive couple crossed and eventually reached Canada — via the railroad to Cleveland and a schooner across Lake Erie.[31]

In another of the more notorious Kentucky cases, Willis Lago, a free African American living in Cincinnati, was indicted in Woodford County in 1859 for "enticing away" a "mulatto girl named Charlotte who belonged to Claiborne W. Nichols of Versailles." Charlotte paid Lago $50.00 to help her escape from slavery and, after making her escape successfully, Kentucky Governor Beria Magoffin demanded that Ohio Governor William Dennison turn over Lago as a "negro stealer" subject to Kentucky justice. Dennison refused and the case eventually reached the U.S. Supreme Court. In *Kentucky v. Dennison* (December 1860), the dispute was resolved by the denial of "a motion for a rule on the Governor of Ohio … commanding him to cause Willis Lago, a fugitive from justice, to be delivered up, to be removed to Kentucky." Lago was never extradited. Charlotte was never found.[32]

Harboring

Whether in private urban residences, rural farmhouses, barns and other outbuildings, or even in caves and other natural hiding places, fugitives sought and were given sanctuary by sympathetic whites and African Americans. Rendering of this particular type of aid was deemed the crime of "harboring fugitive slaves" and complemented that of enticing or assisting runaways slaves to escape. There are numerous examples of this crime, actual or implied, in various regions of Kentucky — a great many of which refer to Louisville given its size, its urban setting and the infrastructure of its free black community.

$500 Reward.

RANAWAY from the subscriber, on Sunday night, the 8th inst. about 10½ o'clock, the following described slave : MARY, aged 25 years, and her three children, SAM, JOE, and a child two years old. Mary is rather dark, pleasant countenance; Sam and Joe are very light mulattos, aged 9 and 7 years; the child is black. Also, EDDA, mulatto, aged 18 years, well-formed and sprightly.

Two white men were seen with them just before they left. and I suppose they have stolen the negroes.

I will give $300 for the return of the slaves, and $100 each for the white men, if taken out of this State.

aug 9 b1&d3&w4   CH. Q. ARMSTRONG.

Fugitive slave notice: "Mary and children," *Louisville Journal*, August 11, 1852. Example of an escape of a woman and children, with the suspicion of assistance.

As early as the 1820s, Louisville was still a small town with a small free black community, but had already become a sanctuary, convergence and crossing point for fugitives from western and central Kentucky. Both fugitives and those who wished to overtake them understood these attractions. For example, in July 1822, Udorah "ranaway, or was stolen or coaxed away" from George J. Johnson, to whom she had been hired, of Newcastle, Kentucky. Since her mother was enslaved in Louisville, her owner supposed that thirteen year-old Udorah would find her way into the town and had "made diligent inquiry respecting her" — to no avail.[33] On January 25, 1823, Ellick ran away from John Hagan of Washington County. Hagan stated that Ellick "…was raised by a Mr. Lightfoot, near Louisville, who sold him to Mr. Richard Payne of Washington County, and it is probable he will endeavor to make his way back to Louisville and cross the Ohio River."[34]

On September 17, 1825, Reuben escaped from Francis Taliaferro of Oldham County. Taliaferro offered a 50 dollar reward and added that Reuben "has a wife at Mr. Fitzhugh Thorton's in this county and, no doubt, will make the principal part of his stay in that neighborhood, being uncommonly fond of his family."[35]

On June 1, 1830, Lewis fled Samuel Law-less' farm near Louisville. Lewis was be-lieved to be hiding "in or about Louisville, where his mother and sisters live."[36] Wil-liam Talbut of Louisville sought the return of Charlotte, a sixteen year old young woman. Talbut stated "it is my opinion, founded upon good circumstantial au-thority, that she has been persuaded off, or concealed in this city by some white per-son." The advertisement continued, "She was raised in the State of Maryland, and it is probable that she will endeavor to make her way back — perhaps by the aid of some white man."[37]

Similarly, on January 9, 1831, John ran away from Jesse Smith of Danville. In seeking his return, Smith stated that "it is probable that he will make for Louis-ville."[38] William escaped from M. Lang-horne of Louisville on February 27, 1831, and Langhorne stated "it is probable he is lurking about the city."[39] Hiram, who ran away from George Triplett of Spencer County in September 1831, was also be-lieved bound in the direction Louisville because "his mother lives somewhere about" the city.[40] Sealy, a "quite likely 13 or 14" year old, escaped from James Prather of Louisville on December 12, 1831. She, too, was believed "lurking somewhere about the City."[41] Sam fled Henry Robb of Jeffer-son County on May 27, 1832 and Robb be-lieved that "it is probable that he is in the City of Louisville."[42] Reuben, described as "a sleek black, 24 or 25 years old," escaped from James Brown of Jefferson County in 1844. In the advertisement for Reuben's apprehension, Brown added that, "as he left in haste, it is supposed that he is in the neighborhood of Louisville."[43] Likewise, when Melinda escaped from John Price of Louisville on July 9, 1845, he naturally as-sumed that "she is lurking or concealed in the city."[44] The same suspicion was ex-pressed when Harriet "ranaway" from Mrs. E. Castleman of Louisville on New Year's Day 1851 and it was assumed that she was "secreted in this city."[45] Similarly, when John "ranaway from Henry Norton, resid-ing 6 miles South of Louisville, on Satur-day, 27th September," the advertisement stated that "he is probably somewhere in Louisville."[46]

The term "station" in Underground Railroad parlance has one of two mean-ings. The first, and better known, refers to a specific site such as a house or church, where fugitives could find sanctuary and from which they would often be "con-ducted" to the next "station." As many of the cases reviewed in this study, this type of station was usually associated with a particular individual, more often than not a free person of color, or a white anti-slav-ery activist, or the pastor of a church.

Although most stations were tempo-rary stops on the Underground Railroad, free African American communities such as those in Louisville and Cincinnati afforded fugitives the rare opportunity to "hide in plain view"— to blend in, at least for awhile, with free African Americans and often urban slaves (in the case of Louis-ville) who were usually faceless and invis-ible to whites. Thus, as noted previously, the free African American community it-self was a "station" or junction of sorts— in essence, a nest or cluster of individual stations— where many people were capa-ble of making various arrangements for the short- or long-term concealment of fugitives.[47] Before 1850 and to some extent thereafter, harboring fugitives in such communities was not the work of an orga-nization, but simply the consequence of African Americans helping other African Americans— often family members.

This type of station was sometimes a community or rural settlement in which free African Americans lived in close prox-imity to anti-slavery whites, such as the Quakers in southeastern Indiana. Under-ground Railroad lines, many of which ran through individual stations, converged on and radiated from these communities. The

Louisville, Madison, Cincinnati and Maysville areas were stations—or junctions—of this sort and will discussed in detail in Chapter VI. As such, the more elaborate coordination possible within these junctions facilitated crossing the Ohio River and the movement of fugitives through Indiana or Ohio.

To address this perceived problem, laws were enacted requiring that freed blacks leave the state and prohibiting the migration of free African Americans into Kentucky.[48] To enforce these laws, there were periodic searches to identify and subsequently remove free people of color with no legal right to reside in the Commonwealth. Those caught and found guilty of "illegal migration" were given the option of posting bond to leave the state or being "hired-out" (which meant being sold into virtual slavery) by an agent of the Court. Of course, these "round-up's" were also effective means of identifying fugitive slaves who, if apprehended, were jailed and either returned to their owners or sold.[49]

Slave Escapes and Inter-racial Relationships

In urban areas as large and complex as Cincinnati and Louisville in the 1850s, the "color-line" was not always a well defined and impermeable barrier between the races. Poor and working class whites, particularly the Irish and German immigrants who flooded the mid-west and border region beginning in the 1840s, free African Americans and hired-out slaves often lived and worked in close proximity to one another. This "blurring of the color line" created several opportunities for fugitives to secure sanctuary. For example, if they had money or "friends" with money, they could simply rent a room. Furthermore, because local ordinances prohibited

African Americans from engaging in a range of business activities, white businesses developed—such as groceries and grog-shops—that actually catered to and often depended on trade with African Americans, even when such trade was illegal.[50] Particularly in urban areas, people interacted across racial and status lines—enslaved African Americans interacted with whites and free African Americans who, in turn, interacted with one another.[51]

In other words, the color line was more a construct than a barricade and many of the interactions across racial and status lines produced relationships that violated, to varying degrees, the accepted racial norms of antebellum American society. Some of these were "business" relationships, but others became personal and sometimes intimate if and when the African American party was viewed and treated as a person, not as a servant or an object unequal in power and value. When a truly human relationship developed, it became difficult to think of someone as a person, equal to oneself, and then treat him or her as livestock—in contrast to relations between whites and favored slaves that had the character of relations between pet-owners and beloved pets. Thus, when such relationships did become personal—and often sexual as well—the color line would often be breached and either the law or the accepted standards of racial etiquette, or both, would be violated.

Intimate inter-racial relationships often produced a special type of assisted slave escape unrelated or only loosely related to the Underground Railroad. How often such relationships figured in slave escapes cannot be ascertained based on the available evidence. However, given the sensitivity of the topic, a few illustrations—typically from failed escape attempts—are revealing. For example, on February 21, 1856, an article entitled "Elopement Extraordinary" appeared in the Louisville press that illustrated how such relationships often led to slave escapes. The article stated:

> Yesterday between the hours of breakfast and dinner, a runaway couple were captured in New Albany. One of them was a likely black woman, the cook of Mr. Newland, in this city, and the other a white gentleman from the East somewhere, bearing the name of Elisha Hillyer. It was a regular love match.... The particulars of this romantic negro stealing affair are these: The white man was deeply enamoured of the black cook, and, no doubt, persuaded her to run away, having before hand provided a couple of through tickets over the New Albany railroad to Michigan City.... The woman, after getting breakfast for her master's family as usual, packed up her duds, took the omnibus to Portland, where she joined the white man, and together they crossed the river on the ferry boat. The woman was closely veiled, and excited the suspicion of Mr. Conner, the ferryman, who noticed her pretty closely, and after she entered the ladies' room on the ferry boat, saw the man go up to her, raise her veil, and imprint a sweet kiss upon her pouting lips, when to the great surprise of the ferry master, he discovered the woman to be a negro.

The woman, twenty-two year old Mary Jane, was arrested and returned to her owner. Hillyer, described elsewhere as a "big fellow, and good looking, with bushy whiskers," escaped, but was soon captured hiding in a New Albany cellar.[52]

Similarly, in a July 1857 case in which a personal relationship is suggested, J. R. Sprinkle, "a light complexioned and chunky man ... a genteel looking fellow from Memphis" was arrested on the charge of attempting to "runoff" Caroline, an enslaved woman from the Federal Hill ("My Old Kentucky Home") plantation of Bardstown. Along with a Police Court report, an accompanying article entitled, "Negro Stealing" stated that:

> Officer Bligh last evening arrested a chap who is suspicioned very strongly for an attempt to steal away a negro woman, the property of Dr. Buchanan. The man was seen before 5 o'clock yesterday morning at the Jeffersonville ferry landing, on this side of the river, in close confab with the woman. One of the officers of the ferry boat sent for a watchman, and the woman was taken to jail. The man dodged off, but was subsequently taken.

The ferryman, Henry Cooney, "...was convinced from their talk and actions that they met by agreement, for the purpose of traveling through Indiana together."[53]

Hillyer and Sprinkle may not have been Underground Railroad agents in any strict sense. However, they were willing to assist fugitives for seemingly personal reasons and, to consummate their plans, were also willing to work with those with connections to established escape networks. A more detailed and dramatic example of such a relationship is included in Chapter VII.

Coordinated Escapes

Slave escapes such as these entailed elaborate planning and sustained effort on the part of both fugitives and those who assisted them. The records of such escapes reveal the existence of extensive local and regional networks that could be activated under favorable circumstances. Based on the evidence reviewed in this study, it was this degree of coordination and collaboration that distinguished escapes with true Underground Railroad involvement from those that were either unaided or nearly so.

In some cases, as noted previously, early networks consisted of strategically located family and friends. For example, on November 1, 1825, fifteen year old Marilla escaped from Elisha Athy of Middletown. Athy stated that her "mother lives ... in Louisville, and I think she must be somewhere at that place or in the neighborhood" being hidden by her family or others.[54] Lewis ran away from Samuel Lawless of Jefferson County in June 1830. In advertising for Lewis' return, Lawless stated that, "when last seen, he is supposed to be in or about Louisville, where his mothers and sisters live ... and has the appearance of daily laborer on the Street."[55] Martha Jane escaped from "the Widow Mary Barbee" of Middletown in January 1832 and was thought to have secreted "herself in Louisville."[56] In May 1832, Aunt Sarah escaped from David Watkins of Jefferson County and Sim escaped from Henry Robb of Louisville. The escapes were unrelated, but both fugitives were thought to be "loitering about Louisville."[57] In 1836, Diana fled James B. Huie of Louisville and, according to Huie's advertisement, was "no doubt lurking about the city or county, as all of her relations reside here."[58] Nancy escaped at roughly the same time from J. Clarke and was "supposed to be in Charleston, in the State of Indiana."[59]

When Kitty ran away in 1842, her owner, B. F. Morse of Jefferson County, stated that "she will attempt to cross the river, or secrete herself in Louisville, where she has a free brother, and may have obtained a free pass,"[60] much as when Ellen escaped from J. S. Penn of Louisville in 1844, she was thought to be "harbored by some one in the city."[61] Similarly, Harry, who escaped from P. Chamberlin of Jefferson County in 1849, was thought to be "lurking about town, and he has a wife living with Julius Howard, on Market Street."[62]

Many of the lawsuits for the recovery of the value of lost slave property referred to assistance received by fugitives that involved some degree of planning and coordination. For example, *Edwards v. Vail* (April 1830) involved a suit for the value of a "negro who came on board from Jeffersonville, Indiana, with a white woman, and left the boat upon its arrival in Cincinnati."[63] Similarly, in *Graham v. Strader* (October 1844), Graham sued "to recover

damages for the unauthorized transportation of his three slaves, Reuben, Henry and George, on board the steamboat, 'Pike', from Louisville to Cincinnati, whence they escaped to Canada." The slaves were described as

> ... three yellow men between nineteen and twenty-three years of age, well trained as dining room servants and as scientific musicians. Complainant allowed the slaves to go to Louisville to live with Williams, a free man of color, to learn music, and afterwards gave them written permission to go to the State of Ohio.... [I]t appears that the boys, while under the care of Williams, were with him once and perhaps twice in Madison, Indiana, and two or three times in New Albany, Indiana, playing as musicians.[64]

Rendering aid could sometimes be quite costly in monetary terms. For example, in May 1849, the U.S. Circuit Court heard the case of George Ray of Trimble County vs. Luther A. Donnel and William Hamilton of Decatur County, Indiana. The suit was "to recover the value of certain slaves—a mother and four children, the latter nearly white—who had run away from their master in Kentucky, and, as was alleged, had been harbored by the defendants." The Judge ruled in favor of the plaintiff and the award of "not less than $2,500," including court costs, was deemed high "enough to use up almost any man detected in giving 'aid and comfort' to runaway slaves."[65]

The "Quiet Insurrection" of the 1850s

The 1850s were a decade of mounting conflict and deepening divisions between North and South. Beginning with the debates that produced the Compromise of 1850 and the Fugitive Slave Act that took effect in September of that year, the decade moved from crisis to crisis—with slavery at the heart of each. The publication of *Uncle Tom's Cabin* in 1852 challenged the Southern view of both slavery and the character of the Negro, and created a public relations nightmare from which the South would never recover entirely. The furor precipitated by the Kansas-Nebraska Act (1854) and its explicit nullification of the 1820 Missouri Compromise offered the South the hope that the political balance upset by the territorial acquisitions of the Mexican War might be restored by the creation of new slave states. However, the determination of the South to extend slavery was matched by the determination of the North (and, now, the West) to contain it as evidenced by the political shifts that undermined the Whig Party and created the Republican Party in the mid–1850s.[66] New crises soon followed — "Bleeding Kansas," the Dred Scott case (1857) and John Brown's Raid (1859) — eventually bringing Abraham Lincoln to the presidency of a "house divided against itself" in 1860 and culminating in Civil War in 1861.[67]

Those wishing only to limit slavery to the existing slave states, such as Abraham Lincoln, were hardly abolitionists. Yet, to southern politicians, particularly from the deep southern interior, opposition to the extension of slavery was synonymous with opposition to slavery itself. From their perspective, if slavery could not grow, it would die — or be destroyed at the whim of a new American majority. Because this new majority was created by industrialization, European immigration, urbanization in the northeast and midwest, and the drive to settle the Great Plains and the West — its needs and worldview, and the attendant forces of change and modernization swelling its numbers were only beginning to manifest themselves. In other words, although still profitable and deeply embedded in the lifeways of the South, slavery was becoming as obsolete in the industrializing United States as it had become in the British Empire where the institution was abolished in 1838. Of course, what seems obvious in retrospect was certainly not obvious to most Americans in the 1850s.

Still, the institution of slavery could be only so strong and only so secure in such a divided nation. In the borderland, where the structure of slavery was weakest and most porous, these many factors, taken together, sustained what O'Brien termed a "quiet insurrection" on the part of enslaved African Americans. She concluded that, among white Kentuckians, the

> fear of a slave rebellion was uppermost in their minds and so preoccupied were they with thoughts of a wildly impractical and useless uprising by their slaves, that they apparently did not notice, or else could not stop, the quiet insurrection their slaves were mounting under their noses... Armed, not with guns, but with tenacity, courage, patience, and above all, incisive intelligence, slaves waged a continual war against slavery.[68]

Slave escapes became more, rather than less, frequent. Conspiracy scares became routine and, beyond the efforts of enslaved African Americans, this "quiet" but not always bloodless "insurrection" was complemented, aided and abetted by a broad conspiracy of conscience on the part of free African Americans and white anti-slavery activists throughout the region. The Underground Railroad emerged as the organized expression and instrument of that conspiracy. In other words, the totality of these factors forced the imposition of some semblance of order and structure on efforts to assist fugitive slaves.

There were numerous indications that Kentucky slaveholders felt increasingly pressed both by the sustained outflow of fugitives and by the willingness of others to assist those fugitives. In November 1852, shaken by the steady stream of slave escapes in the area bordering Maysville, slave-holders from Mason and neighboring counties met "for the purpose of devising means to better secure the slave property of Kentucky." The article, reprinted from the *Maysville Eagle*, urged " the formation of slave protection societies in each county of the State, especially those bordering on the Ohio." Each county was "to have a pursuing committee, to act on the instruction of the President ... to have a permanent fund, to pay expenses of pursuit; to pay a stipulated reward to those who capture."[69] In essence, the plan of action recommended by these harried slave-holders was to create an organization to pursue fugitives more efficiently to combat a more organized Underground Railroad. Similarly, in September 1855, "the slaveholders of Henderson county" met at Henderson to "take steps as to the better security of slaves in that county." Echoing the views of slaveholders in the eastern and central border regions, they condemned "the acts and doings of northern Abolitionists and fanatics" and proposed the creation of "a league or association" to protect their property.[70]

Thus, by the mid 1850s, the frequency of slave escapes, the numbers of fugitives, the more visible involvement of "friends of the fugitive," black and white, both in Kentucky and on the northern side of the Ohio River border — caused considerable frustration, consternation and, at times, almost mild hysteria in some sections of the state. Extreme and usually impractical remedies were proposed. For example, in 1856, a state representative from Henry County introduced a bill in the Kentucky General Assembly stating that "all persons convicted of tampering with negroes, and attempting their abduction, shall be punished with death." This bill was only defeated by ten votes.[71] During the frigid winter of 1856, the *Cleveland Leader* reported that "According to the best information which we have been able to obtain, more than two hundred and fifty slaves escaped from Virginia and Kentucky during the month of February, 1856."[72] Against

this backdrop, later in the same legislative session, the Kentucky General Assembly spent "much time" debating a bill to provide for patrols on the Ohio River "for the protection of the slave population." The bill proposed would

> ... make it the duty of the County Judge and a majority of the Justices in the counties upon the Ohio river to appoint patrols ... [and] require that all water crafts at the Kentucky shore and not in the immediate charge of the owner, &c., shall be chained and locked and the oars removed....[73]

To many in the state, this bill seemed both desperate and foolish. The editor of the *Louisville Courier* confessed that he had "very little faith in the plan proposed. It may prove efficacious, but we doubt the virtue of any remedy that can be invented." He concluded that "we are a prey to the thieving scoundrels of the North, and legislation can effect but little...."[74] The bill was rejected by a vote of forty-three in favor, fifty opposed.[75] By the late 1850s, different factions were blaming one another for the seeming inability of local and state authorities to stem the tide of slave escapes. Referring to a recent rash of runaways, another *Louisville Courier* editorial stated, "We should not expect anything else, so long as we have so many Abolitionists among us. Black Republicans are as thick in these parts as wolves in a prairie."[76]

Other examples of how these attitudes were expressed could be found in reports of fugitive slaves who returned to Kentucky, ostensibly, of their own volition — reports that reveal, often inadvertently, much that they were intended to conceal. As an example, in October 1850, Alfred Taylor "who had been abducted some four weeks ago by the managers of the underground railroad, and run off to Canada" returned to Mrs. Butler, his owner in Louisville, convinced that "freedom and

Canada are hard."[77] The article added that "a white man in the city … persuaded him off, and no doubt caused him to rob his kind mistress of … $200 or $300, all of which he took away with him, but returned with nothing but rags."[78]

The risks to friends of the fugitive were different, but as real as those to fugitives themselves. Abolitionists, real or suspected, were wholly unwelcome in the South by the 1830s and, by the 1850s, those with anti-slavery sympathies and any hint of an inclination to assist fugitive slaves were viewed as enemies and were treated accordingly.[79] One of the better-known and more interesting Kentucky cases concerned Mr. and Mrs. Thomas Brown, mentioned previously as two whites who worked as Underground Railroad agents in the Henderson area. On June 7, 1854, a mass meeting was held at the Henderson County courthouse and the following resolution, which described many of the facts of the case, was adopted:

> Whereas, it has come to the notice of the citizens of this city that Thomas Brown and his wife have been engaged in unlawful traffic with the negroes of this city and county; also, in making arrangements with them to run them off to Canada; and whereas the said Brown has been arrested on a charge of running off negroes; wherefore be it Resolved, That Mr. Brown being now confined in jail in Union county for stealing negroes, and this it is believed that his wife is particeps criminis in receiving stolen property, a committee be appointed to request Mrs. Brown to leave the city and county of Henderson in ten days from this date.[80]

Thomas Brown was eventually sentenced to the Kentucky penitentiary.

Southern whites who wrote letters or articles for the anti-slavery press were wise to use pseudonyms or to do anonymously. If not, they risked the fate of J. Brady, a white teacher in Lexington who wrote a highly critical account of slavery in the Lexington area that was published in an Ohio newspaper in 1856. Brady foolishly signed his initials (J. B.), which made him a target for hundreds of angry white Lexingtonians. He was subsequently mobbed, "conducted to the courthouse yard, and there stripped," then tarred and feathered, and forced to flee to points north.[81] Only a month later, the citizens of Flemingsburg acted outside the law when they tarred and feathered an Abolitionist, name not given, "for tampering with slaves."[82] These cases also indicate the presence of a few Underground Railroad operatives on Kentucky soil. It is reasonable to assume the presence of at least a few others who eluded discovery.

Another important, but obscure case, describes the inner-workings of the Underground Railroad in Cincinnati in some detail and the fate of one of its agents. On June 13, 1957, a husband and wife from Kentucky, Irvin and Angeline Broadus, the property of Colonel C. A. Withers, were arrested in Cincinnati at the residence of William A. Conolly "at No. 18 on Vine Street." Conolly was one of the editors of the Cincinnati *Daily Commercial* and had been suspected as a "member" of the Underground Railroad for some time.[83]

After being informed that the Broadus couple was being harbored in Conolly's home, six U.S. Deputy Marshalls descended on this hiding place while Conolly was absent. Irvin Broadus was armed and prepared to defend himself and his wife. A desperate and violent confrontation ensued in which Broadus and John C. Elliott, one of the marshalls, were stabbed and seriously wounded. With a white man injured, a large mob formed, quite probably with the intention of lynching Broadus. However, both fugitives were conveyed safely to jail. Broadus and Elliott recovered from their wounds—and Broadus and his wife were eventually returned to Kentucky. The news report added:

> Recently the managers and agents of the Underground Railroad have been tampering with the slaves and, on Saturday

evening, June 10th, they made their escape.... It is well known that there is a regularly organized vigilance committee of the UGRR directors in this city, and, in fact, in all the Northern and most of the Southern cities.... A meeting of the Vigilance Committee was held on Friday, and money raised to run the slaves off.[84]

Conolly eluded capture and it is likely that the same apparatus primed to smuggle the fugitives north was used to smuggle Conolly out of Cincinnati.[85] The Vigilance Committee mentioned in the article was the organization behind which Levi Coffin was the moving force.

There were also more spontaneous expressions of the outright refusal of many blacks and whites in the northern states to obey the Fugitive Slave Act of 1850. As one manifestation of this defiance, free blacks and white anti-slavery groups sometimes engaged in dramatic rescues— or rescue attempts— of fugitive slaves captured in the North. For example, an article from the *Cincinnati Enquirer*, reprinted in the *Louisville Courier* in December 1852, described "an attempt ... by a party of Kentuckians to recover some of their runaway negroes, who were about starting on the cars for Cleveland. The Kentuckians were knocked down by a gang of Abolitionists and the slaves rescued, and then run off."[86] Similarly, in May 1854, a Kentucky slaveholder pursued a fugitive to Akron, Ohio. However, before seizing the runaway, "the owner told the marshal, if there shall be any fuss, let the nigger go. There was a 'fuss' and 'the nigger' went." The article continued, "The owner of the negro ... knew that his life would be in danger if a mob should be raised for the rescue of the negro... The fugitive slave law cannot be executed in Ohio, and probably never will be."[87]

In Cincinnati, "gangs of negroes interspersed with a few whites" attempted to rescue "sixteen slaves" on the steamboat *Falls City* en route from Wheeling to St. Louis in March 1855. The crowd made several futile attempts to free the African Americans and, through the efforts of anti-slavery attorneys, "a writ of habeas corpus" was obtained. However, before this writ could be executed, the owner moved the enslaved African Americans to Covington — with the understanding that "they will remain in Covington until the Falls City is ready to leave, when she will go over and take them on board."[88]

In announcing a "grand celebration" planned in Cincinnati for Washington's birthday in 1856, the *Louisville Courier* cautioned the many Kentuckians who had been invited: "Before the latter leave home they should take care to properly secure their negroes, or, judging from recent events, their host will arrange for them a journey on the underground rail road."[89]

Not all escapes were successful and both the apprehension of fugitives in the immediate aftermath of an escape and the recovery of fugitives long given up for lost were widely reported in the southern press as victories over the forces working to destroy the southern way of life. For example, a July 1853 article celebrated the recovery of a fugitive in Louisville. The fugitive was a " pastry cook on the steamer Sam Snowden known by the name of Tom Steel, who had run away from Frankfort some 5 years ago." Steele escaped by steamboat to Cincinnati and eventually settled in Pittsburgh where "he has a wife and several children." Unfortunately, after his capture, Steele's owner "took charge of his long lost property, and will no doubt send him South."[90] Similarly, in July 1854, officers of the steamboat, Alvin Adams, "arrested a fugitive, or runaway slave, on the boat, at Madison" and brought him to jail in Louisville. The news article stated:

It appears that the slave in question ranaway in company with another from Jno.

H. Page, of Bowling Green, and had managed to reach Washington, Ind., together, when this fellow left his partner and went to Madison, in the full expectation of taking a boat at Madison for Cincinnati; and once in Cincinnati, he thought he would be perfectly safe. The rascal, however ... fell into honest hands....[91]

Escape attempts sometimes failed tragically, as was the case in December 1855 in Bourbon County. As described in the *Louisville Courier,* "there was a negro stampede from Millersburg, Bourbon county, on the night of the 16th." Seven fugitives fled in a carriage "driven by a white man, who represented the inmates as a runaway match on their way to Aberdeen ... to get married." The article continued,

> They proceeded in the carriage to near Washington, whence they went on foot to East Maysville, where they attempted to cross the Ohio in a skiff. The skiff leaked and sunk, and the three women and child were drowned. The men cried for help and were rescued by a market man going from Aberdeen to Maysville, who ... took them to jail in Maysville. There is great excitement at Millersburg, and if they can get possession of the free negro, he will probably be hung. The white man, if he is discovered, will be pretty apt to meet with the same treatment.[92]

The common thread linking these many examples is the steady escalation of tension and determination on both sides of the fugitive slave question. The issues and stakes for fugitives were the same as a century before — freedom or the consequences of capture. However, friends of the fugitive grew in number and their willingness to defy federal and state law often assumed the trappings of a crusading movement. Defenders of slavery responded by raising the barricades and augmenting their judicial and police power. In many respects, the battle between North and South began in the borderland.

Before the Bar: Friends of the Fugitive in Court

In the 1850s, many friends of the fugitive ran afoul of Kentucky authorities. Some were prosecuted as felony offenders; others had their cases adjudicated in city and county courts. Among these many cases, some are particularly informative and illustrate how local and regional assistance networks evolved into a more organized Underground Railroad.

In January 1850, such a case was tried in the Louisville Police Court. John Cain, a free African American, was arraigned for "enticing Mary, a slave girl of Mr. Thos. J. Read's, to attempt to runaway." In court, Mary testified that "Cain had been talking to her on the streets about freedom; and said that he could take her clear off without any danger." She added that "a colored man by the name of Whiting brought her to town, and she stopped at Cain's house until he could take her across the river." The arresting officer inserted that he

> ... learned from Edward Trueman, a slave man that had been arrested over in Jeffersonville, that John Cain had been in the habit of running off slaves, and had succeeded in many instances. This induced the officer to visit Cain's house where he found the girl Mary. The court held Cain to bail in the sum of $1,000 to appear and answer the charge of attempted abduction. The case of the slave man Trueman was laid over. He crossed the river on the ferry boat, and was arrested in Jeffersonville and brought back.[93]

Had Trueman not been caught and persuaded, by whatever means, to testify against Cain, there would have been no impediment to Mary's escape.

In a case that aroused tensions between Kentucky and Indiana over white involvement in the Underground Railroad, "Norris Day, sometimes a preacher, was arrested some days ago at Madison" after the Governor of Indiana issued a warrant in response to a requisition for Day from the Governor of Kentucky. The article, reprinted from the *Frankfort Commonwealth*, continued that Day was charged with "enticing slaves from their masters." Day "had a hearing before Judge Walker, of Madison" and was discharged on a technicality. However, "he left in haste for parts unknown — fearing, it is said, both mob violence and a new warrant."[94]

Alexander Hatfield was one of the truly mercurial characters in the free African American community of Louisville and a fixture in the local courts, having a taste for alcohol and a tendency to rowdiness. Hatfield was often caricatured as a buffoon in the Louisville press, but he also had a propensity for being around fugitive slaves and "places" important to the Underground Railroad. What makes Hatfield intriguing is the difficulty in determining whether he was a crafty Underground Railroad operative or a fool and occasional informant.

For example, in February 1854, the following court report appeared. Alexander Hatfield "a free negro barber, was up for drunkenness and disorderly conduct, and drawing a pistol on one Maria, a slave of Mrs. Mullen. He had only just arrived from Canada via Cincinnati, and was only bluffing a little." A companion article added that Hatfield found Canada "a hard road to travel, had just got back yesterday, and was so overjoyed that he got drunk right away."[95] If nothing else, Hatfield had journeyed to Canada for reasons unknown and had returned — behaving in a manner, calculated or not, that certainly deflected suspicion.

In September 1856, Hatfield figured in an unusual criminal case, as indicated in excerpts from the court report:

> Samuel Cole and James Armstrong were arrested … for attempting to run off Jack, a slave of Wm. C. Kidd … that notorious rascal, Alex Hatfield, a free negro, gave information that these men were to meet

at his house to wait for Jack, who was to run off with him and his wife. Alex made all the arrangements, first hiding the officers under the bed, and then going out after the white men, soon returned with them. They, then, in the hearing of the officers under the bed, made their arrangements, by which Hatfield and his wife, and the boy Jack, were to all go off together. The white men assured Hatfield, who pretended to fear that he would be caught, that they could get off safe and clear. They would cross the river at Second street in a skiff, and then the road would be plain and easy.[96]

In the end, Jack did not appear and may have been forewarned. The officers wearied of hiding under the bed, and "rolled and pitched into the white men," eventually lodging the two in jail. Cole and Armstrong "denied all attempts to run off a slave, said they came here to buy a boat, got drunk and were taken in by Hatfield." Since no escape occurred, Jack could not be held guilty of any offense. Hatfield and his wife were viewed as having performed a public service in their own blundering way. However, whether Hatfield was cunning or foolish, by informing the police he betrayed the whites involved and protected the African Americans — including himself.

A case involving a family relationship was tried in February 1855. As stated in the court report, "Charles Taylor, a free man of color, was up for enticing away Frank, a slave" of William R. Adams of Louisville. Frank escaped in June 1854 and was "supposed to be in Canada." According to testimony by witnesses, Charles Taylor was Frank's father "and had spent $200 to get him away."[97] A month later, "Charles Smith and Henry Porter, a couple free negroes, were arrested for aiding and abetting Charles, a slave of Edward Holbrook, to escape." Charles worked with Porter as a cook on the steamboat, Sultana, and escaped from the boat "going to Terre Haute, since which time he has not been heard of." Smith was accused of representing Charles as a free man and "was considered guilty."[98] In November 1855, Porter was apprehended in New Orleans and returned to Louisville.[99]

One of the more important men in the free African American community of Louisville was tried in City Court in April 1855. The report of this case, quoted below in its entirety, offers unusual insights into how some Underground Railroad agents operated:

> James Cunningham (f.m.c.), the musician, was arrested on suspicion of running off slaves. Kirkpatrick has suspected him ever since Mr. Shotwell's slave was run off three years since. Letters from Fairbanks addressed to him and his wife were found in his possession. K. had reason to suspect that the clothing of Shotwell's slave was deposited there. Other negroes belonging to Mr. Thomas, Capt. Rudd, and Mr. Brannin had been run off since, and some of their clothes were found in Cunningham's house. The latest case occurred about a year ago ... Officer Hamlet arrested a negro named Shadrach Henderson a year or two ago for running away negroes, and Henderson, in his statement, implicated Cunningham.[100]

While Cunningham's past history was problematic in the eyes of local authorities, there was no specific crime for which he was arrested in April 1855. The arresting officer, Kirkpatrick, claimed, in essence, that he "meant to arrest Cunningham sometime before," but had not done so—as "he had been waiting for a more favorable opportunity to send both Cunningham and his wife to the penitentiary." In the absence of a specific, actionable charge, Cunningham was still held to bail in the amount of $500 "to be of good behavior for one year."[101] Cunningham posted bail promptly. Although convicted of no crime, Cunningham's profession enabled him to travel and acquainted him with African Americans and whites throughout the region. Also, the significance of finding

the clothes of fugitives in Cunningham's house was that provision was made for clothing changes or disguises in the early stages of these escapes.

One of the more convoluted cases of this kind involved John C. Long, who was examined several times on the charge of aiding Alfred, "a slave of Mrs. Butler," to escape from slavery in September 1855 while Mrs. Butler was visiting Carrollton. At the heart of this case was the theft of a valuable watch by Alfred—which was given, presumably, to Long. The watch, used presumably to finance Alfred's unsuccessful flight to freedom, found its way nonetheless to Columbus, Ohio. Alfred's testimony was incriminating, but "the testimony of a slave cannot be received." However, the most damning evidence came from letters found in Long's home,

> ... one or two of them ... were dated, one from Westport, and others from Chillicothe, Ohio. The letters from Chillicothe were written by a brother of Long's asking about some one, evidently a runaway, requiring a description, &c., in order that the writer could have free papers made out for him by the county clerk of that district. On the back of the same letter was written in pencil a full and most accurate description of the boy Alfred.[102]

The case was continued given the inconclusive nature of the evidence that could be admitted, then continued yet again awaiting the arrival "of a free negro witness from Eminence" who could prove "that Mrs. Butler's watch is now in Canada under pledge for board."[103] Of particular interest in this and many other cases are references to the use of regular mail in coordinating escapes.

In October 1857, John Knight, "said to be a free man of color," was arrested and tried in Louisville for "running off a slave of L. Thompson" by the name of John William. Knight employed an interesting, although unsuccessful, deception. According to the court record, John William

... stated that some time last July he met the accused on Brook Street. The latter had a couple of buckets and a brush, and asked witness if he wanted a job. He said yes, and then the other told him to come along with him, and they went across the river together on the ferry, took the plank road to New Albany and there he staid all night under a beech tree. The next morning, they went to the depot, the witness having the white-wash buckets. The accused then went away somewhere, and in the meantime a white man came along and arrested witness and brought him over to Kentucky.

The Court concluded that it was difficult to prove Knight guilty of anything other than a misdemeanor since Williams did not actually escape and it was unclear whether escape was his goal.[104] However, the ease with which Williams was able to cross the river — and the confidence Knight seemed to place in this gambit — suggest, as corroborated by other cases cited in this study, that this was not the first time an enslaved African American crossed from Louisville to Jeffersonville simply by pretending to be free.

In May 1858, William Tatum, "alias John Jones was arrested" for "trying to dodge over into Indiana with a slave named Hugh, the property of Peyton Meekin of Nelson County." Tatum and Hugh attempted to cross the river at the Portland ferry and, when questioned separately, their accounts did not agree. Tatum first claimed that Hugh was free, then that Hugh was his slave. Hugh never denied being enslaved. Both had " big pair of saddle bags" as if packed for a long journey. The two were arrested and Tatum "was required to answer the charge, a very serious one" of assisting a slave to escape.[105] Tatum was indicted a few months later.[106]

One cannot but wonder if Tatum,

150 Dollars Reward.

RANAWAY from the subscriber on Saturday the 9th of June last a negro man, named

CÆSAR,

About 24 years of age, 5 feet 8 inches high, slender made, a little stoop shouldered, quite black, well dressed, and probably has with him a number of clothes formerly worn by gentlemen. Said boy was employed for a considerable time as a house servant by Mr. A. Allan, tavern keeper, Louisville: is intelligent and speaks softly. He went off in company with a negro man named BUCK, who has since been taken and brought back. Said negro man Cæsar was seen in Chillicothe, Ohio, about the 20th of June, and is probably lurking about there at this time. His object it seems, when he started, was to go to Philadelphia, but he may change his route. He has changed his name to that of GEORGE The above reward will be given if returned to the subscriber, residing near Louisville, Jefferson county, Ken or seventy-five dollars if secured in any jail in the United States, and information given so that he can be obtained.

H. HAWLEY.

July 3.   286—ow

☞ The editors of the Gazette, Chillicothe, Gazette, Columbus. Ohio, and the Gazette. Pittsburgh, Pa; will insert the above three times in their respective papers, and forward their accounts to this office for payment.

Fugitive slave notice: "Cæsar," *Louisville Public advertiser*, March 2, 1822. An early example of an escape from the Louisville area through Chillicothe.

alias Jones, was the mysterious "Jones" to whom Levi Coffin referred in 1876 — who, in one year, aided twenty-seven fugitives in their efforts to escape from the Louisville area. "Jones'" modus operandi was to conceal fugitives in his home and then send them to Cincinnati by steamboat, sometimes accompanying them himself.[107]

Shortly thereafter, a more complex and far more serious case was brought to court, again in Louisville. The case began with a "charge of theft and abetting slaves to runaway" against William Lewis, a middle-aged white man. Lewis was arrested after the local watchmen found numerous "suspicious things, including wearing apparel" and even a daguerreotype of en-slaved African Americans who had es-caped from the Louisville area sometime before, "all nicely packed in a new chest" in Lewis' sleeping room. Since these fugi-tives had been apprehended at the "house of Dick Buckner, the free negro," Buckner was arrested, years after the fact, on the same charge as Lewis—which ended the first phase of the case.[108]

Additional testimony was taken against Lewis the next day. One witness, Jacob Deal, testified that Lewis rented rooms from him and "that negro women are in the constant habit of going into his room at unusual hours. This was consid-ered irrelevant to the case in hand, but it goes to prove that he is an agent of the un-derground railroad." In the end, Lewis was "held to bail of $800 to answer a charge of felony, and in default, was committed" to jail. The court report added, "He may not be guilty of an attempt to run off the slaves, but he looked mean enough to be guilty."[109] Two days later, Dick Buckner was brought to trial on the same charge and the testimony entered into evidence, along with that in Lewis' case, was both revealing and potentially damning:

> Several of the police have been on the trail of the hoary old villain for some time, being pretty well convinced that he and Lewis ... are agents of the Black Republi-can party and conductors of the under-ground railroad.... In the house of said Dick Buckner was found ... five carpet sacks filled with runaway nigger's duds, also a family bible, and other books, which belonged to Harrison Laville, a slave, the property of J. B. Bowles. In the bible was recorded the marriage of Har-rison, who got off with his wife and a child named Eliza. A letter was also pro-duced, which deeply incriminated and doubly d — d Buckner, as the active agent of runaways. Said letter was written from Chatham, Canada West, by one J. West-ley Ray ... a runaway from Shelby county, Ky.... As the evidences of his guilt thick-ened upon him, his counsel, to stop the dreadful clamor, admitted everything

and submitted the case. He was held to $800 bail to answer a felony, and in de-fault, was committed.[110]

Buckner was later indicted on two counts of "aiding and abetting the escape of slaves." He was found guilty and sen-tenced to two years in the Kentucky pen-itentiary.[111]

In September 1858, another free Afri-can American in Louisville was charged with the same offense. Once again, the court report is instructive and the escape strategy familiar:

> Miles Wilson, a free man of very black color, and hair so kinky that it is tied into knots, was in arrest on the dark and dire-ful charge of aiding and abetting the es-cape of Charles, the slave of F. A. Moore.... Mr. Wright, a collector on the Jefferson-ville ferry boat, testified that he saw ac-cused and the slave Charles together on the boat last evening, on the way to Jeffer-sonville, and Miles paid the ferry for him-self and Charles, saying the latter was all right. This didn't suit the collector, who questioned Charles, and finally arrested and brought him to the city.[112]

Charles testified the following day and stated that he and Wilson were "going across the river to a ball, with the intention of coming back again at nine o'clock." The defense also "set up that Miles got crazy on whisky." However, the report added that, "after getting on the other side the chances are nine out of ten that he would disappear on the underground railroad."[113] Wilson was later indicted, found guilty and sen-tenced to ten years in the Kentucky peni-tentiary.[114] When sentenced formally on January 20, "he owned up that he was guilty, but stated that John Lancisco, a coffee-house keeper of Jeffersonville, was the prime mover and instigator in the mat-ter, and that the plan was concocted by the white man."[115]

As these and other cases indicate, the sheer number of African Americans and whites having some role in assisting fugitives reflects the growing magnitude and coordination of efforts of this kind in the borderland in the 1850s. However, there was also a larger regional network to which local efforts were linked. The available evidence suggests that evolution of the very linkages that created this larger network represented the critical threshold in the evolution of the Underground Railroad in the west and that the maturation of free African American communities in the borderland was an essential catalyst in this process.

The Free African American Community

Fugitives and free people of color west of the Appalachians followed the same "pattern of black chain migration" from south to north, often settling in the same mid-western cities or Canada.[116] This similarity with regard to patterns of movement was not coincidental. As noted, free people of color were unwelcome in most regions and faced the constant dilemma of finding a relatively safe place in which to live and work. Where free blacks clustered in various towns, cities and rural enclaves, their sheer numbers created possible havens and sources of aid for fugitives. Further, the bonds between free and enslaved African Americans were far stronger and far more complex than often supposed and represented "the African American community's propensity for collective self-help ... bonds of blood, of culture, of common experience, and of a common world view that recognized the injustice of American racial inequality."[117]

Many free people of color had experienced slavery. Others had parents who had been enslaved and/or relatives who remained so. Because of frequent kidnappings and limited legal protection, free people of color were also fully aware that "no African American was safe from slavery" as long as slavery was permitted under American law. In a more immediate and practical sense, intricate networks of communication linked blacks in the North and South. Such networks were created by interregional movement driven by the travel and employment patterns of free blacks, slave-hiring and, to a lesser extent, even domestic slave trade. Each entailed the movement of African Americans sometimes over great distances—for example, being sold "down the river" to the cotton states, being hired out to work on steamboats plying the Ohio or Mississippi Rivers, or as sailors or even teamsters. In more fully developed free black communities, such as Louisville and Cincinnati, African American churches and fraternal organizations created "safe spaces" and opportunities for information exchange beyond the easy reach of white surveillance. Moreover, although most African Americans were illiterate, many were not and urban free blacks were most likely to have access to minimal education. Thus, having a small but critical mass of literate free people of color (and some enslaved African Americans) in these small communities also facilitated the circulation of black and anti-slavery newspapers and even communication by United States mail using coded language.[118]

Neither the information exchanges that often facilitated escapes nor the other forms of assistance rendered more directly to fugitives required any formal organization. Most free African Americans were simply predisposed to assist fugitive slaves and/or to work with others committed to the goal of freedom, black or white. In this sense, it was not necessary to create or join an organization to become part of a movement—or to express and act on the values of a community. Fugitive slaves were similarly predisposed to trust other African Americans and to be wary of whites.[119]

Some free and enslaved African

[Reported for the Louisville Courier.]
Trials in Criminal Court.
FRIDAY, July '13.

HARBORING SLAVES.

Commonwealth *vs.* Stephen Latapie (f. m. c.) This was an indictment for harboring and concealing a slave of Mr. Hornsby, of Shelby county, Ky., in June past. To this indictment the defendant plead not guilty. The proof tended to show that the negro girl was concealed in the hack-house of the defendant and was there found by her owner, but it was not perfectly clear that defendant knew she was a runaway, and had harbored her for the purpose of concealing her from her master. He proved an excellent character by those who had known him for years. There being some doubt about his guilt, the Jury found him not guilty. The case was ably and eloquently argued by Messrs. Pope and Wolfe, for the defendant, and Mr. Craig, prosecucutor, and Capt. Rousseau, for the State.

Commonwealth *vs.* Wm. Jeter.—This was an indictment for harboring and attempting to conceal a slave, the property of Col. George Young, of Shelby county, Ky., but in the employ of Dr. Johnson, in this city, where the offence was committed, for which the prisoner is indicted. Defendant plead not guilty. The proof was conclusive that he had taken the slave to an obscure portion of the city and there obtained temporary lodging for her, but subsequently removed her to his own home, where the watchman found her. He appeared before the jury with a bad character, having been in the Penitentiary of the State once. Some proof was introduced touching upon his insanity but it was not reliable and established to the satisfaction of the jury. He was found guilty and sent to the Penitentiary for the term of three years.

The case of the Commonwealth *vs.* Johnson, for killing Ben. Lawrence, was next taken up, and they are now engaged in selecting a jury. This case will probably consume several days.

Louisville Court Report: *Louisville Courier*, July 14, 1855. Two cases: Stephen Latapie, a free man of color, found not guilty of harboring a fugitive; William Jeter, sentenced to the penitentiary for the same offense.

Americans reached into or worked in the southern interior to assist fugitives. However, people of color and whites associated with the Underground Railroad provided the greatest assistance once fugitives neared or reached free territory. The preponderance of the evidence reviewed in this study supports Horton's conclusion that "fugitives were most likely to plan and execute the initial phase of their escape on their own or with the aid of associates in the South, but for those lucky enough to reach the free states, local black communities became critical to maintaining freedom."[120] Noted African American historian, Benjamin Quarles, presented a classic account of this "Black Underground" in his seminal study of African Americans in the anti-slavery movement[121] in which he traced the origins of these patterns to black reactions to the Fugitive Slave Act of 1793. Quarles also noted that this Act "offended the popular sense of fair play" in that it "legalized kidnapping" and created "a great reservoir of sympathy for those who made the dash for freedom" among whites as well.[122]

This sympathy had deep roots and a long history among free African Americans. For example, African Americans who betrayed fugitive slaves to slave catchers and other authorities were viewed — and treated — as traitors by the vast majority of their kinsmen. When such treachery was revealed, reprisals were often swift and violent. For example, in 1852, several fugitive slaves from Louisville were apprehended after another African American informed the police of their whereabouts, presumably to collect the reward. Once this betrayal became known, "at a recent negro camp meeting near Charlestown, Ind., a black man was tied to a tree and severely lashed ... having given information ... of the whereabouts of Mr. Armstrong's negroes who had run away from this city."[123] As another example, in February 1853, there was a similar "lynching affair" in Alleghany City, Pennsylvania, where

> A free negro was charged with betraying the placed of refuge of a runaway slave. He was waylaid by two men, who threw a bag over his head, leading him out to the woods about a mile and half from town, where they beat him in a most cruel manner…. The whipping was inflicted with a rattan, which was broken almost to splinters.[124]

Even in the cases of greater Louisville and greater Cincinnati, the free black populations were large only in relative terms. Neither community was home to more than a few thousand free African American residents. It is difficult to imagine that the passage of so many fugitives and the identity of so many of their "friends" were not generally known. This being the case, it is equally difficult to imagine that fugitives could have flowed through — and their "friends" could have lived and operated in — these communities over so many decades had sympathy for runaway slaves not been both broad and deep.

There are several rich veins of evidence to support this conclusion. For example, the observations of African Americans recorded during the antebellum period, and the recollections of African Americans recorded after the end of slavery — all describe the nature and conditions of slavery in Kentucky, the phenomenon of slave escapes and the presence of the Underground Road north of the Ohio River in substantially the same terms. Slave escapes were more common than rare occurrences. African Americans who escaped from bondage generally did so on their own initiative, using their own resources. Those African Americans who chose to flee slavery were described as either exceptional individuals or very ordinary individuals faced with extraordinary

circumstances. When they sought and received assistance, such aid usually came from other African Americans. When the Underground Railroad developed, existing slave escape routes through such African American communities usually became Underground Railroad lines. Thus, the population distribution of African Americans in the lower north was not determined by the location of Underground Railroad lines. Rather, Underground Railroad lines were determined largely by the location of African American communities. The difference is subtle, but important.

That one African American would help another, whether in the country or city, or on a steamboat, was not considered exceptional. However, African Americans and whites seemed to view the act of aiding a fugitive in very different contexts. Ironically, most of the African Americans who rendered or received such aid considered it unrelated to the Underground Railroad. In other words, most African Americans in the Kentucky borderland viewed assisting runaway slaves as an extension of their community values, but viewed the Underground Railroad as an organization "staffed" by whites and other African Americans who lived "somewhere else." Even the few renegade anti-slavery whites who lived in or ventured into Kentucky seemed connected to "something" in free, not slave, territory.

There was also a problem of perspective that cannot be ignored. As described in these many cases, a fugitive slave might have only fleeting contact with one or more Underground Railroad agents along his or her escape route — and spend much of his or her journey alone or with fellow fugitives. If the agent was another African American, help from that source was not usually viewed by fugitives as being related to the Underground Railroad. From the perspective of these fugitives, then, the Underground Railroad was peripheral, rather than indispensable, to the success or failure of their escapes. To others, it played no role at all. However, the friend of the fugitive might perform the same act and render the same type of aid hundreds of times, each time to assist a different fugitive — for example, rowing runaways across the Ohio or transporting them by wagon from one station to another. From the perspective of the friend, this single act could become magnified in importance the more often it was repeated over the years.

Thus, those who were the bulwarks of the Underground Railroad movement seldom perceived themselves, and were seldom perceived by fugitives, as part of any Underground Railroad organization. These perceptions, however paradoxical, fit the available facts quite well.

In summary, the conditions that prompted slave escapes before 1850 were ubiquitous and rooted in the contradictions of slavery itself. However, the preconditions that favored the evolution of an organized Underground Road network after 1850 were more complex and rare. First, it was necessary that the physical geography for a slave escape route or corridor be present. Second, it was necessary that the human geography complement the physical geography to guarantee the availability of assistance along the escape corridor.

Third, it was necessary that circumstances— political, social or cultural —create the clear and compelling need for more formal and better organized assistance. In this regard, the involvement of blacks and whites as friends of the fugitive in or near Kentucky must be understood in the context of deepening sectional conflict in the 1850s. As the metaphorical barricades were raised to protect their way of life, southern whites often found themselves trapped by their own system. Honest differences of opinion regarding slavery were not tolerated and whites who did not support the institution of slavery and its racial

ideology were forced either to leave the South or remain cautiously silent. A few colorful but essentially conservative figures such as Cassius Clay (who favored the hardly radical scheme of gradual, compensated emancipation followed by the removal of African Americans) were the only exceptions. Not surprisingly, free African Americans in the midst of or near slave territory were held inherently suspect, but whites who acted against slavery were viewed as traitors, if not dangerous nonconformists and heretics.

Fourth, it was necessary that several unusual individuals, willing to risk their freedom and often their lives by violating both American law and social convention, emerge and assume leadership in the task of transforming a passive into an active assistance network. Such involvement was not without cost or risk as there were severe penalties for whites and African Americans convicted of "assisting" or "enticing slaves to escape" or "harboring fugitive slaves."[125] As the evidence reviewed thus far suggests, those who willingly risked imprisonment or worse by defying the law seldom acted through highly structured or formal organizations, but rather through loosely structured networks. Some individuals played decidedly passive roles; others committed their lives to clandestine groups such as the Anti-Slavery League that operated in south central Indiana in the decade before the Civil War.[126]

Ironically, the available evidence also suggests that, while northern anti-slavery groups may have been multi-racial in their composition, friends of the fugitive in or near slave territory usually operated in racially separate networks. As shall be elaborated in Chapter VI, there was often substantial coordination, collaboration and cooperation between these groups, but even friends of the fugitive were sometimes divided by the color line and the racial attitudes it implied in antebellum America.[127]

Still, friends of the fugitive, taken together, represented a small, powerful and persistent social movement. Organizations are sometimes spawned by such movements, but are not essential to their purpose. For example, one could abhor slavery, sympathize with fugitive slaves and, in the spirit of "practical abolitionism," act to assist them without ever joining an informal group or a more formal organization. However, organizations are often essential to marshalling and concentrating the forces needed to achieve the purpose of a movement. The Underground Railroad emerged in the Kentucky borderland when this social movement broadened its political and participatory in the crucible of the 1850s.

CHAPTER VI

The Underground Railroad: Escape Routes, Corridors, Crossing Points and Junctions

> Chapman Harris, a huge free Negro, black as the ace of spades ... is a preacher from some where back of Madison, Ind., where he is said to be an active member of the Freedom Party.
>
> Outside his home at Eagle Hollow, three miles east of Madison, Harris placed an iron plate or anvil in the trunk of a sycamore tree; when the time came to go across the Ohio to pick up fugitives, he would hammer on the anvil.[1]

Where fugitives crossed the Ohio River and how they moved north are documented far more reliably than how and by what routes they reached the Kentucky borderland. Even the men and women who assisted fugitive slaves north of the Ohio River had little knowledge of how those runaways reached free territory. The conventional scholarly and popular wisdom was that fugitives "usually kept to the woods and fields" and that "few if any land routes, such as existed north of the Ohio, could be traced in the South." In essence, the only "traceable routes from the South were by steamboat up the Mississippi and Ohio Rivers to Cincinnati, Ripley, and other river towns."[2] However, an examination of source materials created by those with more direct knowledge, primarily fugitive slaves themselves, suggests that this generalization is far too broad and that there were important exceptions.

Through Kentucky

Comparatively few fugitive slaves escaping from or through Kentucky were conducted or led from slave to free territory. Rather, most faced the formidable task of negotiating their passage through hostile territory of which their knowledge was often decidedly limited, where the least misstep could result in disaster. As noted in Chapter IV, fugitives were forced to use those fragments of information they could accumulate before and during their journeys—information that helped them locate and navigate a route toward freedom. In this respect, runaway slaves had little interest in being pathfinders and were vulnerable to hunger, the vagaries of the weather and their pursuers if their movement through slave territory was not well-paced, purposeful and efficient. Instead, they seemed to prefer, more often than not, routes that were already defined, relatively simple to understand, locate and follow.

There is strong evidence that, because of these factors, fugitive slaves escaping from or through Kentucky tended to follow natural and man-made routes to freedom. If possible, they did not wander aimlessly toward the "North Star," but followed the "North Star" purposefully along or in the shadows of established paths: the Ohio River and its tributaries; canals; paths forged by large migratory animals through the primeval wilderness; and the roads and railroads created by other humans. The regional river system was discussed in Chapter II; the nature of the land-routes must now be examined in some detail as well.

Millennia before the first European settlers and enslaved Africans crossed the Appalachians, a "road system" of sorts existed in Kentucky. The buffalo were the chief road-makers. Their migratory trails, known as buffalo traces, wound from Illinois and Tennessee through the then heavily forested regions of Kentucky connecting feeding and watering places, and salt-licks. Given their size and weight, these large animals were powerful and effective trail-blazers. Thus, these traces also—probably after millennia of bovine trial and error—followed the highest, driest, most stable and most direct routes through the state. Not surprisingly, the Native Americans, when they entered the region, appropriated the major buffalo traces as their long-distance highways for travel, war and hunting.[3]

Many buffalo traces converged at and passed through Cumberland Gap. The legendary "warriors' path" of the Native Americans followed this route. For this reason, as Daniel Boone, the Long Hunters and other early pioneers found their way west in the 1760s and 1770s, they did not invent the routes by which they traveled. Rather, they discovered routes already in use by others or found persons who knew the whereabouts of such routes. As these paths were widened, the more strategically located buffalo traces and "Indian trails" became the wagon roads that brought thousands of settlers (and enslaved African Americans) to Kentucky. Several of these important traces criss-crossed the state and

> ... possibly the greatest of them all crossed the Ohio River at the present site of Maysville. It led straight up the hill to the high ridge and on to the Lower Blue Licks. Here a branch led up Licking River to the Upper Blue Licks, and thence on through the country to Cross Plains, the present site of Athens, Fayette County. From the Lower Blue Licks, the trail ran southwest.... Another big branch crossed the Ohio River and came by Stamping Ground to North Elkhorn, passing on to

Cross Plains, and then across the Kentucky River near Boonesboro to the lower Cumberland region.... Another branch from Stamping Ground passed through Great Crossings and on to the site of Lexington, and then down what is now South Broadway and on to the Kentucky River.[4]

For settlers wishing to reach the Falls of the Ohio (the present site of Louisville) by an overland as opposed to a water route, several buffalo traces and Native American trails were available as well. For example, from the Central Bluegrass to the southeast

> The most commonly used road ran from Harrodsburg to near Bullitt's Lick, then northward to the Fish Pools and on to the Falls. A portion of this road was a large, well-worn buffalo trail that was identical with the present Preston Highway. Closer to the Falls, the path turned westward and followed a route which is now Fifth Street. Another fork of this same road skirted the "wet woods" to the east and led to the south fork of Beargrass Creek; this route was identical to the original Shepherdsville Road.[5]

Several other traces snaked their way to and from the Louisville area. "Harrod's trace" passed through Jeffersontown and Chenoweth Run and, in Shelby County, "ran parallel and near the existing Interstate 64." "Boone's trace," forged by Squire Boone in 1779, was a more northerly variation.[6]

Judging by fugitives' points of origin and where they crossed the Ohio, and documents reviewed in this study, runaway slaves sometimes traveled the roads that evolved from the original traces and trails, particularly through sparsely populated areas where they could travel unobserved. More often, these routes could be followed on foot from a safe distance. However, while long-distance travel relied on long-distance routes, there were numerous local trails forged by smaller animals that made permanent homes in Kentucky. Unlike the migratory buffalo traces, these "deer and varmint" paths seldom became the wagon or stage coach roads or turnpikes of later years.[7] They remained short routes, the "ghost roads" through forests and over hills, and could be extremely useful to fugitives as means of avoiding patrols, and circumventing unwelcoming towns and more densely settled areas.

Andrew Jackson's escape illustrated both the use of such paths and the dangers of traveling through unfamiliar country with minimal information. Born in 1816, Jackson fled slavery in Bowling Green and set out for "Shakertown in Logan County." He followed the road, pretended to possess a pass, then fled into the woods when a white traveler "demanded to see his papers." He soon lost his way, hid in the woods again, followed streams and trails—then returned to the road, walking all night and dodging into the forest whenever other travelers drew near. Jackson was pursued several other times by men and dogs, fought off his pursuers with stones and evaded them with guile. He continued traveling stealthily by night, hiding by day, eating berries for sustenance and alternating between forest paths and established roads to check his direction and estimate his rate of progress. Eventually, Jackson reached the Ohio River in Union County and crossed into southern Indiana.[8]

The evidence also suggests that fugitive slaves made frequent use of early stage-coach lines that could bear them across the state with considerable rapidity. Using forged passes or certificates of freedom and few dollars, fugitives could sometimes cover great distances in comparatively little time. By 1838, this problem had become sufficiently acute the Kentucky General Assembly passed an Act making it "unlawful for the owner and proprietor of any mail stage or stage-coach" to transport enslaved African Americans "without a written request of their owners"—and making stage-coach

AN ABOLITIONIST AND RUNAWAY CAPTURED.
A man named Ed. Williams was arrested on the ferry boat yesterday with a negro belonging to Mr. J. W. Ferris, of Memphis, Tenn. They had traveled all the way by stage, the expenses being paid by the negro, who was flush of funds. After the arrest Williams made a full confession, and both were lodged in jail to await a requisition from the Governor of Tennessee.

News article: "An Abolitionist and Runaway Captured," *Louisville Courier,* May 11, 1858. A failed escape from New Orleans by steamboat.

owners liable "for the full value of all slaves which may thereby escape from their owners."[9] This law seems to have had little effect.

As an example, on May 2, 1841, Peter, an enslaved African American held in Paris, Kentucky escaped on the stagecoach to Maysville. Peter worked in the "harness and saddle shop" of his owner, William S. Bryant and, immediately prior to his disappearance, was given the task of repairing the harness of a stage-coach. When the coach resumed its journey, Peter was somehow permitted to ride alongside the driver. Once he reached Maysville, he "quietly climbed down off the stage-coach and slipped off into the darkness, toward the Ohio River."[10] Peter's owner then sued the stage coach company to recover the value of his lost property. In *Johnson v. Bryan* (May 1841), the Kentucky Court of Appeals approved damages and stated that "slaves availed themselves of the facilities afforded by stage lines and steam cars to escape from their masters. The rapidity with which they were carried ... enabled them to elude pursuit and detection. The evil was growing, as stage lines were increasing."[11]

While fugitive slave escape routes and Underground Railroad lines north of the Ohio River can be delineated in much greater detail than the broad corridors leading to, across and from Kentucky, some escape accounts offer some additional insight into how fugitives moved through the state. One was recounted by the Rev. Jacob Cummings in an 1894 interview with Wilbur Siebert. Cummings had once been the property of James Smith, living near Chattanooga, Tennessee. In July 1839, Cummings escaped and hid first on a nearby island, then moved to the mainland "and came out on north side of the Cumberland Mountains." There, Cummings was captured, but soon escaped again. This time, he "found a horse ... and rode 14 miles ... crossed Kentucky to the Ohio River, and used a rail to break a lock fastening a skiff." Cummings finally "reached the Indiana shore just before daylight in the last days of September."[12] Precisely where Cummings crossed the Ohio cannot be ascertained. However, he then

... turned up the Ohio River, and atNew Albany, in Floyd County, Indiana, met his first abolitionists ... Uncle Charley Lacey, William Finney and Uncle Zeke Goins. He worked for them a couple of weeks, then moved on to the little town of Charleston, in southeastern Clark County.... Two miles above there Cummings was arrested and taken down to Jeffersonville. The judge said he had no right to hold him. Several men hurried him out and they escaped with horses.

After many harrowing adventures, Cummings eventually reached Canada West.[13] Also worth noting is the clear implication that Indiana routes were far more attractive at this relatively early date than would be the case in the 1850s.

To Kentucky from Tennessee and Points South

Given the geography of North America and the distribution of enslaved African Americans in the South, many of the fugitive slaves escaping through Kentucky originated in Tennessee, with smaller numbers from farther south in Alabama and Mississippi as indicated in Chapter III. These regions were the heart of the "Cotton Kingdom" and contained some of the heaviest black population concentrations in the nation. That escapes from the southern interior were common is understandable considering the rigors of slavery in the cotton (and rice and sugar) growing states. However, slave escapes over long distances had relatively low rates of success—the probability of success being, perhaps, inversely proportional to the distance from free territory.[14] Consequently, runaways from Tennessee and farther south who reached Kentucky had already beaten the odds—but still faced an arduous and perilous passage through the state.

Fugitives from central Tennessee had but two alternative routes in a broad and general sense. They could escape overland, following (or shadowing) more or less the old traces and trails, and the newer roads that led from northern Tennessee through the Bowling Green area, past Mammoth Cave and then to north central Kentucky. As indicated previously, central Tennessee slave owners were well aware of these routes and, consequently, it was not uncommon for advertisements for the return of fugitive slaves from Tennessee or northern Alabama to appear in Louisville or Lexington newspapers. As Franklin and Schweninger noted,

30 percent of the fugitive slave advertisements placed in the *Nashville Whig* between 1812 and 1816 gave Kentucky or Ohio as the probable destination of the fugitive in question, as did 61 percent of the advertisements placed in the *Tennessee Republican Banner* between 1840 and 1842.[15]

Alternatively, they could follow the unusual course of the Cumberland River—which has its source in eastern Kentucky, then flows in a gentle southwesterly loop through northern Tennessee, past Nashville, then loops to the northwest until it returns to Kentucky and ultimately empties into the Ohio River. In other words, fugitives from central Tennessee who followed the river to the east would find themselves in southeastern Kentucky—almost due south of Lexington and over one hundred miles from free territory. Fugitives who followed the Cumberland to the west would find themselves in or near the Jackson Purchase, with the choice of crossing into southern Illinois or southwestern Indiana, or attempting to escape by steamboat on the Ohio.

Fugitives from the far eastern and far western sections of Tennessee had fewer options. As noted, eastern Tennessee was situated in the Appalachian region and its valleys. Fugitives could either follow the

---

Fifty Dollars Reward.

RANAWAY from my plantation in Rutherford county, on 31st ult., a mulatto fellow named Ben (*Alias*) Ben Singleton, aged about twenty seven years, five feet five or six inches in height, a serviceable sprightly fellow, has lived in Nashville for the last fifteen years, presumed to be lurking about the city or neighborhood as he was seen there on the evening of the 31st. I will give twenty dollars for his apprehension in the county of Davidson, or State of Tennessee, or the above reward if taken out of the State and secured in any Jail so that I can get him.

Je9, 1846, d1m&w2   ROBERT L. WEAKLY.

☞The Courier, Louisville, Ky., will publish the above to the amount of $5, and charge this office.—*Nashville Union.*

Fugitive slave notice: "Ben," *Louisville Courier,* June 1, 1846. An escape from the Nashville, Tennessee, area.

mountains and exit in eastern Kentucky or Ohio—or flee west to follow the routes leading from central Tennessee. In the west, escape by the Tennessee or Cumberland Rivers into western Kentucky was an attractive prospect to many fugitives, as was escape by steamboat on the Mississippi River. Many of these fugitives passed through the Jackson Purchase area and were mentioned in a few of the surviving issues of antebellum Paducah newspapers.

As examples, James escaped from A. C. Gillespie of Columbia, Tennessee in 1832. Gillespie stated that "Since his elopement I have understood that he intended going to Ohio, Indiana, Pennsylvania or out of the United States ... taking the stage or steam boat at Nashville, and going to Louisville, Cincinnati, Wheeling, Pittsburgh, &c."[16] Stephen escaped from Henry Dunn of Pontotoe, Mississippi in late 1854. On January 22, 1855, he was captured and committed to the McCracken County jail.[17] On February 24, 1855, John ran away from F. G. Moore of Hamburg, Tennessee. Moore indicated that John was "well acquainted with the river" and, presumably, felt that the fugitive was likely to pass by or through western Kentucky.[18] Similarly, Prince escaped from northern Mississippi and was captured and jailed in McCracken County in May 1855.[19] If nothing else, these few notices suggest that both fugitive slaves and those who sought to apprehend them were quite well acquainted with this corridor through western Tennessee into western Kentucky by the 1850s.

$500 REWARD.—Ran away from the plantation of Dr. Drane, four miles from Clarksville, on the road leading to Hopkinsville, negro man RICHARD black complexion, fully 6 feet in height, large frame, and muscular, between 40 and 50 years of age; it is thought he has a scar under the angle of the lower jaw, perhaps the right side; when spoken to so as to excite him, the skin wrinkles thick about the centre of the forehead, giving the expression of pain; wore an old fur hat with a high crown, gray sack or frock coat, lined with red calico; black corded cassimere pantaloons; also, a loose roundabout of light drab fulled cloth, lined throughout with domestic dyed purple, and coarse brown jeans pantaloons, and brogan shoes; other clothes not recollected, and may exchange the above.

He left home on Monday morning last, the 28th of February, without any known cause; can read and write tolerably well, and may have furnished himself with a pass or free papers, or he may be under the guidance and protection of some white man. If so, I will give a reward of $500 for his arrest and conviction in a court of justice. If said negro is taken at a distance over 100 miles from home I will pay a reward of $200. If taken north of the Ohio river and secured in jail so that I can recover him I will give a reward of $300. Any information from persons having seen such a negro, communicated through the Post-office, at Clarksville, will be thankfully received.

mar 8 eod2 w3 .   DAVID L. SMITH, Manager.

☞Louisville Journal insert twice tri-weekly, and three times weekly, and forward accounts to this office for collection.—*Clarksville Chron.*

Fugitive slave notice: "Richard," *Louisville Journal,* March 8, 1848. Another example of an escape from western Tennessee of a literate fugitive, one in which assistance is suspected.

These far eastern and far western routes had some advantages. In the west, the key advantages were proximity to the Mississippi River and, even more fundamentally, to free territory. In the east, a corridor of small free black communities led into and through the more protected terrain of the mountains—a more difficult journey, but one with natural barriers as potential allies. As some of the documentation for crossings into Ohio indicates, there were a number of intrepid fugitives who followed this upland path.

A February 1853 article reprinted from the *Clarksville Jeffersonian* provides some insight into the machinations of friends of the fugitive in northern Tennessee along the routes that led directly to and through Kentucky. The article concerns H. F. Painter, who moved to

Clarksville in August 1852 and established himself as a chair maker. After accumulating debts, he moved to Nashville in December 1852 and his actual purpose in Tennessee was revealed.

> Since his departure revelations have been made by negroes here and in Robertson county, which prove that he had been tampering with the slave population. He promised a number of slaves safe passage to the free-States, upon the payment to him of twenty dollars, and authorized the same proposition to be made to the entire slave population.... Quite a gang of the negroes assembled in Robertson county during the holidays awaiting his return.... A vile attempt has been made upon the life of a respectable lady, masters have been robbed, and a rebellious spirit aroused in the hearts of the negroes by his villainy, and it behooves all good citizens to exert themselves to bring him to justice.[20]

Although not stated in this article, Painter's actions were fairly consistent with those ascribed to Underground Railroad operatives in slave territory. The reaction of his neighbors was typical as well.

Crossing Points: An Overview

By 1850, the South's determination to recapture fugitives and, if possible, punish their friends necessitated that those friends become far better organized. The documents reviewed in this study indicate that escape routes to, through and from the Kentucky borderland became more clearly defined. The means by which fugitives were aided on their journey became more systematic and routinized. Because crossing the Ohio River was essential to reaching free territory, such crossing points served fugitives escaping alone, fugitives seeking help and those who provided such aid. However, in the 1850s, river crossing points became far less random and organized assistance often centered around

them — and along the escape routes that converged on and radiated from them.

As a fascinating example, in 1851, "a man named Hansen" made the southern Indiana farm of Colonel James W. Cockrum "his headquarters" and remained with Cockrum "for more than five years." Hansen posed as "a representative of a Philadelphia real estate firm" with an "interested in natural history." Colonel Cockrum's youngest son, William, ran errands for Hansen and eventually became his confidante "and to this personal acquaintance Indiana is indebted for the most explicit account of the work of the underground Railroad."[21] According to William Cockrum, Hansen was no ordinary migrant from the east, but was actually John T. Hanover,

> ... an agent of the Anti-Slavery League, and the superintendent of its work in Indiana. The organization was extensively controlled by men of ability and well supplied with funds... There were as many as fifty educated and intelligent young and middle-aged men on duty from some ways above Pittsburgh, Pennsylvania, along down the Ohio, both sides of it to the Mississippi River. These men had different occupations. Some were book agents ... some were singing teachers, school teachers, writing teachers, map makers carrying surveying and drafting outfits for that purpose; some were real Yankee peddlers; some were naturalists and geologists...[22]

River crossings were not left to chance given Hansen's penchant for organization and subterfuge. Based on his association with Hansen and other members of the Anti-Slavery League, William Cockrum later identified the location of twelve major Ohio River crossing points along the northern border of Kentucky. These crossing points were spaced roughly fifty miles apart — from the Jackson Purchase in the west to the Virginia border in the east.[23] Before proceeding, it is important to note that a significant number of

NOTICE.

On the 18th day of Aug., 1860, a negro man calling himself JIM, was committed to the Jefferson county Jail as a runaway slave. He is about 22 years of age, mulatto color, 5 feet 6½ inches high, weighing 100 pounds, grey eyes, small goatee, fresh cut on the back of the head, large scar on the left wrist, heavy made and a little bow-legged, holds his head uncommonly high. Says he is a Stonemason by trade, and belongs to Tolbert Fanning, near Nashville, Tenn., and the keeper of Franklin College. Was taken up in the State of Indiana. The owner can come forward, prove property, and pay charges, or he will be dealt with as the law requires.

au21 d3&wtf

W. K. THOMAS,
Jailor Jefferson co., Ky.

NOTICE.

On the 16th day of August, 1860, a negro man calling himself ANDY, was committed to the Jefferson county Jail as a runaway slave. He is about 28 years of age; brown skin; 5 feet 9¾ inches high; weighing 178 pounds; heavy bushy hair; trim and well made; good countenance and intelligent; thin whiskers and mustache; right arm has been broke above the elbow. Says he is a Blacksmith by trade, and belongs to John Dean, of Lexington, State of Mississippi. He was taken up in Indiana. The owner can come forward, prove property, and pay charges, or he will be dealt with according to law.

au21 d3&wtf

W. K. THOMAS,
Jailor Jefferson co., Ky,

Fugitive slave notices: "Jim" and "Andy," *Louisville Public Advertiser,* August 21, 1860. Fugitives from Nashville, Tennessee, and Lexington, Mississippi, respectively, caught and jailed in Louisville.

fugitive slaves continued to escape on their own. Thus, these were not the only points at which runaway slaves crossed the Ohio, but rather the points at which—based on both antebellum and postbellum evidence—fugitives could receive assistance.

1. In far western Kentucky, a region embracing Cairo, Illinois and Paducah, Kentucky.

2. At Diamond Island, near Posey County, in southwest Indiana, leading northward along the Wabash River.

3. In the Evansville, Indiana and Henderson, Kentucky area, a "very popular route as there were many free negroes" in Evansville among whom the refugees could be easily hidden. This work was done at night by Fishermen who supplied fish to the market."

4. Near the mouth of the Little Pigeon River in Warrick County, Indiana,

and then north through Oakland City to Petersburg.

5. In the Owensboro, Kentucky and Rockport, Indiana area where "there used to be a little fisherman's hut on the south bank of the Ohio river and two men who put in much of their time fishing, living in that shack. The real business of the men was to carry refugees that were brought to their shack at night, across the Ohio river."[24]

Routes in the western third of the state led eventually to Chicago and Lake Michigan for fugitives bent on reaching Canada.

In the middle third, between Meade and Carroll counties, there were three major crossing points centering around Louisville through which a substantial number of fugitives escaped in the decades before the Civil War. Typically, these crossings drew fugitives from the slave-rich Bluegrass region and led ultimately through Indiana or western Ohio to Lake Erie:

6. In the Leavenworth, Indiana (near the mouth of Indian Creek) and Brandenburg, Kentucky area, leading northward to Corydon, Indiana.[25]

7. In the greater Louisville region, including New Albany, Jeffersonville, Clarksville and Charleston, Indiana—with Louisville as a major junction.

8. In the Madison, Indiana and Trimble and Carroll Counties, Kentucky area.[26]

In the eastern third of Kentucky, there were four crossing points, the first two of great consequence as they, too, were exit points for escape corridors leading from the Kentucky Bluegrass:

9. The Cincinnati, Ohio and Covington, Kentucky area, the well-traveled and extensively researched "Grand Central Station" of the Underground Railroad[27]—with Cincinnati as a major junction.
10. In the Maysville, Kentucky and Ripley, Ohio area, also well-traveled and researched extensively.[28]
11. In the Portsmouth, Ohio area, leading toward Chillicothe and then to central Ohio.
12. In the Ashland, Kentucky and Ironton, Ohio area, and the Kentucky/Virginia/Ohio border in the Appalachians.[29]

Map VI-1 identifies the approximate location of these river crossings. The remainder of this section will explore these crossing points, the escape routes that wound toward them and both the fugitives and friends of the fugitive whose paths often intersected there as well.

From Kentucky to Illinois

Kentucky's long Ohio River border begins, in the west, in the vicinity of Cairo, Illinois. This section of Illinois was settled earliest and largely by migrants from the South who brought their slave-holding proclivities to the western frontier. Through their influence — although slavery was prohibited by the 1787 Northwest Ordinance — long-term indenture arrangements simulated slavery until the 1840s.[30] As a special case, Shawneetown, the "easternmost Illinois city on the Ohio River," was even exempted from the anti-slavery clause in the 1818 Illinois Constitution in order that slave labor would be available for its saltworks. Legends and rumors abound regarding ill-treatment received by enslaved African Americans at this site and kidnappings of free people of color as a means of supplementing the workforce. There is also a rather macabre connection to fugitive slaves. Atop a hill near Shawneetown, stands a

> … Southern Colonial house … built in 1834 by John Cranshaw, an Englishman, and has a sinister air heightened by its

Map VI-1. Kentucky Fugitive Slave River-Crossing Points.

lonely site. Local opinion is divided as to the buildings original use. Some believe that it was a station on the Underground Railroad; others that it was a prison for captured runaway slaves who were resold in the South. Available evidence favors the latter belief; Cranshaw it is said, gave elaborate parties on the lower floors with profits he gained from the terrified slaves he kept imprisoned in the upper part of the building.[31]

Three major fugitive slave escape routes extended across Illinois. One began at Chester, another at Alton and the other at Quincy. These served fugitives crossing Illinois' much longer Mississippi River border with Missouri and all converged ultimately at Chicago.[32] The third route from far western Kentucky contributed far fewer fugitives. This section of Illinois was simply smaller both in area and in African American population—and movement eastward by land or river to Indiana or Ohio was more attractive. Still, the flow of fugitive slaves from Kentucky into Illinois was not altogether insignificant. These runaways used two lesser branch routes. The first led from Cairo northward to Springfield. The second and probably more important followed the course of the Wabash River into Indiana.[33]

After 1820, the pro-slavery element in southern Illinois was joined by a new wave of settlers from the east with decidedly anti-slavery views. These newcomers "were quite willing to assist a slave escaping from bondage" and, by 1837, some loosely organized assistance was available to fugitive slaves.[34] John Jones, writing from Chicago, described the sentiments of African Americans in Illinois in the early 1850s. Jones stated that "there are a few lingering skeletons lurking about through" the conservative southern part of the state, but that "they will be swallowed ... in the great Anti-Slavery flood which is now sweeping over the mighty West." He added that "the Underground Railroad is doing a fair business this season. We received

eleven passengers last night ... and there were others on the road.... We will take care of them, and see that they are snugly shipped to Queen Victoria's land."[35]

While Illinois witnessed the passage of thousands of runaway slaves, surviving records indicate that most did not originate in or pass through Kentucky.

From Kentucky to Indiana

Southwestern Indiana

While the raw number of African Americans living in Indiana was negligible, African Americans "were congregated in a few counties along the Ohio River," with growing numbers in a few more northerly counties such as Wayne and Marion after 1840.[36] This distribution of the state's small black population had important implications for fugitive slaves and those who wished to assist them.

African Americans tended to settle in small Indiana townships and farming communities. In Knox County in western Indiana, for example, African Americans represented 10 percent of the population of Vincennes (221 of 2,070 persons) and the Lyles settlement was a sizable black community in Patoka Township.[37] Emma Thornbrough noted that the Lyles family migrated from North Carolina and purchased 1200 acres in Indiana. Similarly, other early black settlers migrated from the South, particularly from North Carolina "in the company of white Quakers." For example, African Americans moved with the Quakers into Washington County and, "by 1850, there were 252 Negroes in the county, mostly in Posey and Washington townships." In Jackson County, African Americans clustered in Jackson and Redding Townships—and, in Orange County, blacks lived near Quakers in Orleans, Chambersburg and Paoli Townships.[38]

As Siebert observed, far more fugitive slaves escaped into the states of the Old Northwest than into any other region of the United States and Indiana's black population included a great many fugitives.[39] Many of these fugitives merely "passed through" Indiana en route to another free state or Canada. Others settled in Indiana, at least temporarily, and usually blended into existing African American settlements. For example, Vernon Township in Jennings County, Salt Creek Township in Franklin County and Fugit Township in Decatur County all contained small but significant black settlements that were home and haven to fugitive slaves. As both a consequence and as evidence of the fugitive presence, these small black settlements either shrank considerably or literally melted away after the passage of the Fugitive Slave Act of 1850 — as African Americans fled to Canada to escape the operations of this new law. Thornbrough concluded "the Negro settlements in Indiana ... in every case were located on one of the routes of the Underground Railroad" because "runaways tended to seek out members of their own race"[40]

As escape became more difficult after 1850, assistance grew in importance. In such fluid circumstances, these settlements along the border and in the "lower north" became the superstructure for a more sophisticated network of escape routes:

> The first ... was a continuation of the routes from Cincinnati and Lawrenceburg which converged in Wayne County. Thence a main line ran north through Winchester, Portland, Decatur, Fort Wayne, and Auburn into Michigan. The second main line originated from three branches which crossed the Ohio River at Madison, New Albany, and the vicinity of Leavenworth. These converged near Columbus and passed north through Indianapolis, Westfield, Logansport, Plymouth, and South Bend. The third main route crossed the Ohio at Evansville and followed the Wabash River through Terre Haute and then up to Lafayette.[41]

With Evansville to the west, on the Indiana side of the Ohio, and Henderson to the east, on the Kentucky side, the first crossing point from Kentucky to southwestern Indiana witnessed a steady flow of fugitives as "free territory lay just across the river" and "there certainly were people sympathetic to slavery in Indiana."[42] The location of this route was appealing to fugitives from western Kentucky wishing to avoid southern Illinois — and those from western Kentucky and Tennessee following the Cumberland or Tennessee Rivers. An early history of Henderson County stated that "In 1843 began and in 1844-45 was steadily developing the systematic enticing away, or stealing, of slaves from Kentucky and running them off to Canada by a cordon of posts, or relays, which came to be known as the underground railroad."[43]

Perhaps the most interesting case in the Henderson area concerned Thomas Brown, an Underground Railroad agent operating in Henderson County itself — which was discussed previously. Nearby Evansville also had a small free black community known for aiding fugitives in crossing the river and moving northward. Echoing Cockrum's recollections, "...legends hold that 'fishermen' ferried the runaways across the river at night. Once across the river, white businessmen (most notably Willard Carpenter) and the free black community helped them on to Canada."[44]

Another indication of receptivity to the anti-slavery message and support for the Underground Railroad was the rate of subscription to and circulation of anti-slavery newspapers in a given area. Clearly, such publications could only circulate clandestinely in slave territory, but no such limitation applied on the northern banks of the Ohio River. Frederick Douglass often published lists of subscribers to his newspaper that included persons from southern Ohio, Indiana and Illinois — and, in Evansville, A. L. Robinson requested that "large quantities of four-page Anti-Slavery tracts printed for gratuitous distribution" be sent to him in 1852.[45]

An illuminating account of the role of this crossing point was published by Alexander Ross. Ross was a native of Toronto who became a committed anti-slavery activist and ventured into the American South in 1856 after reading *Uncle Tom's Cabin*. His purpose was to facilitate slave escapes and, before his journey, he arranged a code with his friends to coordinate the "shipment" of "hardware" (male fugitives) and "dry-goods" (female fugitives) to free territory. He reached Nashville in 1857 and, with the help from "a Quaker lady" and "an old free negro" preacher, arranged the escape of seven young men. Ross did not accompany them, but instead gave them information regarding the route(s) they should travel and gave each of them a gun, a knife, shoes, a compass, food and money. Ross then sent letters to "friends" in Evansville, Cincinnati and Cleveland "to keep a sharp lookout for packages of hardware."[46]

Once fugitives actually consummated their escape, Ross typically fell under suspicion and moved to another town. Although he operated throughout the South, his route of choice for fugitives from central and western Tennessee, and Alabama was through Evansville (probably following the Cumberland River from Tennessee), then to Cincinnati (by river or overland), then to Cleveland (by railroad).[47] Unlike Calvin Fairbank, Ross was never apprehended despite several "close calls."

The fugitive slave crossing points in Meade County, Kentucky represented the western limit of the Louisville region. These crossings centered around the towns of Brandenburg on the Kentucky side of the river and Leavenworth, in Harrison County, on the Indiana side. As Saulman notes, "Harrison County has 42 miles of frontage with Kentucky along the Ohio River. If slaves could reach the Harrison County border, they could generally find someone who would help them further north."[48] Given its location between Owensboro and Louisville, the Meade County crossing served as an alternative slave escape route for African Americans fleeing from the Bluegrass region and from far western Kentucky. This escape route led next to Corydon and then converged at Columbus with branch routes leading from Louisville and Madison.

While "the majority of those who settled in early Harrison County were strongly opposed to slavery," they "were also strongly opposed to white masters emancipating and setting slaves free" in their midst.[49] Still, Indiana was free territory and, as such, was attractive to free people of color despite the hostility of whites. For this reason, Harrison County and Corydon were viewed as viable options for free people of color seeking safe haven — particularly for those hoping to purchase land. For example, in April 1822, Shelton Morris, one of the architects of the free black community of Louisville, "...a boy of colour, emancipated by Richard Morris of Jefferson County, Kentucky and made choice of Edward Wilson as his guardian and had this act, along with the text of the will that freed him and his siblings, entered in Harrison County records."[50] This entry suggests that Morris and his newly emancipated siblings may have chosen southern Indiana as the place to invest their small inheritance. Why none became long-term residents of Harrison County is unknown.

The black population remained small, but not inconsequential. By 1820, there were 99 free people of color in Harrison County, 8 of whom lived in Corydon. However, by 1850, the black population declined to 60 as many free African Americans were drawn away, presumably, to other nearby towns.[51] Also, by the 1850s, if not much earlier, an Underground

Railroad network existed in this region. The "Bell-Wright" affair in 1857, one particularly well-documented account, illustrated how this network was organized and how it operated — and identified some of its major maps. Because of the richness of the evidence, this incident is included in Chapter VII.

The Louisville Region

For reasons as much geographic as demographic, the role of Louisville was critical both to the passage of fugitive slaves and to the work of friends of the fugitive in the trans–Appalachian west. As Cockrum concluded on the basis of his own experience:

> There were probably more negroes crossed over the Ohio river and two or three places in front of Louisville than any place else from the mouth of the Wabash to Cincinnati. The reason for this was that the three good sized cities at the Falls furnished a good hiding place for runaways among the colored people. Those crossing at these places were all conveyed to Wayne county, Indiana, and thence on to the Lake.[52]

Growth in the free African American population, coupled with the presence of smaller but relatively stable free black communities in the Indiana towns facing Louisville — for example, in 1860 there were 757 African Americans in Floyd County (New Albany) and another 520 in Clark County (Jeffersonville and Clarksville) — made the greater Louisville area a major refuge and crossing point for fugitive slaves.[53] However, free people of color were an anomaly, people who were black but not enslaved in a slaveholding city. As such, they were objects of both fear and scorn as reflected in the memorable language of an occasionally incoherent, but profoundly revealing, 1835 Louisville newspaper editorial entitled "Local Evils":

> We are overrun with free negroes.... Their impudence naturally attracts the attention of slaves, and necessarily becomes contagious.... We are not alarmists — but we do believe prompt measures to drive the vagrant negroes from among us, to prevent servants from hiring their own time, and to subject the entire slave population to rules sufficiently rigid to preserve order and insure perfect subordination, are necessary to our security.[54]

Given such a hostile environment, the evolution of a cohesive community required wise leadership and two individuals figured prominently in the community formation process — Shelton Morris (1806–1889) and Washington Spradling, Sr. (1802–1868), both of whom will be discussed in Chapter VII. African American churches were products of this transformation and means of moving it forward. Among the most notable of the early African American churches was Quinn Chapel A. M. E., established by local free people of color in 1838. As Gibson noted, "it was considered by the community as an abolition church," but "the idea of an abolition church established in this city among the slaves could not be tolerated by some slaveholders; hence they forbade their slaves visiting that Free Negro Church."[55]

Quinn Chapel was a lynchpin of organized A. M. E. activity along the Ohio River border. As such, it was connected closely to other small A. M. E. congregations in southern Indiana and Ohio — and to the "Quaker friends of Indiana" who "gave liberally" to assist in the construction of a new church edifice in 1854.[56] In essence, Quinn Chapel, probably more than any of the other seven antebellum black churches in Louisville, was part of the network associated with Underground Railroad activity in north central Kentucky.[57]

In contrast, the First African Baptist Church (later renamed Fifth Street Baptist Church) was founded as a separate branch of the First Baptist Church in 1829 and became wholly independent in 1842. Its pastor, the Rev. Henry Adams, was a devoutly religious but largely apolitical leader and, as such, was highly regarded by local blacks—and whites. Adams left First African briefly in the 1850s to become pastor of Cincinnati's Baker Street Baptist Church, the leading black church in that city. However, his conservative philosophy soon precipitated conflict with his new church members, since

> The sentiment of that church was strongly anti-slavery, and many of its members were connected with the Underground Railroad. Politics was discussed and prayer meetings held for the liberation of the slaves. Brother Adams was not accustomed to mixing politics and religion; hence there was a divergence of opinion. He resigned and returned to his old flock in Louisville.[58]

More specifically, Adams expressed his belief that aiding fugitive slaves was "man- stealing." Loring Moody castigated him in *Frederick Douglass Paper*, stating that "it is bad enough for a white man to ... sanction crime, and robbery and blood... But for a colored man — one of the proscribed and enslaved race to do it, and thus virtually consent to the enslavement of himself and his race — the guilt is doubly damning."[59] The sentiment at Quinn Chapel and perhaps at a few other antebellum Louisville churches was similar to that of Baker Street Baptist.

Perhaps, most intriguing and most paradoxical with respect to the role of the Louisville area as a key nexus of the Underground Railroad is the striking contrast between the significance of the area, on one hand, and its virtual invisibility in the standard histories of the region, on the other. The roles of the Madison, Cincinnati and Ripley areas as fugitive slave crossings and Underground Railroad centers are reasonably well known, at least to students of the antebellum era. These places are associated with Underground Railroad activity. Louisville has not been in standard historical accounts.[60] Still, there are a few important but obscure exceptions that focus on the unique urban environment that existed in border state cities such as Louisville and Cincinnati and the unique challenges and opportunities it offered. For example, O'Brien noted that

> By the end of the antebellum period, slavery in Louisville had evolved into a very different system than the slavery practiced on the plantation. The wider area of employment for slaves, the presence of free blacks, and the shifting, frenetic pace of the city all contributed to a decline in white surveillance and greater freedom of movement for slaves... The pace of city life also had the effect of making slavery more difficult to use as a means of race control... Also, there was simply no way in the city to maintain that proper distance between the races that was necessary for strict maintenance of the slave system... There was even a better chance in Louisville, via the river, for a slave to become a successful fugitive from the institution that bound him.[61]

These were precisely the factors that drew fugitives to Louisville — that made Louisville and its neighboring towns a temporary refuge and crossing point for runaway slaves.

In such a densely populated urban area, fugitive slaves could only cross the river at certain spots and under certain conditions. The busy Louisville area riverfront extended both east and west of the Louisville and Portland canal (opened in 1830). For fugitive slaves hoping to cross the Ohio secretly, neither the wharf areas of Louisville — nor Shippingport and Portland (small towns at the eastern and western "ends" of the canal eventually annexed by Louisville) — nor the canal itself were advantageous locations. Crossings from downtown Louisville to Jeffersonville were often attempted, but only by the use of deception and disguise. East of Louisville, clandestine crossings were possible at or near the numerous ferries and small settlements such as Charleston (Indiana) and Westport (Kentucky) that dotted the Ohio riverbank for roughly fifty miles to Madison and then to Carrollton. These crossings were not as active, but were viable alternative routes.

For example, "tradition holds that there were slaves brought across the Ohio River at the Charlestown Landing and brought over to Charlestown to join the New Albany route to Bloomington ... there were very strong abolitionists who lived in Charlestown." A bit farther to the east, the three Adams cousins built homes near Bull Creek in the early 1800s and "there was a landing at Bull Creek and these homes, so tradition says, were places where negroes were sometimes hid..."[62] As shown in Map VI-2, there were no settlements of note west of the Louisville area until Westpoint — miles to the south in Bullitt County where the Salt River empties into the Ohio. However, there is also evidence of an occasional random crossing in this area as well.[63]

The most important crossing point in the greater Louisville area was located west of Portland — leading from Louisville across the Ohio River to New Albany. How this crossing figured in the plans of fugitives and their friends is revealed in several documents, one of which was an 1855 article entitled, "Daring Attempt of Five Negroes to Runaway." In May 1855:

> Sunday night a bold and systematic, though unsuccessful attempt was made by five slaves in this city to runaway.... Henry, a very likely negro man belonging to Mrs. Cocke, who had been permitted to hire his own time and had been the same as a free man for years... Violette and her two children, slaves of Mr. Jack ... and a slave man the property of Judge Nicholas.

Violette was a "favorite servant" and Henry's wife. Henry had a "room on Mr. Jack's property." Their escape was well planned, as:

> The whole party had taken a hack about midnight, first providing themselves with all their good clothing and a supply of eatables. The negro of Judge Nicholas acted as hackman, and with his load proceeded to Portland, or rather below the lower ferry, designing to cross the river in a skiff.

Unfortunately, they attracted "the attention of the Portland watchmen" and all were arrested, except for Henry. However,

> ... At this juncture, a skiff was seen rapidly nearing the Kentucky shore, apparently from New Albany. The occupant became alarmed and fled back again to the other side of the river before any effort could be made to catch him.

Violette, her children and the other fugitive were all lodged in jail. Henry remained at large and was able to return to his "room" unobserved, where " ...a pair of boots, all bespattered with mud, were found."[64]

This foiled escape attempt required considerable planning and coordination. Supplies and a hack had to be obtained. Arrangements with someone in New Albany were necessary as were communications between parties on both sides of the river throughout the enterprise. In other words, Henry, Violette and company had to arrange to reach a certain point, "below the lower ferry," on a certain day, at a certain time. Someone from New Albany had to secure a skiff and cross the river on the same day, at the same time — and, presumably, someone was waiting to receive and conceal the fugitives in New Albany, and then "pass them on" to the north or east.

West of the "lower ferry" (at the foot, more or less, of 36th Street in modern Louisville) was a large tract of forested wetland. This area (see Map VI-2) stood in relatively close proximity to heavy con-

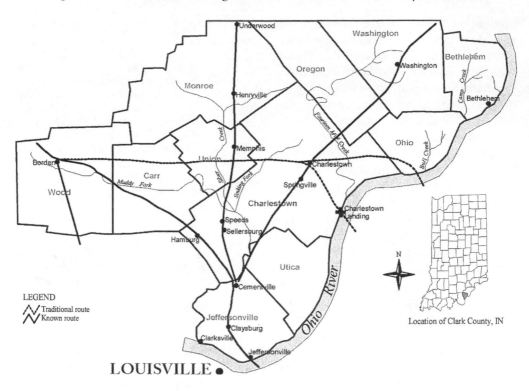

Map VI-2. Louisville and Southern Indiana.

centrations of potential fugitives, faced New Albany and served as a crossing and hiding place for fugitives on other several occasions. In October 1855:

> We learn that one of two slaves who escaped from Mr. Arterburn a few nights since, was discovered by a hunter Saturday evening in a hollow log, well provisioned, in the wards of lower Portland. The hunter had a double barrelled gun and ordered the negro to come out and surrender. He came out promptly, and just as promptly seized the gun of his capturer and started off the direction of Salt river, with the speed of a quarter horse, carrying the gun with him. The hunter returned to the city, give the alarm, and soon after a posse went in pursuit of the runaway, with what success we did not learn.[65]

Again, in 1857, another news account focused on an escape that made use of this section of the county:

> ...four Negro men suddenly disappeared from the city, and it was soon ascertained that they had runaway. Liberal rewards were offered for their apprehension, and on Saturday they were captured over in Indiana, between Hanover and Madison.... A couple of white men, it was ascertained, had taken them across the river below the falls to New Albany, where they were received by a third white man, who planned their escape. Two of the runaways belonged to parties in Bardstown, and the others to Warren Mitchell and Mr. Ballard of this city.[66]

The origins of the systematic use of this crossing point date to the 1850s, although unassisted crossings were reported in earlier years. In 1850, several free African Americans of Louisville, New Albany and Cincinnati met to discuss the formation of a Masonic Lodge. While the group agreed on the desirability of establishing a local lodge, they disagreed over the advisability of establishing "a lodge in

Louisville while the prejudice was so strong against free Negroes." The group decided to locate the lodge in New Albany and, after receiving a charter from the Grand Lodge of Ohio, "set Mount Moriah Lodge No. 1 to work on June 12, 1850." William Gibson was a member and recalled that "for three years, they remained at New Albany, Ind." During this time, the Masons "labored under many disadvantages, such as crossing the river in skiffs at midnight … at the risk of their lives, and then walking five miles up to the city." Eventually, the Lodge moved to Louisville.[67]

These facts mean little in isolation. However, there are other references to a "Black Masonic Lodge" that met "west of Portland" — not in a building, but in a place directly across from New Albany. Both primary source evidence and the recollections of elderly African Americans interviewed in the 1930s attest to the importance of the Lodge and its relation to this crossing point. For example, Sarah Merrill was born in Munfordsville, Kentucky, and settled in New Albany after the Civil War. In an interview with Iris Cook in the 1930s, Merrill shared some family history that confirmed several of these other sources regarding slave escape routes in the Louisville region:

> My great uncle, Lewis Barnett, was a slave, and he was brought to Louisville from the South to be sold at auction. He escaped and crossed the Ohio River at about where Portland is. He came to New Albany with 12 other Negroes. He came out State Street, and down where Cherry Street is now and went west on Cherry Street till he hit the knobs west of town. The slaves were covered up in a wagon full of corn....

Barnett and the others were caught and returned to Louisville. Barnett was

CHASE OF A RUNAWAY.—We learn that one of two slaves who escaped from Mr. Arterburn a few nights since, was discovered by a hunter Saturday evening in a hollow log, well provisioned, in the wards of lower Portland. The hunter had a double barrelled gun and ordered the negro to come out and surrender. He came out promptly, and just as promptly siezed the gun of his capturer and started off the direction of Salt river, with the speed of a quarter horse, carrying the gun with him. The hunter returned to the city, give the alarm, and soon after a posse went in pursuit of the runaway, with what success we did not learn.

News article: "Chase of a Runaway," *Louisville Courier,* October 1, 1855. An escape from Arterburn's "slave pen" in Louisville. The fugitive hid near the Portland to New Albany crossing point.

then "sold on the block … and taken to New Orleans." He survived and visited Merrill and her family in New Albany after the Civil War where he told his story to Merrill and her siblings — who, ironically, lived on State Street.[68]

There were few African Americans living or enslaved in Portland, and no record of an African American Masonic lodge — at least as a physical structure — in or near Portland during this period. However, this "northwestern" section of Jefferson County, where the Ohio River bends to the south, was largely below the floodplain and, consequently, was sparsely settled. Thus, this unusual area had the significant advantages of being, as mentioned previously, forested and marshy, relatively close to local African American centers of population and directly across the river from New Albany. Henry Webb of New Albany was told by his father, who was born enslaved in the Louisville area, that a major fugitive slave route ran through Louisville and New Albany. Webb, when interviewed by the Federal Writers' Project, stated simply that:

... runaway Negroes used to come across the Ohio River from Portland.... Plans for escapes were hatched in a colored Masonic Lodge, located in Portland. The Negroes would cross the river in a skiff, manned by fishermen (supposedly) and if the coast was not clear on this side they would go up the river for a short distance.... Many that crossed hid with friends in the hills back of New Albany and then after all danger was past made their way north by way of Salem."[69]

Across the Ohio, there are long-standing community and family traditions that "several New Albany houses were used to hide escaping slaves, including one at 1401 State Street" believed to have a basement below its basement. New Albany's modern-day Second Baptist Church, the Second Presbyterian Church before the Civil War, is also believed to have hidden fugitives in its basement. George Washington Carter, an influential businessman, and William Harding, who worked on the river, were key African American friends of the fugitive in New Albany with close ties to the free African American community in Louisville. For example, Harding was reputed to have "smuggled" copies of *The North Star* to free black musicians living in Louisville — who "would hide the newspaper in their sheet music" to avoid detection and then share it with others.[70] As Thornbrough observed, "after being carried across the Ohio in skiffs, the slaves took refuge with Negro families on the Indiana side."[71]

After negotiating a river crossing, fugitives could follow several routes leading from New Albany and/or Jeffersonville to Salem, or an alternative "station," and then northward (see Map VI-3). As Cook observed:

One of the most notable routes was that which was conducted by Quakers and Covenanters and a few other abolitionists through Harrison and Washington Counties.... One of the most remarkable leaders in the business was "Little Jim-

mie" Trueblood, ably assisted by his wife. He was only five feet two inches tall and never over 110 pounds, and his wife was also very small.... Many of the fugitives came by way of New Albany, but more by way of Harrison County, the main line running through Palmyra and the vicinity of Salem and thence north to Sparkville and Bloomington. This was known as the "west line," and was the most used.... Besides "Little Jimmie" Trueblood, others believed to have been leaders along the route were Thomas H. Trueblood, a Quaker; Matthias Marks, Isaiah Reed and Dr. Mary Lusk....[72]

Peters' research on the Underground Railroad in New Albany and southern Indiana yields important corroborative insights — one of which concerns the relationship between the Underground Railroad and the actual Railroad in the 1850s.[73] In September 1855, this relationship stirred up considerable controversy in Louisville when one of the conductors on the New Albany and Salem Railroad, a Mr. James Haynes (or Hines), was accused of "endeavoring to assist in the escape of a runaway slave." The article presented the following facts:

Officer Meeker and another New Albany officer had arrested the runaway negro at the cars; that the man acknowledged he was a runaway; that some Abolitionist and a big negro attempted to rescue him, and that he succeeded in getting away from the officers and getting in the cars; that the officers attempted to re-arrest him, when Conductor Hines, backed by the Abolitionists, got on the platform, declared that the cars were theirs and the officers should not enter it, and forcibly prevented them from doing so; that they heard the big negro, who had assisted in his release, give the fugitive directions how to proceed in order to escape successfully, and that the cars moved off with the runaway on board.[74]

Officials of the New Albany and Salem Railroad assured irate Louisvillians that "employees of the N. A. & S. R. will not be permitted to aid runaway negroes

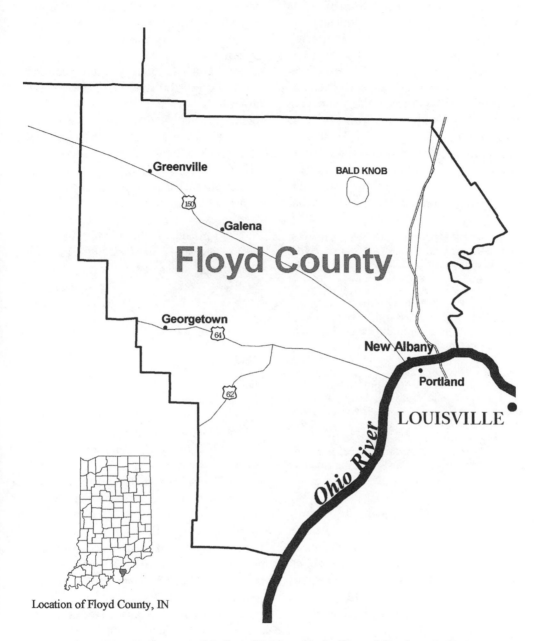

Location of Floyd County, IN

Map VI-3. Underground Railroad Routes: Louisville and Southern Indiana.

to escape." However, they defended the conductor, prompting the following response:

> We know there are plenty of nigger stealers about New Albany, for the repeated escapes of slaves from here, recently, abundantly shows it. No one will be more rejoiced than ourself to hear that the N. A. & S. R. has relieved itself from all suspicion of having employees who aid negroes to escape from their masters....[75]

As yet another example, Julia Ward King was born in Louisville in the 1850s and, when interviewed on June 10, 1937, recounted — from a combination of memory and often repeated family history — a fascinating escape adventure that attested to the presence of white friends of the fugitive operating in Louisville. Ward's parents, Samuel and Matilda, were owned apparently by different slaveholders and were each permitted to hire their time. For reasons unknown or undisclosed, Ward's father "run away to Canada on the Underground Railroad." By some arrangement, Ward, her older sister, Mary, and her mother soon followed. Ward recalled that

> Mama went down to the boat. A man on the boat told Mama not to answer the door for anybody, until he gave her the signal. The man was a Quaker, one of those people who says "Thee" and "Thou." Mary kept on calling out ... and Mama could not keep her still. When the boat docked, the man told Mama he thought her master was about. He told Mama to put a veil over her face, in case the master was coming. He told Mama he would cut the master's heart out and give it to her, before he would ever let her be taken. She left the boat before reaching Canada, somewhere on the Underground Railroad — Detroit, I think — and a woman who took her in said: "Come in, my child, you're safe now!" Then Mama met my father in Windsor.[76]

This escape, remembered vividly although through the eyes of a child, used a necessary and familiar combination of river and overland routes. Black involvement in Louisville was possible; white involvement, although the identity of those involved cannot be established, was certain.

More problematic is the task of identifying specific sanctuaries, the houses and other structures occupied or used by friends of the fugitive. Given the poverty and poor quality of housing available to the vast majority of free blacks, the physical reality and much of the material culture of the antebellum free black community of Louisville disappeared long ago. In other words, the neighborhoods occupied by African Americans in the decades before 1860 have been razed and rebuilt several times — even the old churches. Current research can identify where probable Underground Railroad sites "were," but only rarely have actual African American owned and occupied antebellum sites survived. Thus, while fortunate for fugitives, Louisville's role as a junction is unfortunate from the standpoint of the historic preservationist. The Louisville region may prove to be as poor in Underground Railroad sites as it is rich in Underground Railroad history — which lends the oddly pristine crossing point west of Portland an even greater sense of significance and authenticity.

The Madison Crossings

The fugitive slave escape corridor leading through Trimble and Carroll counties to Ohio River crossing points in the vicinity of Madison, Indiana was one of the most active and well-known in Kentucky. This corridor and its many branch routes defined the eastern limit of the Louisville region and also channeled fugitive slaves toward Columbus, Indiana where it converged with those branch routes from the west. As the origin of numerous fugitives associated with this crossing suggests, the location of this route roughly midway between Louisville and Cincinnati made it an oft-traveled alternative route for fugitives escaping from the central Bluegrass. Further, as noted previously, Madison, although a small town by contemporary standards, was one of the larger urban centers along the antebellum Ohio River border. Although this area has been researched in greater depth[77], this study would be wholly incomplete without at least an overview of its history and major maps.

By the 1820s, a number of free

African Americans in the Madison area had begun assisting fugitive slaves. In these early years, "George Evans, Joe O'Neil, John Carter were the early leaders" and "from Graysville, Fountain Thurman and William Crosby provided leadership," while "at Greenbrier Jim Hackney was the acknowledged activist."[78] In 1834, E. S. Abdy, an English traveler, visited Madison and noted that a small African American farming community had developed near the town. Most of the black settlers were "from Virginia and Kentucky" and some were "liberated slaves."[79]

Ironically, one of the keys to understanding the Underground Railroad in this region was found in the recollections of one of its key operatives, Freman Anderson, as an elderly man. In September 1891, Anderson was interviewed at his home in Hanover, Indiana, and recounted how, while enslaved in Trimble County, he guided fugitives to the Ohio River and ferried them across "the Dark Line" to Indiana "where they would be taken charge of by underground agents and ultimately conducted to Canada."[80] His recollections were both colorful and fascinating.

For example, he recalled spending the night in the top of a tree with a fugitive couple from Bourbon County while bloodhounds and slave-catchers passed underneath. He spoke of how he himself killed a slave-catcher whose dogs had killed a runaway young woman from Lexington. Anderson even recalled meeting John Brown in Madison before the Harper's Ferry Raid (October 1859) — and how Brown dissuaded him and other discontented African Americans from launching an uprising until Brown's general revolt had begun.

While some portions of Anderson's reminiscences may seem the inventions or exaggerations of a old man, Anderson mentioned several people, places and events that can verified, lending greater credibility to his account. For example, he

identified quite accurately much of the African American leadership of the Underground Railroad in the area: Simon Gray, Elijah Anderson, Chapman Harris, John R. Forcen and Mason Thompson. He also mentioned the arrest and incarceration of Elijah Anderson in 1850s for aiding several fugitive slaves. Each of these statements can be confirmed through other sources.[81]

John Lott was another early African American leader in the struggle against slavery and one with an unusual but important historical connection to Kentucky. Lott was born in Pennsylvania and worked on the river before settling "in the beautiful, hilly country at Madison, Indiana." He, Chapman Harris and George Anderson were "powerful mates" in organizing the black Underground Railroad network in the area. In 1846, when proslavery whites attempted to drive African Americans from the Madison area, Lott followed the Underground Railroad himself and moved his wife and three children to Chatham, Canada West.[82]

Lott never returned to Madison. However, his daughter, Mary, married John E. Meyzeek of Chatham. Their son, Albert Ernest Meyzeek, would return to Louisville in the 1890s — and would become one of the leading educators and arguably the leading civil rights activist in Kentucky for the next generation. The younger Meyzeek learned of the Underground Railroad from his grandfather and took great pride in carrying on the activist tradition of his family.[83]

Another major map in the early black Underground in the Madison area was George DeBaptiste. DeBaptiste arrived in Madison in 1838 and was hired, in 1840, as the personal attendant of William Henry Harrison. In this capacity, he served as a steward in the White House during Harrison's brief term as President of the United States. DeBaptiste opened a barbershop after returning to Madison and became actively involved in aiding fugitives, also venturing across the river into Kentucky to conduct some runaways to freedom. In fact, his barbershop became the "nerve center" of the Madison Underground Railroad — much as was probably the case with Washington Spradling's barbershop in Louisville. After repeated pro-slavery attacks, DeBaptiste relocated to Detroit in 1846. There, he prospered in business and became a leader in the Detroit black community while continuing to work with the Underground Railroad.[84] Other African American Underground Railroad workers in the region included George Evans, "credited with conducting slaves from Hanover to Decatur County as early as the 1830s." Griffith Booth and John Carter were active as well, and Booth was among the free people of color driven from Madison in the 1840s.[84]

Still, of these many formidable and admirable men, two individuals — Elijah Anderson and Chapman Harris — played the most pivotal, conspicuous and well-documented roles. The exploits of both are discussed in Chapter VII.

The Madison area also stands out as home to the most visible and consistently active group of anti-slavery whites at any point on the Indiana side of the river. This presence in Madison and its surrounding area had a long history. As early as 1809, Benjamin Whitson (1761–1829), a Methodist minister, moved to Madison from North Carolina, via Kentucky, and expressed open opposition to slavery. Others followed, including "James and Daniel Nelson, from Vermont, who settled in Lancaster township in 1820; the Hoyt and Tibbets families ... and Thomas and Lewis Hicklin." The Hicklin brothers were also ministers. Thomas was particularly zealous and, before moving from Kentucky, "there was a reward of $100 offered for him dead or alive, on account of his anti-slavery work." Lewis was centrally involved in organizing the first anti-slavery meeting" at nearby Nells Creek in 1839.[85]

Amelia Hoyt was the daughter of Benjamin Hoyt, one of the more active members of this society. As an elderly woman, she recounted its work with fugitive slaves and recalled how her father and his comrades often left "their comfortable homes at dead of night to help the poor slave on toward the north star, and to treat him as a man and a brother."[86] When interviewed in 1880, Hoyt described an especially memorable incident that involved Louisville and Madison in the 1840s:

> A slaveholding family from the far south was accustomed to spending the summer north — at Louisville.... They brought a trusted man-servant along. He overheard it said on one occasion: "This is our last visit." To himself, he said: "This is my last opportunity to escape." When the time came for the family to return home he was told to load their goods onto a waiting boat. He did so, but before the family appeared he walked down to the water, took a canoe fastened there, and paddled up the river. On a Saturday evening, he entered the town of Madison and enquired for a respectable colored family with whom he might spend the Sabbath, and was directed to the home of DeBaptiste.

DeBaptiste delivered the fugitive to Hoyt's father, who assisted him on his northward journey.[87] As this incident suggests, at least by the 1840s, white anti-slavery activists began to support the work of and coordinate their efforts with local free people of color. For example, during this period, John Sering "opened the Clifty Falls route for fugitive slaves," a "rugged ravine and series of waterfalls ... located just a mile and a half west of Madison." Much as Mammoth Cave in south central Kentucky, "Clifty Falls provided a measure of cover for runaway slaves for some years."[88]

Other activist whites included John C. Todd, Jacob Wagner, John Carr, Will Ryker, James Stewart and James Baxter. Nearby, the Nell's Creek Anti-Slavery

Society, organized as noted in 1839, had seventy members by 1850. Through anti-slavery Baptist churches, some of its members contributed funds to Thomas Craven's Euletherion College at Lancaster, Indiana — one of the few institutions in the antebellum United States committed to educating both blacks and whites.[89]

Finally, the African American and white anti-slavery cells in Madison had counterparts in some parts of Kentucky by 1850s. Along with Delia Webster's brief residence in Trimble County in the 1850s (see Chapter VII), there were anti-slavery sympathizers and friends of the fugitive slightly to the south in Henry County as described in an article from the *Shelby News* reprinted in *The Provincial Freeman*. Specifically, in October 1856, three African Americans from the vicinity of Newcastle "were enticed away, and made their escape by help of the underground railroad." Once in Canada, the fugitives "attempted to communicate the good news of their arrival ... to some of their colored friends" by mail. Unfortunately, their letter was intercepted and opened, and both a larger escape plot and the names of their accomplices were revealed. Now alerted, local authorities bided their time in hopes of gathering more incriminating evidence.[90]

One local slaveholder soon "discovered his negroes conspiring with some of their neighboring brethren to make a start for Canada," implicating "a man named Stewart, living in Newcastle." From this evidence, it was determined that "Stewart had sent the party in October" and "was to go down to Madison ... and make arrangements for them to cross the Ohio, and for all services was to receive fifty dollars." Stewart was arrested and the enslaved African Americans were sold "to the land of cotton and sugar." Another white man, George Mahoney, was mentioned in the correspondence from Canada and was "believed to be as guilty as Stewart," but could not be linked to the most recent conspiracy.[91]

Both angered and frightened, Henry County residents held "a mass meeting at which several resolutions were adopted, the last "...calling upon the Legislature to pass more stringent and effective laws guarding this species of property." The group added that "it will be found, in nine cases out of ten, where slaves are persuaded off, that the Abolitionists engaged are residents in the community. These are the dangerous class, as they have constant intercourse with the negroes."[92]

From Kentucky to Ohio

The Covington/Cincinnati Region

From the standpoint of fugitive slaves, the role of Ohio was comparable in importance to that of Kentucky. According to Siebert, "Ohio was the foremost state in the abolition business, being peculiarly located for this purpose," with "thirteen ports of entry on the Ohio River" and "a network of from 2800 to 3000 miles of road throughout the state." This complex network of routes extended toward "five termini or ports of embarkation on Lake Erie."[93]

Five Ohio counties shared an Ohio River border with Kentucky: Hamilton, Clermont, Brown, Adams and Lawrence (from west to east). A number of southern anti-slavery families and free people of color settled in Hamilton and Clermont counties before 1810. Already predisposed to aiding fugitives, their presence attracted and they often assisted thousands of runaways who passed through the region before 1830.[94] Brown and Hamilton Counties, in particular, were known as bastions of anti-slavery sentiment along the river.[95] Much as the crossings and routes from Kentucky to southern Indiana, the major

Ohio crossings had an underlying structure:

> At the western edge of the state the routes originated at Cincinnati or North Bend, fifteen or twenty miles down the river, whence the fugitives were practically always taken to College Hill (now a part of Cincinnati), where Lane Seminary was located. From College Hill the principal routes went either northwest through Hamilton ... to Richmond or Newport, Indiana, both Quaker towns, or northeastward through either Wilmington or Xenia to Springfield and thence to Bellfontaine, Kenton, Tiffin and Sandusky. From Xenia a second set of routes reached Mechanicsburg, Marysville ... passing on to Sandusky ... Cleveland or some other lake port.[96]

As early as 1820, Cincinnati boasted an embryonic anti-slavery movement organized around a congregation of Quakers and a small African American community of 400 people. By 1829, the African American population increased to 2,258. The resulting heightened competition for jobs and living space triggered a race riot in 1829 that prompted an exodus of more than one thousand African Americans who then formed the nucleus of the first major black settlements in Canada West.[97] This sobering event also led to the call for the first Convention of Free People of Color — which met in Philadelphia in September 1830 and inaugurated the first American "civil rights" movement.[98]

Still, mob violence did not deter African American migration to Cincinnati and certainly did not stem the tide of fugitive slaves. As Siebert notes, "from far and near fugitive slaves entered the city" and "numerous fugitives crossed over from Covington and its vicinity." Once in Covington, "escaping slaves were harbored by Thomas Carneal in his mansion, which he erected in 1815."[99] By 1850, Cincinnati gained the distinction of being the "Grand Central Station" of the Underground Railroad.

Once across the Ohio River, fugitives were often harbored in Cincinnati's African American community. Although largely invisible in the published literature concerning the Kentucky and Ohio Underground Railroad, several African Americans played significant roles in this respect. For example, "a splendid Negro named Boyd" maintained "Station A on the south side, containing a secret room big enough for five persons between his parlor and kitchen." Boyd worked closely with "Mrs. Annis, a free woman who sold chickens in the market and induced slaves to flee from Kentucky."[100] The Dorum family "were capable colored stationkeepers," as were the Hall, Lewis and Burgess families. Shelton Morris, who played such a pivotal role in the formation of Louisville's free African American community, moved to Cincinnati in 1841 and, according to Levi Coffin, became one of the most "efficient operators" of the Underground Railroad in southern Ohio. African American churches such as Zion Baptist and the Cincinnati African Methodist Episcopal "were active Underground centers" and "helped refugees for decades."[101]

Henry Bibb's many escapes, described in Chapter VII, all passed through Cincinnati in the late 1830s and early 1840s. As another early example of fugitive traffic through the region, Anthony Bingey recounted how his brother and family escaped — quite opportunistically — from Kentucky in 1836 after having

> ... the good luck to find on the Newport road a driver's pocket-book containing $500. The Bingeys promptly decided to spend most of this money in leaving for Canada. They entrusted $400 to James Williams, a friend in Cincinnati, to buy horses, a wagon and firearms. From their master, General Taylor, they got a pass "to attend a camp-meeting up the river," but instead went to the landing and stole the ferryboat. On this they crossed to Cincinnati, took their purchases from

Williams ... and that night drove fifty miles north. They drove through Springfield and Columbus to Sandusky, and there embarked on the steamboat "Michigan."

The family eventually reached Amherstburg in Canada West.[102]

In 1848, Martin Delany visited Cincinnati seeking support for the anti-slavery movement (and subscribers to *The North Star*). He spoke to many groups, met many free blacks individually and had ample opportunities to observe their social world. Delany found most black Cincinnatians warmly receptive to his message, and noted that "whenever our principles are fully made known, they meet with many who readily subscribe to them, practical anti-slavery being that which the people desire." However, Delany concluded that those strong sentiments required organization and direction, adding that "the harvest in the West is truly ready, but the laborers are few." Interestingly, Delany was most impressed with the African American "women of the west" and found them more strongly opposed to slavery than their counterparts in the "east."[103] Further, he observed that inter-racial relations in Cincinnati had a distinctly "Southern" flavor and commented that "the anti-slavery people of Cincinnati and the colored people, have no intercourse or acquaintance, only being brought together on great or extraordinary occasions ... when the colored people take no part among the whites." Delany then expressed his chagrin at witnessing "respectable colored residents of this city ... thus duped and imposed upon by the mock anti-slavery of Cincinnati."[104]

From Delany's description, a picture emerges of a community nearing political maturity, strongly anti-slavery and strongly pro-fugitive slave — awaiting some catalyzing event(s) to force it toward greater organization and unity of purpose. Thus, by 1850s, the African American community was organized and committed overtly to the anti-slavery cause. There were many symbols of this political "coming of age." For example, public celebrations of West Indian Emancipation (August 1, 1838) were especially popular as the end of slavery in the British Empire was viewed as the beginning of the end of slavery throughout the world.[105] Blacks in Cincinnati also mobilized to rescue or raise funds to purchase the freedom of captured fugitive slaves.[106]

White abolitionists were quite active as well and played roles that are far better known historically. Among the best-known, Harriet Beecher Stowe harbored fugitives in her home from 1836 until she moved in 1850. By the 1840s, there were at least thirty rather visible Abolitionists in Cincinnati. Underground Railroad activity reached a new pitch of intensity when Levi Coffin and his family moved from the Richmond, Indiana area to Cincinnati in April 1847. Coffin believed that more formal organization and management were needed since some of the older Abolitionists had either died or relocated and, in his view, few of the local African Americans, other than those mentioned above, were "shrewd managers." As an immediate result, Coffin organized a Vigilance Committee that included blacks and whites and transformed his free labor store (that sold no slave-produced goods) at the corner of Sixth and Elm Streets into a weigh station for fugitives. Women were also involved in key roles through an Anti-Slavery Sewing Society.[107] Coffin was soon considered the "President of the Underground Railroad."

One indication that the Underground Railroad had become a more formal organization by this time was that the Vigilance Committee had a board of directors and, most importantly, a budget. To defray the costs of "running" the Underground, Coffin is believed to contributed "over $50,000 of his own earnings and to have collected twice that amount from local business and professional men to support the secret movement." Among the "stockholders in the Underground" were future Governor and Senator Salmon P. Chase and John J. Jolliffe, the attorney who would defend Margaret Garner.[108]

Laura Haviland, the noted Abolitionist, also worked closely with Coffin and his associates in Cincinnati to coordinate escapes that passed first through Cincinnati and then moved north through eastern Indiana.[109] On the strength of such efforts, fugitive slave traffic through southwestern and south central Ohio was heavy over the four decades preceding the Civil War. However, source materials from Kentucky and Ohio, the records and recollections of fugitive slaves and Underground Railroad workers agree that "the greatest movement of fugitives through Ohio came after the passage of the Fugitive Slave Law of 1850 and, judging from newspaper reports of escapes and arrests, reached its highest point about the years of 1855 to 1857."[110] The most famous, and most tragic, of all slave escapes through the Cincinnati region occurred during this period — the Margaret Garner incident, which will be discussed in Chapter VII. Furthermore, as was the case in the Madison area, some active "friends of the fugitive" were also based on the Kentucky side of the borderland. One, Dr. T. J. Trimble of Boone County, was arrested in 1853 and "accused of being an abolitionist and of kidnapping slaves." His bail was set at $15,000. The news article added, "so great is the excitement in that vicinity that they threaten violence against any person who shall offer to become his surety."[111]

African Americans often lived along Underground Railroad lines that branched in several directions from Cincinnati. One route stretched north through Preble and Darke Counties — with a branch-line that crossed into Indiana through "a colored settlement in Israel Township, where Nathan Brown, Ebenezer Elliott and others had stations." Another western route passed through West Fork, "a damned abolition hole," then north to Dunlap "...a Negro settlement from which Hansel and Wade Roberts passed them to Hamilton.[112] In eastern Cincinnati, the "Old Stone Jug Tavern" was used to hide "hundreds of liberty-seekers." Other routes from Cincinnati were "the Miami Canal, completed to Toledo in 1842, and the Cleveland, Columbus and Cincinnati Railroad, which was running through trains by March 1851." As in Indiana, "these new means of transportation were promptly utilized by leading abolitionists of Cincinnati and towns along the way."[113]

Another well-known operative was Abraham Allen of Oakland in Clinton County where escape routes from both Cincinnati and Ripley converged. Allen assisted fugitives with "a special, six-seated, covered wagon built for Underground use, which became famous throughout southwestern Ohio as the Liberator."[114] These few examples reflect the extensiveness and the density of the Underground Railroad network in the environs of Cincinnati. This did not mean that the majority of whites held anti-slavery views — or even that the majority of African Americans, who were staunchly opposed to slavery, were also active friends of the fugitive. What did exist in Cincinnati — and could exist above ground as at Madison and Ripley, in contrast to Louisville — was a critical mass of both blacks and whites who were inclined toward practical abolitionism.

African Americans and whites were well aware that Louisville and Cincinnati were favored destinations of fugitive slaves. In a letter to the famous white Abolitionist, William Lloyd Garrison, reprinted by Frederick Douglass in 1853, a correspondent from Cincinnati stated, "the Ohio River is no impassable barrier between freedom and slavery. It is a fence along the Northern side of our great plantation, which thousands of breachy slaves jump over every year."[115]

Clermont County

In Clermont County, Ohio, immediately east of Hamilton County (and Cincinnati), a similar network existed — adapted to the realities of a less populous and more rural area. There were noteworthy conductors. One was Jacob Ebersole, who was born in 1812 and became an early pioneer in the work of assisting runaway slaves. Ebersole inherited four hundred acres south of New Richmond from his father. In 1851, he added more than another one hundred acres and "built a new residence commanding a charming view of the beautiful Ohio Valley." This relative isolated area, "with skiffs available on signal," became an important crossing point between the major crossings at Covington and Maysville.[116] Once fugitives were safely across the Ohio River,

> ... they were cared for and soon driven fourteen miles northeast to Williamsburg, where Charles B. Huber, a sturdy tanner, and Dr. L. T. Pease harbored them.... At least two conductors made night trips with them from Williamsburg, viz., Mark Sims, a mulatto with many years in Huber's employ, who made deliveries to Quaker settlements in Highland and Clinton Counties; and Samuel Peterson, who ... transported these people to Mt. Orab and to Isaac Brown's farm near Sardinia, both in Brown County.[117]

Another route extended east from New Richmond to Lindale, where the Coombs family played a prominent role both in the Gilead Anti-Slavery Society (established in 1836) and in aiding runaways. This route merged with a western line leading from the Ripley/Maysville crossing. In the southeast corner of Clermont County, the small town of Moscow was another alternative crossing point where "Robert E. and W. M. Fee, anti-slavery Democrats, kept open house for colored arrivals." Fee's mansion "looked out over the Ohio River, and in one of its windows a light burned all night to guide liberty-seekers across."[118]

To the east, the same escape routes leading from crossings into Clermont, Brown and Adams Counties merged at Wilmington or Xenia with the branch lines leading northeasterly from Cincinnati. However, "the important gateway of Ripley sent its fugitives straight northward to Wilmington, or over to the line into Adams County, where they were taken along the Maysville-Chillicothe pike (Zane's trace)."[119]

The Maysville/Ripley Crossing

The fugitive slave escape route leading from Lexington and the densely populated central Bluegrass region to Maysville was one of the earliest and most heavily traveled in Kentucky and was mentioned frequently in fugitive slave notices and articles. As examples, Chew ran away from Benjamin Buckner of Winchester in June 1836. Changing his name to "John," he "had been carried in the stage to Maysville" and, presumably, from Maysville across the Ohio River.[120] Andrew escaped from John T. Lyle near Versailles on December 24, 1836. The advertisement for his return declared that he "left Lexington, as I have been informed, on the 28th of December, in the Maysville Stage, and entered his name ISAAC on the way bill.[121] Following the same route, Lewis Clarke escaped from Madison County on a Saturday night in August 1841. He fled on horseback, with clothes and traveling money to ease his way. Clarke journeyed first to the home of his brother, Cyrus, in Lexington twenty-five miles to the north. He then traveled to Maysville, crossed the Ohio River and then continued to Cincinnati. Friends in Cincinnati advised him to travel by steamboat to Portsmouth and then by canal boat to Cleveland. He finally reached Canada six weeks after his escape journey began.[122]

Ripley, Ohio, stood opposite and a few miles to the west of Maysville and, much as Madison, Indiana, was home to numerous anti-slavery whites who had "chosen or been forced to leave the South." By 1840, more than three hundred whites belonged to the Ripley Abolition Society led by men such as "U.S. Senator Alexander Campbell (Ohio's first Abolitionist), Theodore Collins, Tom Collins, Eli Collins, Tom McCague, Dr. Beasley, the Rev. James Gilliland." Ripley was also home to two black settlements established before 1820. To the north, there were many friends of the fugitive in towns such as Red Oak "where Reverend James Gilliland and his congregation formed the core of the largest concentration of Underground Railroad conductors in Ohio." These anti-slavery activists were surrounded by adamantly pro-slavery neighbors on both sides of the Ohio River.[123]

In 1850, Martin Delany visited Ripley, Ohio, where he held a "meeting in the church of the famous Dr. John Rankin, long and favorably known ... as a firm friend of the panting fugitive." Delany observed that Rankin's house was a beacon, but that the actual "underground depot is ... situated in a cavern about two miles south, the whereabouts of which none but abolitionists are aware." Ripley itself was described as a "small village," with several colored families, all of whom are industrious and well-doing.... They have a church and a literary society there, and colored and white children go to the same schools."[124]

Transcending the importance of this anti-slavery infrastructure were the roles

> ☞ Some ten or twelve slaves have, within the last week, made their escape from Maysville and its vicinity. Several have also escaped from Covington. Since the Know-Nothings and Free-soilers carried Ohio, the underground railroad through that State has been doing a largely increased business. The late overthrow of the Know-Nothings in Indiana seems to have pretty effectually stopped the operations of the U. G. R. R. in that State.

News article: "Fugitive Slaves," *Louisville Courier*, December 14, 1855. Report of a mass escape from the Maysville and Covington areas.

and work of two extraordinary individuals—one white, the Rev. John Rankin (1793–1886), aforementioned, and one black, John Parker (1827–1900), both of whom will be discussed at length in Chapter VII. In essence, the work of Rankin and his associates, while in the foreground of Underground Railroad history and legend, was made possible by African Americans laboring in the background. The relationship between Parker and Rankin is illustrative of the type of relationship that existed between black and white friends of the fugitive throughout the borderland. Specifically, Parker stated that he "revered Mr. Rankin but did not work with him" directly. Perhaps, implicit in this statement is another, more fundamental message: Parker and men like him did not work "for" Rankin or anyone else.

Another important, but largely unknown, working relationship developed between anti-slavery whites and John W. Hudson, another free person of color. Hudson lived in Sardinia, a small settlement twenty-five miles to the north and was a key conductor between 1834 and the Civil War. Described as "a powerful man with courage," he routinely traveled "on foot, horseback or by wagon" to assist fugitives and was paid wages by white Abolitionists.[125]

Thus, two of the key Underground Railroad operatives in this key borderland region were African American. Moreover, the most heavily traveled routes from these river crossings snaked toward and through small African American communities scattered throughout south central Ohio. These facts do not minimize the roles and contributions of truly admirable men such as John Rankin or the anti-slavery society at Red Oak, but simply reflect the actual relation between the efforts of both groups in the same movement.

Southeastern Ohio

The Ohio counties bordering the eastern and more mountainous sections of Kentucky witnessed the crossing of fugitives from Kentucky and some, as noted previously, who followed routes from the southern interior through the Appalachians. In 1840, *The Colored American* published a lengthy article on "Colored Inhabitants of Ohio" that offered a rare description of the black population of southeastern Ohio — apart from the bare essentials reported customarily in the U.S. Census. Focusing on Jackson, Gallia, Scioto, Shelby, Mercer and Darke Counties, the editor described a network of scattered, but similar, rural black farming communities, with an occasional small concentration of African American population in or near one of the larger towns such as Portsmouth and Chillicothe. Beyond gross demographic patterns, discussed to some extent in Chapter II, these scattered hamlets were also described as havens for industrious, relatively prosperous and temperate free people of color. Virtually all had been founded by African Americans from Virginia or Kentucky — most of whom had been emancipated and some of whom had migrated to Ohio with sufficient funds with which to purchase land. Each community had established a school for its children; most had also established at least one church, usually Baptist or African Methodist. Each was also surrounded by whites who were hostile to varying degrees.[126]

WPA research on slavery in Boyd County unearthed numerous accounts of slavery and slave escapes in a section of the state deep in the Appalachians from which fugitives escaped to southeastern Ohio. As one telling example,

> a young Negro saw his own sister stripped naked and unmercifully whipped by one of these over-seers. He gathered up all of his small belongings and tied them in a bundle and securing a club of wood, laid in wait for the cruel "boss" until after dark, when he killed him with the club. He then escaped, via the "Underground Railroad." ... He succeeded in making his way to Canada and freedom where he stayed until after the war, when it was safe to return.[127]

The earliest recorded slave escape through Adams County occurred in the summer of 1822 when Joseph Logan fled slavery in North Carolina. Logan "swam across the Ohio near Ashland, Kentucky, tramped northwest to Portsmouth, and west to ... Adams County." There, he reunited with his wife and child. Logan settled in the area and committed himself to aiding other fugitives. A formidable figure, he "...carried a club to ward off men and dogs...."[128] Manchester, in southeastern Adams County, was another key entry point from which fugitives could follow "Simon Kenton's trace" northeast to Highland County. Numerous safe-houses "staffed by staunch anti-slavery Presbyterians" dotted the route. Further the northeast, "...runaways were harbored in the Negro settlement of Roxabell ... and hauled from there to Washington Court House."[129]

The Scioto River bisects Scioto County and flows into the Ohio at Portsmouth. The earliest records of slave escapes from

Kentucky into this region of southern Ohio date to 1820. However, the borderland in Scioto County was unusually hostile. Portsmouth was a strong pro-slavery center and, by 1830, had driven out most of the hundred or more African Americans once resident there. Still, fugitives escaped through this region and often found assistance from white Underground Railroad workers such as James M. Ashley. In one of his more memorable and formative adventures:

> In 1840, when seventeen years old, James was near Greenupsburg, Kentucky. With the aid of an old slave, he rescued a group of five Negroes and took them across the river to a man named Goodrich, living just ... ten miles southeast of Portsmouth. A reward of $500 was offered for the recovery of the slaves. James strolled through Portsmouth to learn whether suspicions were afloat. Two local abolitionists knew what he had been up to. A merchant handed him a ten-dollar gold piece and said he might need it; an old Quaker gave him a hundred-dollar bill, with an approving look.

Ashley continued his daring rescues until 1851, when he moved to Toledo.[130]

As Ashley's account suggests, a few white abolitionists operated secretly in Portsmouth and coordinated their work with nearby free people of color. For example, Joseph Ashton used his wagon to transport fugitives into Pike County. Fugitives were also moved north on the "Chillicothe pike and left with two colored men, Joseph Love and Dan Lucas. They, in turn, drove with them ten miles northwest of Waverly to the Barrett family, also colored people in Pee Pee Settlement."[131]

Also drawing fugitives from eastern Kentucky and the Appalachian escape routes, Lawrence County witnessed a moderate but steady flow of runaways beginning in the 1830s, if not earlier. Ironton was founded in 1840 at what was already a principal crossing point. There, Joseph H. Creighton, a Methodist minister, and John Peters "befriended fugitive slaves, who came across in skiffs and joe boats."[132] Lawrence County was also home to one of the most effective and colorful African American Underground Railroad leaders:

> James Dicher, colored, was the most fearless local conductor. He and his wards were often pursued, but they shifted routes and resorted to other tricks. Dicher, tall, thin and of copper complexion, was called the "red fox" of the Underground. His co-worker, Gabe Johnson, marveled at the risks he took.... Together they operated along the river from Portsmouth up to Proctorville, a distance of about sixty-five miles.[133]

From this point, another route branched northeast, through a chain of stations operated by black and white agents to "Poke Patch Colored Settlement" in Gallia County along the Ohio/Virginia border. Given this location, Poke Patch was a crossroads for fugitives bound north from both Kentucky and Virginia.[134] Friends of the fugitive were committed and well organized, even holding a "convention of the colored citizens of Gallia County in 1851" at which they articulated, among other resolutions, their sympathy with fugitive slaves.[135]

In general, fugitives crossing from Kentucky into Scioto and Lawrence Counties followed routes through southeastern Ohio—perhaps the most important of which passed first through Chillicothe—that converged ultimately at Columbus in central Ohio. For example, "Richard Chancellor and his son Robert, Jesse and John Fiddler and Andrew Redmond" were key operators in the Chillicothe area. In Columbus, fugitives were harbored and moved "by colored drivers, including Shepherd Alexander, Lewis Washington, his son Thomas and others." Washington himself owned "several teams and wagons, being in the excavating business.[136]

As in the other regions of the borderland, the movement of runaways depended on the coordinated efforts of African American and white friends of the fugitive. Given the distribution of African American population in the southern half of Ohio, the roles of African Americans as conductors and African American settlements as havens were crucial, if not wholly indispensable.

Fugitive slaves crossing from Kentucky into Ohio found more and better organized sources of aid and comfort on their journey north than in any other region of the borderland. The existence of an organized Underground Railroad in many sections of the country may be questioned — and questioned legitimately based on the evidence or lack thereof, but there was unquestionably an Underground Railroad in the borderland, particularly in southern Ohio. Designating this merely a "local" network requires considerable interpretive license — since it channeled fugitives escaping from or through much of central Kentucky through much of southeastern Indiana and southwestern Ohio. When the Anti-Slavery League of southwestern Indiana described by Cockrum, the Louisville and Madison regions are taken into account as well, this network expands to include much of the upper south and lower north by the 1850s, as depicted in Map VI-4.

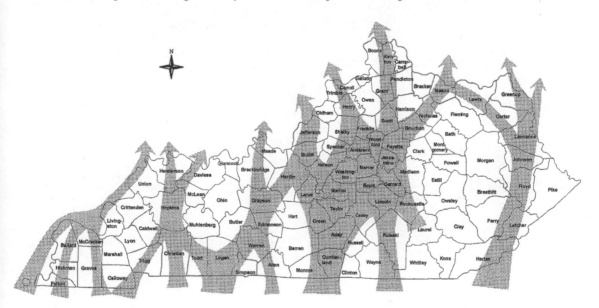

Map VI-4. Fugitive Slave Routes through the Kentucky Borderland.

CHAPTER VII

Individuals and Cases of Note

Beyond the broad patterns described empirically in the Kentucky Fugitive Slave Data Base and illustrated by the hundreds of examples cited in preceding sections of the study, sufficient information is available in a few instances to illuminate the lives of actual fugitive slaves and/or those who assisted them in much greater detail. Of the individuals discussed below, some are well known; others are more obscure. Some are fugitives. Others are friends of the fugitive. A few are fugitives who, after reaching free ground, became friends of their fellow runaways and leaders in the anti-slavery struggle. Many important individuals have been omitted — for example, Josiah Henson and Levi Coffin — although they are mentioned elsewhere. There omission here should not be construed as a judgment regarding their importance.

The brief overviews that follow, presented only in chronological order, add an anecdotal dimension to the historical record and may now be viewed in a larger historical context.

Fugitive: Eliza Harris

While accounts of slave escapes from or through Kentucky are strewn throughout antebellum historical sources, few have been immortalized in significant works of American literature. One of the rare exceptions concerns Eliza Harris, a famous fugitive whose daring escape from bondage in Kentucky was central to *Uncle Tom's Cabin* — so much so that she is often presumed to be a fictional character.

The "real" Eliza Harris was enslaved in the region surrounding Maysville, Kentucky "about 1830." She was "married" to an enslaved African American on a neighboring farm and, after the deaths of two children in infancy, was strongly attached to her remaining child, a two-year old son. When Harris learned that her owner was in dire financial straits and planned to sell her son, "she became frantic and decided to take her baby and escape to Canada." It was winter and there was no time for planning or other preparations. What followed was one of the most harrowing and memorable slave escapes in American history:

> She did not wait, but slipped out and went several miles to the Ohio River; she found the ice broken up and was at a loss as to what to do. There were no bridges those days, and of course no raft could cross in the ice jam.... She picked up her baby and clasped it to her bosom and ran for the river. Reaching it, she jumped on an ice cake and as it sank, got onto another. Thus, by crawling, jumping and lifting herself and baby from one cake of ice to another she finally crossed the river.[1]

Harris was guided to the home of the Rev. John Rankin in Ripley. After she and her son recovered from their ordeal, she was conveyed to Cincinnati and then to the home of Levi Coffin in Newport, Indiana where she remained for the next two weeks. With Coffin's assistance, she was transported next to Underground Railroad stations in Cabin Creek, near Georgetown in Randolph County (Indiana), then to Pennville in Jay County, then to Greenville, Ohio, then to Sandusky — and then "across the Lake to Canada and located in Chatham."[2]

Although little is known of Harris' life after slavery, what is known suggests that her story, unlike so many others, had a comparatively happy ending. In 1854, Levi Coffin, his wife and daughter visited some of the African American settlements in Canada West and encountered many of the thousands of fugitives they had assisted over the previous thirty years. At one meeting,

> ... a woman came up to Mrs. Coffin, seized her hand and exclaimed, "How are you, Aunt Katie? God bless you!" Mrs. Coffin did not recognize her at first, then found it was Eliza Harris, whom she had befriended at her home in Newport years ago.... The Coffins visited Eliza in her home and found her comfortable and contented.[3]

Fugitives: Thornton and Lucie Blackburn

Thornton and Lucie Blackburn were two notable fugitives from Louisville in the early 1830s. Thornton Blackburn was born about 1814 in Maysville, Kentucky. He moved to Louisville with his owners in 1830 and escaped on July 3, 1831. In the fugitive slave advertisement placed after his flight, Blackburn was described as "about 5 feet, 9 or 10 inches high; stout made, and of a yellow complexion; light eyes, and of good address."[4] His wife, Lucie Blackburn — called "Ruth" or "Ruthie" — described herself as "a Creole from the West Indies." She was purchased by Virgil McKnight, later President of the Bank of Kentucky, only a few weeks before she fled with her husband.[5] The possibility that Lucie would be sold to settle the estate of her former owner might have precipitated their flight.

The Blackburns crossed the Ohio River to Jeffersonville and, posing as free people of color, boarded the steamboat Versailles. Disembarking at Cincinnati, they traveled to Sandusky, Ohio, by stage coach and reached Detroit on July 18, 1831. The relative ease with which they escaped suggests that they had a sound plan, possibly contacts in Jeffersonville and Cincinnati — and that they had funds.

They remained in Detroit, living humbly but happily by all accounts, until discovered by a member of the Oldham family in 1833. They were arrested and jailed, and a trial ensued to determine whether or not the couple should be returned to bondage in Kentucky. The presiding judge ruled in favor of their owner(s). However, Detroit's free black community refused to accept this decision and "took matters into their own hands." First, Mrs. George French and Mrs. Madison Mason, wives of ministers of Detroit's "Black Baptist Church" were allowed to visit Lucie Blackburn.

While unobserved, Mrs. French changed clothing with Lucie, who then escaped the jail in this disguise and was "spirited ... across the Detroit River and into Canada."[6]

Not surprisingly, Lucie's escape tightened the restrictions on her husband. On June 17, when he was bound in chains for his long return journey to Kentucky, the black and now also many white citizens of Detroit became so incensed that four hundred of them marched on the jail where he was held captive. They wrested Thornton from custody after beating the Sheriff so severely that he died of his injuries a year later. Thornton was then placed in a wagon and a wild race began toward the Detroit River with a posse in hot pursuit. Thornton's entourage thought it best to abandon their wagon and hastened through the forest to the riverbank on foot. There, one of Thornton's eight rescuers sacrificed his gold watch to pay his passage across the river.[7]

The Blackburns settled eventually in Toronto and became pillars of the Canadian anti-slavery movement.[8] Interestingly, the "Blackburn case" remained in the Kentucky court system long after the Blackburns left the United States. In *McFarland v. McKnight* (June 1846), several related suits were brought

> ... against the owners and master of the steamboat, Versailles for having taken on board, in the Circuit of Jefferson ... a female slave called Ruthy ... and a man slave (her husband) called Thornton Blackburn.... The owners of the slaves resided in Louisville, the slaves ran away from their owners ... and were taken on board and registered as passengers on the books of the Versailles, conveyed on board to Cincinnati, and there landed, whereby they have been lost to their owners.[9]

Fugitive and Friend of the Fugitive: Henry Bibb

Several fugitives left gripping accounts of their bondage in Kentucky and their flight therefrom. Some offer extremely valuable insights. However, the *Narrative of the Life of Henry Bibb* (1849) is arguably the most important of these due to the eloquence and probity of its author, and his subsequent stature in the national anti-slavery movement. Bibb's extraordinary and often ignored account opens several windows through which life in antebellum Kentucky can be glimpsed with great clarity.

Henry Bibb — known as Walton to his owner — was born enslaved in 1815 in Shelby County near Louisville. In Bibb's words, he "was brought up in the Counties of Shelby, Henry, Oldham and Trimble. Or, more correctly speaking, in the above counties, I may safely say that I was flogged up."[10] Bibb attempted his first escape in 1835 when hired to a Mr. Vires in Newcastle. Hoping to reach Canada and freedom, he was caught, whipped, soon escaped again and was caught and flogged yet again, then returned to his increasingly exasperated owner.[11]

Bibb's determination to escape subsided temporarily while he courted and subsequently "married" Malinda, a lovely young African American woman enslaved in Oldham County — the daughter of a free woman of color living in nearby Bedford. Fatherhood soon followed, but the inherent contradictions of being a husband and father whose wife and child were the property of another man rekindled his longing for freedom, this time for himself and his family.[12] Promising to return for them, Bibb escaped on Christmas day in 1837 and described the ensuing events as follows:

> I was landed in the village of Madison, Indiana, where steamboats were landing every day and night ... which afforded me a good opportunity of getting a boat to Cincinnati. I secreted myself where no one could see me, and changed my suit ready for the passage. I then stepped boldly on the deck of this splendid swift-running Steamer.... I crowded myself back

from the light among the deck passengers, where it would be difficult to distinguish me from a white.[13]

Bibb reached Cincinnati and, through the good offices of a free man of color, was put in contact with Abolitionists who fed him and told him how to reach the next safe house on his journey northward. He progressed with difficulty as far as Perrysburgh, where he "found quite a settlement of colored people, many of whom were fugitive slaves." Bibb remained in Perrysburgh through the winter and, "about the first of May," began the journey back to Kentucky to free his wife and child.[14] He found his family and arranged for them to escape by steamboat and meet him in Cincinnati. Unfortunately, they failed to appear at the appointed rendezvous point and Bibb, after having been betrayed by slave-hunters passing as Abolitionists, was captured and taken to Louisville to be sold. However, he managed to escape from his captors once again and stated:

> Before I left the city, I chanced to find, by the way, an old man of color. Supposing him to be a friend, I ventured to make known my situation, and asked him if he would get me a bite to eat. The old man most cheerfully complied. I was then about forty miles from ... where my wife, whom I sought to rescue from slavery, was living. This was also in the direction it was necessary to travel in order to get to the free North.[15]

Bibb left the state and returned again in search of his family in 1839. Malinda was closely watched and he was betrayed yet again, probably by an enslaved African American, and imprisoned along with his wife and child. Before being transported again to Louisville and Matthew Garrison's slave pen, Bibb related what was certainly, under the circumstances, an unusual encounter:

> ... two slaves came to the dungeon gates about the dread hour of night, and called

me to the gates to have some conversation about Canada, and the facilities for getting there.... I of course took great pleasure in giving them directions how and where to go, and they started in less than a week from that time and got clear to Canada. I have seen them both since I came back to the north myself. They were known by the names of King and Jack.[16]

While imprisoned in Louisville, Garrision, one of the more notorious Kentucky slave traders, "made a most disgraceful assault" on Malinda's virtue and had her whipped for resisting his advances. Eventually, they were all loaded aboard the steamboat, Water Witch, bound for Vicksburg and later New Orleans. The family was allowed to remain together to deter Bibb, whose devotion to his family was well-known, from attempting yet another escape.[17] Bibb's next year was filled with a succession of foiled escapes, brutal punishments and, ultimately, separation from his wife and daughter in 1840. Malinda and their child were sold to gamblers and Bibb was sold to a Native American — not surprisingly, from whom he also escaped and then crossed the prairie, reached the Mississippi River and took a steamboat that arrived at Portsmouth, Ohio in early 1841.[18]

After his long ordeal, Bibb gradually settled into the life of a free man and both began his formal education and became involved in the anti-slavery movement. Still, he longed for his family and, against the advice of his friends, returned to Kentucky one last time in the winter of 1845. Retracing his oft-used escape route, he traveled first to Cincinnati and then to Madison by steamboat. Unfortunately, he soon learned that his

> ... wife was living in a state of adultery with her master, and had been for the last three years. This message she sent back to Kentucky, to her mother and friends. She also spoke of the time and manner of our separation ... and that she had given me up. The child she said was still with

her.... This was a death blow to all my hopes.... Poor unfortunate woman, I bring no charge of guilt against her....[19]

Finally, with no hope of recovering his family, Bibb turned his attention and devoted his considerable abilities to advancing the anti-slavery cause. He (re)married in 1848 and, after becoming a noted Abolitionist lecturer, decided to publish his *Narrative* in 1849. On January 1, 1851, with the assistance of his wife, Bibb established the first successful African American newspaper in Canada West, *Voice of the Fugitive*.[20] In addition, Bibb became a true friend of his fellow fugitives and a tireless advocate of black self-help in Canada — stating, in 1851, that African Americans on Canadian soil "do not need aid for immediate relief of want, but they do need the means of helping themselves."[21] He died on August 1, 1854, at the age of 39.[22]

While Bibb's newspaper became an important although short-lived publication, his *Narrative* developed a life of its own. By 1849, given the number of slave narratives in print and their consistently unflattering portrayal of the South, proslavery advocates had devised the strategy of dismissing these first person accounts as nothing more than the inventions or exaggerations of white Abolitionists or free people of color "passing" as fugitive slaves. Bibb's extraordinary courage and devotion to family strained credibility even among his friends. Thus, anticipating charges that he or others simply fabricated his life story, Bibb introduced his *Narrative* with a collection of documents intended to "establish the truth" of his account, among which was even a letter from the son of his former owner.[23] As a result, although Bibb hoped to serve one purpose with his autobiography, he created an unusually reliable source for the study of fugitive slaves and friends of the fugitive in the Kentucky borderland.

Most illuminating were Bibb's descriptions of his many escapes— how he escaped, how and from whom he received assistance, how and by whom he was captured. Bibb's fair complexion gave him the ability to "pass for white" under certain circumstances, an advantage most fugitives, even most mulattoes, lacked. Bibb also used steamboats, consistently, to travel from (and to) Kentucky and various other means to travel from Cincinnati northward through Ohio. In other words, Bibb avoided travel by land through Kentucky and Indiana. Living across from Madison, Bibb would probably have sought assistance there had assistance been available. From his *Narrative*, one would conclude either that Madison's free black and white anti-slavery forces were not yet in place in the 1830s and, perhaps, well into the 1840s— or that Bibb used but avoided mentioning them in his escapes. Bibb's autobiography was published, after all, in 1849 and assisting fugitives was both criminal and controversial. That an anonymous free person of color in Louisville or white antislavery worker in Cincinnati might have helped Bibb would have surprised no one. However, revealing the existence of friends of the fugitive in a smaller town such as Madison risked the inadvertent identification of some of those friends.

Bibb sought assistance, first and routinely, from other African Americans. Even after his betrayal by one of his race, he was still predisposed to trust other blacks far more than any whites. In the same context, other African Americans were inclined to be helpful. Most interesting, this aid was rendered almost at random by ordinary free people of color — folks Bibb often, literally, "met in the street."

Bibb's last glimpse of Kentucky as he beheld it on his final steamboat journey to freedom is a haunting evocation of the ambivalence so many fugitives felt toward a home that was never truly their home:

I was permitted by the smiles of good providence, once more to gaze on the green hill-tops and valleys of old Kentucky, the State of my nativity ... my very soul was pained to look upon the slaves in the fields....[24]

Friends of the Fugitive: Delia Webster and Calvin Fairbank

In September 1844, Lewis Hayden and his family escaped from slavery in Lexington, Kentucky. However, Delia Webster and Calvin Fairbank, the young white woman and man who aided them, came to be far better known than Hayden — at least in Kentucky. Webster was born in Vermont in 1817, studied briefly at Oberlin College, a center for anti-slavery activists in northern Ohio, and migrated to Kentucky in 1842. By 1844, she headed the Lexington Academy, a rather exclusive school for young women. Fairbank was born in New York in 1816 and later became a Methodist minister. Fairbank also studied at Oberlin College, although not with Webster. By 1844, he had gained extensive experience "in the business of rescuing slaves."[25]

Fairbank traveled to Kentucky in 1844 for the purpose of "rescuing" the family of Gilson Berry, a fugitive slave with whom Fairbank became acquainted at Oberlin. Around the first of September, he sought Webster's assistance after depleting his limited funds in the futile search for Berry's family. Webster introduced Fairbank to Lewis Hayden, an enslaved waiter at the Phoenix Hotel who wished to escape with his wife and child. Hayden was hired out and working toward self-purchase, and used his earnings to support Fairbank in Lexington and to finance their escape.[26]

On Saturday, September 28, 1844, Lexington was crowded as the fall horse racing meet was nearing its close. At roughly five o'clock that evening, Fairbank called for Webster in a hired carriage, then continued north, picking up Hayden, his wife Harriet and their son, Jo. The party then drove north along the Lexington-Maysville road and reached Washington in Mason County by four o'clock in the morning of September 29, 1844. Later that day, they drove the four additional miles to Maysville. James Helm ferried them across the Ohio River and they were delivered to the Rev. John Rankin and his famous hilltop Underground Railroad station in Ripley, Ohio. The Hayden family was then spirited north.[27]

By the time Webster and Fairbank returned to Kentucky, news of the slave escape had already spread as far as Maysville. Suspicion soon fell on the two northerners and both were arrested en route to Lexington. The two were indicted in the Fayette Circuit Court for the crime of "aiding and enticing slaves to leave their owners" — and news of the incident and its principal figures spread across the nation.[28] The two were tried separately and both were found guilty. Webster was sentenced to two years imprisonment, but outrage over jailing a woman outweighed outrage over "Negro stealing" and the "petticoat abolitionist" was pardoned by Governor Owsley on February 24, 1845. Fairbank was not as fortunate and was sentenced to five years in the state penitentiary. He served at hard labor until pardoned by Governor John Crittenden on August 28, 1849 — after, it was rumored, $600 was paid to Hayden's owner.[29]

Neither Webster nor Fairbank slipped quietly into obscurity following their release from prison. Fairbank spoke to anti-slavery groups in many northern cities and corresponded with the editors of the anti-slavery press.[30] He soon resumed his one-man Underground Railroad crusade and "on November 9, 1851, he was arrested in Jeffersonville, Indiana, on a charge of having stolen Tamar, a twenty-two year-old mulatto girl — doomed to be sold at auction by her master in Louisville."[31] Fairbank's arrest was publicized widely and, on learning of it, Frederick Douglass expressed deep apprehension that "the evidence may be against him" and "he will be made to suffer the extreme penalty of Slave Laws of Kentucky."[32] Nor was Fairbank himself confident of acquittal as he feared being lynched and lamented that "public opinion" in Louisville "always 'overrides public law' and becomes the lawless rule of action."[33] While no lynch mob appeared, Fairbank found himself beyond the reach of any aid or comfort his friends might offer. In February 1852, he wrote Douglass that

> I am not afraid to die. It does not take long.... Let me be neglected, I shall not complain. If friends do not feel like helping me, like caring for me, truth is no less precious though its standard bearers should desert me.... I hope to see you again. Whether I do or not — for the present, "Good bye."[34]

Fairbank was convicted and sentenced to fifteen years in the Kentucky penitentiary — and when "asked whom he chose to be handcuffed to, selected the only negro.[35] This time, he was not pardoned and, in his autobiography, recounted that he had suffered more than three thousand lashes under the brutal regime of the Kentucky penitentiary.[36]

Webster returned to New England after her release in 1845, but soon found her way back to Kentucky. Although stating that her "delicate and sensitive nature recoils at being thought an intruder,"[37] she purchased a six hundred acre farm in Trimble County in February 1854 — across from Madison and its long active Underground Railroad network. However, enslaved African Americans began disappearing "in considerable numbers, and in less than six weeks Miss Webster was waited upon by fifty enraged slave owners

who ordered her to abandon her project and leave the State." Webster was unmoved, but was soon arrested and jailed for several weeks. She was then released, then subsequently indicted in Trimble County in June 1854, but managed to escape across the river to Madison, hotly pursued by a "posse of bloody hirelings."[38] In the aftermath, Delia Webster's every move was monitored carefully as she traveled periodically to the North — and spoke often of "her sufferings in Kentucky."[39] She continued to operate her farm in Trimble County, although "from the safety of Madison and through the agency of tenants" until 1868. Although she was thought to have died in Jeffersonville, Indiana in 1876, Webster actually relocated to Iowa and died at the home of her niece in 1904.[40]

Fairbank survived the long nightmare of prison and was released on April 15, 1864. He married soon after and, after a stirring round of speeches in which he described his experiences — one of which was even attended by President Abraham Lincoln and most of his Cabinet — Fairbank settled down in New England and sank finally into relative obscurity. Years later, Fairbank published his autobiography, but was deeply disappointed at its reception. His great sacrifice seemed wholly forgotten. He died in 1898 and his "grave remained unmarked for many years."[41]

Fugitive and Friend of the Fugitive: Lewis Hayden

Lewis Hayden, the head of the family assisted to freedom by Delia Webster and Calvin Fairbank, was born enslaved in Lexington in 1811, "...a slave upon a plantation, brought up under the humiliating influences of the slave driver's lash." Hayden's experiences with Kentucky slavery left him an implacable foe of the institution. His mother was beaten into insanity for rejecting the sexual advances of her owner. Hayden himself was sold away from his family and passed through a series of owners over several decades.[42]

Hayden "married" Esther Harvey who was the property of a different owner, in the 1830s. After she bore a son, her owner's business failed and Esther and her child were sold to Henry Clay. Clay soon sold them and Hayden never saw them again. Hayden then "married" Harriet Bell, who already had a four-year old son. By 1844, Hayden, who was then working as a waiter at the Phoenix Hotel, came to fear that he would be sold away. Having lost one family through permanent separation, it was not difficulty to persuade him to attempt a group escape.[43]

Hayden was already acquainted with Delia Webster and confided his desire to escape to her. Webster put Hayden in contact with Calvin Fairbank—who then traveled to Ripley and arranged an escape with the Rev. John Rankin. On September 28, 1844, the Hayden family set out for free territory in a rented carriage accompanied by Webster, Fairbank and another fugitive. The party reached Ripley and moved four miles north to a farm at Red Oak, Ohio, where Fairbank bid them farewell.[44] As noted previously, Fairbank and Webster were apprehended on their return to Lexington, but the Hayden family remained free.

Hayden settled, initially, in Canada West, but moved to Detroit in 1845 and then to Boston in 1846. There, he remained and became a staunch anti-slavery leader—famous (or infamous) in the 1850s for his active opposition to and refusal to obey the Fugitive Slave Act. For example, Hayden defended William and Ellen Craft—the young southern couple who escaped slavery by Ellen posing as a sick white man and William posing as his servant. He led the rescue of Shadrack, in which the "anti-slavery community" of Boston fought to prevent the return of a fugitive slave to his owner. Hayden later assisted in recruiting African Americans for service in the Civil War and remained a highly and widely respected black leader until his death in 1889.[45]

Frederick Douglass became well acquainted with Hayden in the 1850s and described him as "the Kentucky fugitive who has with him all that is noble and gallant of his native state, and has left behind him the last vestige of slavery." For his role in the Shadrack rescue, Douglass deemed Hayden a "warm hearted, fearless man" who, along with his wife, would stand with his "suffering people" to the last.[46]

On February 13, 1855, Hayden engaged in an impromptu debate with John W. Gitchell, an Alabama slave-owner, at a hearing of the Massachusetts Joint Committee on Federal Relations. The following excerpt bears witness both to Hayden's eloquence and his conviction. After Gitchell offered a strong defense of slavery, Hayden responded:

> The principal difference between us is that Mr. Gitchell was born in a free State surrounded by the sweet influence of free schools, free churches, and a free Bible; whereas I was born a slave upon a plantation, brought up under the humiliating influence of the slave driver's lash…. Mr. Gitchell has told you, gentlemen, that God in his own good time will abolish slavery. This is true, and will most probably do this through the free agency of His children….[47]

Friend of the Fugitive? Edward James "Patrick" Doyle

Edward James "Patrick" Doyle, a young Irish immigrant, was at the center of the largest mass slave escape ever recorded in Kentucky. However, for a variety of reasons, Doyle cannot be considered a typical friend of the fugitive—or, at least, not without some lingering doubts as to his motives. The facts of his case are both intriguing and perplexing.

On Sunday, August 5, 1848, Doyle led a band of fugitive slaves, estimated at between forty and seventy-five in number, "for the most part trusted house servants of Lexington's most socially prominent families, on a march to the Ohio River."[48] Doyle was a student at Centre College in Danville and most of the fugitives escaped from nearby Fayette County. Early reports spread alarm that the fugitives were "firing pistols, whooping and singing songs and ditties."[49] Such a massive escape bordered on insurrection and "the entire Bluegrass, with threats of summary violence, turned out to apprehend the fugitives." Hundreds of whites "scoured the countryside" and eventually overtook and captured the runaways in a Bracken County hemp field only fifteen miles from the Ohio River.

Commencing August 30, more than forty fugitives were tried for insurrection in the Bracken Circuit Court. Three of the runaways from Fayette County — Shadrack, Harry and Prestley — were convicted and condemned to death.[50] Doyle was captured as well, then jailed and subsequently tried in Fayette Circuit Court beginning on September 27, 1848. Not surprisingly, he was found guilty on October 9 and sentenced to twenty years in the Kentucky penitentiary. Interestingly, prison records describe this daring interloper as a rather small and unprepossessing man, twenty-two years old, five feet and two inches tall, weighing only 128 pounds.[51]

Assessing Doyle's role in Kentucky history is complicated by two facts. First, a week previous to leading the mass escape, Doyle himself had escaped from jail in Louisville "where he was confined for attempting to sell several free Negroes whom he had induced to accompany him from Cincinnati." As cited in the *Louisville Courier,*

... a very short time since, he was introduced to the police agents of Louisville, by an attempt to sell two free negroes from Ohio, to some of the negro traders the South. The exact felony was not proved against him, but ... he was sent to the work-house. He feigned imbecility in this case, and when he found he had to go to the workhouse, he played the malingerer so well that he was sent to the Hospital. From this place he made his escape, and next turns up in Lexington, engaged in a giant stampede of negroes.... The anti-slavery men should not claim him as a martyr to their cause.[52]

Initial testimony taken in the case also suggested that Doyle offered his services for a fee, as much as $20.00 per fugitive.[53] Clearly, there were men who kidnapped or deceived free people of color, hoping to profit by selling them into slavery. Likewise, there were men who aided fugitives for a price and even men such as Levi Coffin, whose motives were above reproach, were always concerned about funding their operations. However, the conclusion that Doyle was a "Negro rustler" of sorts rests on the more deeply embedded assumption that African Americans were rather easily duped. If one rejects that assumption, it is possible to explain Doyle's activities as those of a friend of the fugitive operating in slave territory — where, according to other sources, it was not unusual for services to be rendered for a fee. For example, Lewis Hayden also paid Calvin Fairbank, whose motives were, by all accounts, unimpeachable. In any case, given the risks he took, one must also conclude that whether he was a "confidence man" or an Underground Railroad agent skilled at dissembling — he was either remarkably foolish and inept or just extraordinarily unlucky.

Whether or not Doyle's motives were pure, the African Americans who followed him on that desperate dash to the Ohio River had freedom as their clear and unambiguous goal. The failure of Doyle's enterprise fell most heavily and tragically upon them. Some may have escaped in the confusion that surrounded their pursuit. Most were captured and, of these, some were sold "down the river."[54] Moreover, as word of the Doyle affair spread throughout the country, the Abolitionist press focused more on the central role of the fugitives themselves in this flight toward freedom that bordered on insurrection. For example, before definitive information was received and Doyle's role became known, Frederick Douglass declared that "the slaves are not headed by white men, but by themselves — black men. This is but the beginning of those scenes to prepare for which we have for years been forewarning the slaveholders." In Douglass' view, Doyle was, at best, a facilitator, but the fugitives themselves were the true leaders in this dash for freedom.[55]

Interestingly, many captured fugitives were accused and convicted of the capital crime of insurrection — since escaping from slavery was not, in itself, a crime.[56] Those sentenced to death were not altogether abandoned to their respective fates. Rather, a series of petitions were submitted to Governor John J. Crittenden requesting that he spare the fugitives' lives. These petitions expressed the practical concerns of several slave holders regarding the impending loss of their property (through execution), but also revealed much regarding the "Doyle affair" that was not recorded elsewhere.

For example, on September 7, 1848, twenty-three petitioners asked Governor Crittenden to spare the life of Shadrach, who "has been sentenced to be hung." They noted that "...said Shadrach has heretofore always been considered honest and faithful." As evidence, they noted that, in 1844, Shadrach's owner "...permitted Shadrach to visit Cincinnati, Ohio, but that he returned promptly and in due time to his master and has never until this occurrence manifested any disposition to be

free." The petitioners concluded that, if Crittenden showed leniency, "the unfortunate condemned Shadrach" would be sold out of Kentucky.[57]

Similarly, L. R. Bullock petitioned Governor Crittenden for a pardon for Jaspar who "...was one of the number arrested upon the charges of insurrection and rebellion and shooting with the intent to kill. He has been acquitted upon the first charges and stands convicted upon the last." Bullock pledged that, if pardoned, Jaspar would be "sold out of the state never more to return."[58]

John McClung of Maysville also petitioned the Governor on behalf of the condemned fugitives. However, McClung's arguments were not those of a slave-owner averse to losing valuable property or a slave trader hoping for profit. Rather, McClung raised some rather nettlesome questions:

> Forty-four slaves ran off together and the seven retained for trial were selected very much at random.... One of the slaves condemned (Prestley) is a mere lad and it is difficult to say why he was retained for trial when so many superior to him in age and intelligence were dismissed.... Shadrach is a negro of intelligence and age, and no doubt taking a leading part.... The boys themselves made a very moving appeal to the court and bystanders when sentence was pronounced and solemnly protested that they were assured by the white man (Doyle) that they would be safely carried across the Ohio in two nights.... The evidence is clear that the main object of the slaves was to escape.

McClung then concluded that the death penalty for insurrection was unsupportable legally and that "in the present state of civilization ... bloody and severe penalties should not be enacted.[59] These arguments had no effect and the three fugitives singled out as "examples" were executed. And Edward J. Doyle died in prison.[60]

Friends of the Fugitive: Shelton Morris and Washington Spradling, Sr.

In Louisville, growth in free African American population, coupled with the presence of smaller stable free black communities in the facing Indiana towns, made the greater Louisville area a major refuge and crossing point for fugitive slaves.[61] Two individuals were largely responsible for transforming Louisville's marginal free black population into a viable community — under decidedly hostile conditions. One was Shelton Morris (1806–1889). He and his family crossed the boundary between slavery and freedom by virtue of the will of Richard Morris of Louisa County, Virginia, entered in Jefferson County records on April 2, 1820. The implied biological relationship, of the "Thomas Jefferson–Sally Hemings" variety, is rather obvious.[62] Shelton Morris, as the eldest of the six Morris progeny, assumed responsibility for his younger brothers, John and Alexander — both of whom were apprenticed as barbers. Morris, who was also a barber, invested his small inheritance in his barbershop, a bathhouse, and in real estate.[63]

The other was Washington Spradling, Sr. (1802–1868). He and his family were freed by the will of William Spradling and the biological relationship it implied. As Spradling himself stated, "I was born a slave.... My father bought me, and I bought my own children, five in number...."[64] Like Morris, Spradling was also a barber and used his inheritance to speculate in real estate. Significantly, the Morris and Spradling families soon became allied when Shelton Morris married Evalina Spradling, Washington Spradling's younger sister, in 1828.[65]

By the time William Gibson arrived in Louisville in 1847, Morris had "closed out business and moved to Cincinnati, O.,

in the forties, being accused of voting for Gen. Harrison for President; from Cincinnati he moved to Xenia or Wilberforce, where he engaged in farming." Still, Morris maintained his ties to the community through his younger brothers who inherited some of his local business interests — and was still well known and highly respected. The children of his first marriage, Horace and Benjamin, returned to Louisville in the 1850s and Horace was among its most influential leaders through the next generation and beyond.[66]

Gibson's memories of Spradling were anchored more firmly on firsthand knowledge and were far more vivid. He observed, for example:

> Washington Spradling was the leading colored man in business and the largest real estate holder. He was a barber by trade, but made his mark as a businessman by trading and brokerage, in connection with his shaving. His mode of making money consisted in buying and leasing lots in different parts of the city and building and moving frame cottages upon those lots. He also built several brick business houses on Third Street. Mr. Spradling had many peculiarities, his dress was very common, as he exhibited no pride in that direction. He loved to converse on law, and, though he was uneducated, was considered one of the best lawyers to plan or prepare a case for the court. He was very successful, and nearly every colored person who was in trouble (more or less) first consulted Washington Spradling; he selected the lawyer and prepared the case....[67]

Spradling also became the first African American — probably in the state of Kentucky — to amass significant wealth. His wealth was based largely on real estate speculation and appreciation of the value of his land holdings as Louisville grew into a major city and, by 1860, approached $100,000. For example, the "unimproved land" that Spradling and Morris bought "cheap" in the late 1820s and early 1830s became the eastern section of the Russell neighborhood, parts of downtown Louisville and the "east end."[68]

Important beyond his obvious business acumen, however, was how he used his wealth. Free African Americans such as Morris, Spradling, David Straws, Henry Cozzens and others were responsible for 48, or 9.4 percent, of all emancipation actions in antebellum Louisville and Jefferson County.[69] While the vast majority of enslaved African Americans owned and manumitted by other African Americans were family members of their owner, "the same process used to free family members could also be employed to assist other African Americans in their pursuit of freedom." In this respect, purchasing and then emancipating enslaved African Americans was one of the more important, but lesser known, strategies of the anti-slavery movement and was often attempted before enslaved African Americans risked escape. Freedom through legal manumission was often attractive to the enslaved African American as it allowed him/her to remain in or near familiar territory — and family and friends— rather than face the dangers and the certain prospect of separation through flight. That this strategy sought to circumvent rather than challenge slavery raised legitimate questions regarding both its ultimate efficacy and its ethical validity, but made little difference to those seeking freedom.[70]

Operationalizing this strategy was simple, in theory. Upon reaching terms of agreement, an enslaved African American would borrow funds from a free person of color. The funds would be applied (by the free person of color) to the purchase of the slave. The new "owner" would then emancipate the slave with the understanding that the loan would be repaid, usually in installments over time. A number of emancipation actions document the existence of this loop-hole in slave law that allowed for the evolution of a legal Underground Railroad channel in the midst of slavery and how this channel was employed by community leaders. Examples of the use of this strategy include deeds of emancipation from Shelton Morris to Savira,[71] from Washington Spradling to Maud,[72] Fanny Hedges,[73] and Elizabeth Davis and her child Julia.[74] When interviewed in 1863 by the American Freedmen's Inquiry Commission, Spradling stated that he alone had bought and freed thirty-three enslaved African Americans. Some had repaid him, but most had not and he was still owed a total of $3,337.50 (which, not surprisingly, he remembered "to the penny").[75]

This same interview represents the only statement by Washington Spradling discovered thus far in the public record or other documents created and/or preserved by blacks or whites. Even in his sixty-first year, his words convey something of his quality as a man — and his abiding sense of grievance and his deep understanding of the plight of free people of color in the Kentucky borderland. When asked by the interviewer to assess the conditions facing free blacks in Louisville, Spradling responded:

> Our principal difficulty here grows out of the police laws, which are very stringent. For instance, a police officer may go into a home at night, without any search warrant, and, if the door is not opened when he knocks, force it in, and ransack the house, and the colored man has no redress. At other times, they come and say they are hunting for stolen goods or for runaway slaves, and, some of them being great scoundrels, if they see a piece of goods, which may have been purchased, they will take it and carry it off. If I go out of the State, I cannot come back to it again.... Another difficulty is this. If a person comes here (perhaps he may have been born free), he cannot get free papers, and if the police find out he has got no free papers, they take him up, and put him in jail.... There are many cases of assault and battery in which we can have no redress.... I know a case here in which a man bought himself three times.... I have to pay taxes to the amount of sixty dollars a year for schools. There is no colored school in any other part of the State

except in this city. Colored children in Lexington, Frankfort, other places, have to come here, if they go to school at all.[76]

Thus, two of the consequences of the steady growth of Louisville's free African American population were, on one hand, the emergence of a class of free black property-owners, personified by Morris and Spradling — and on the other hand, African Americans who used the law and their own resources to assist slaves to freedom. Those who belonged to one group usually belonged to the other.

Equally intriguing, although more difficult to document fully, is the strong probability that, apart from using these legal paths to freedom, Morris, Spradling and other free African Americans were deeply involved in the movement of enslaved African Americans along the illegal path as well. For example, when Morris moved to Cincinnati, he went into business with Michael Clark, the husband of his sister, Eliza, and reputed to have been the African American son of Louisville's William Clark (of the Lewis and Clark Expedition). Morris worked as a barber in Cincinnati and on the steamboats that plied the Ohio and Mississippi Rivers before moving to Wilberforce in central Ohio. Both he and his oldest son, Horace, were active in the anti-slavery movement and in the Underground Railroad in Cincinnati.[77]

Spradling died in 1868, but, when Wilbur Siebert was researching his major study of the Underground Railroad in the 1890s, he found former fugitives who, a generation after Spradling's death, recalled that, "At Louisville, Kentucky, Wash Spradley, a shrewd negro, was instrumental in helping many of his-enslaved brethren out of bondage."[78]

Fugitive: Rosetta Armstead/Anderson

One of the best documented, although little known, slave rescue cases concerned a young enslaved African American woman from Louisville who was "rescued" from slavery in 1855. Between March and June of that year, her case heightened tensions and damaged relations between Kentucky and Ohio, and became one of the many defining moments in the history of the anti-slavery movement in the west. The relation of this case to the Underground Railroad was more technical than actual since, ironically, the person at the center of the case was not a fugitive slave in the strict sense of the word. However, because the Fugitive Slave Act and the status of human property outside the South were the salient issues, the controversy generated by this case revealed some of the fears lurking beneath the familiar myths that enshrouded Kentucky slavery.

The facts of the case were first reported in the Ohio *State Journal* in March 1855 with "the announcement that a female slave, in custody of her master, who was traveling from Louisville, Ky., to Virginia, was to be brought before Judge Jamison, of the Probate Court" in Columbus, Ohio. The "slave girl," designated initially as "Rosetta Armstead," was the property of the Rev. Henry M. Dennison, "an Episcopal clergyman, living in Louisville, Ky." The young woman belonged originally to former President John Tyler, the father of Dennison's recently deceased wife, and had been given by Tyler to the Dennisons. After his wife's death, Dennison asked Dr. Miller, "who was bound for Virginia, to take charge of Rosetta, whom he intended as a nurse for his little girl." The Ohio River was ice-locked and the doctor, being forced to travel by rail, was delayed at Columbus. While there

> The news spread through our city that a slave was in our midst, and the Rev. Wm. B. Ferguson, a colored Baptist minister, made complaint before the Judge of Probate, and the Sheriff was dispatched at 12 o'clock on Saturday night, to take charge of the girl.... Dr. Miller stated to the

Court his agency in the case, and asked, as a favor that the case might lie over until.... Mr. Dennison could reach here and he could take whatever measures he might deem advisable. But the girl declaring that she desired to remain in freedom in Ohio, and the legal question of the rights being conceded, she was, as a minor, permitted to choose a guardian. L. G. VanSlyke of this city, was selected ... and took charge of her person.[79]

Dennison hastened to Columbus spoke with Rosetta at the home of Mr. Vandyke (or VanSlyke). The Ohio *Statesman* reported, as reprinted in the *Louisville Courier*, that

Mr. Dennison told the girl that he had come for the purpose of taking her home with him, if she wished to return, but as she was in a free State, she had the liberty of going or remaining, at her option. The girl ... said she believed she should prefer remaining in a free State rather than be returned to slavery. Mr. Dennison bade her good bye, shook hands with her.... The girl is now in the employ of Dr. Coulter.[80]

Additional details were presented in the *Ohio Columbian* and reprinted in the African American press, noting that "a colored man ... in the cars from Cincinnati ... fell into conversation with a colored girl ... and learnt from her that she was a slave on her way from Louisville, Ky., to Richmond, Va., in charge of a friend of her master." This unnamed gentleman "informed her that she had a right to her freedom." When so informed, "she manifested surprise ... and at once said she wished to be free."[81] However, after having been "declared free" by the Ohio court, Rosetta was then "arrested by the U.S. Marshal to be tried by the U.S. Commissioner as a fugitive from slavery" under the provisions of the 1850 Fugitive Slave Act. The news report noted that "there were serious demonstrations on the part of the mob, white and black, to rescue her from the custody of the marshall, but the marshall was res-

olute and well sustained."[82] Rosetta was then removed to Cincinnati to await a hearing. In Kentucky, there was intense debate over the "right of transit through the free states" with slave property and whether the Fugitive Slave Act could be used to restore persons who became free, as had Rosetta, to their owners. Some commentators even criticized "the Rev. Dennison for the course he had pursued" by allowing Rosetta to remain in Ohio—and not defending the rights of slaveholders. Dennison protested that "his slave did not go to Ohio with his consent, but was taken there in direct opposition to his instructions."[83] As news of this incident spread, many northern papers printed several decidedly unflattering articles referring to "Kentucky man-thieves."[84] In April 1855, U.S. Commissioner Pendery ruled that

... the proof did not show her to be a fugitive from slavery; but that, on the contrary, she was brought into the State by the consent and at the instance of those who held her.... Being brought thus under the operation of Ohio law, without making an escape, she did not come within the provisions of the fugitive slave act. He also held that the alleged right of transit with slaves as property through the State did not exist.[85]

Pendery ordered Anderson's release and her "discharge was followed by cheers of the crowd and ... a large number of persons went up and shook hands with her" and "the freed girl seemed much astonished at the greetings she met, and the congratulations she received on attaining the estate of a free woman."[86] While her release was a cause for celebration in Ohio, it angered and frustrated Kentucky slaveholders. Respecting the "right of transit," much as enforcing the Fugitive Slave Act, was an issue concerning which North and South were becoming evermore deeply and irreconcilably divided. For example, a few days after Anderson's discharge, a meeting was convened in Jeffersontown that brought together most of Jefferson County's largest and most influential slaveholders—including Edward D. Hobbs, Samuel Churchill and William Bullitt. The group produced several resolutions in support of the Rev. Dennison, restating what had become literal articles of faith in the upper south:

> ... the provisions of the constitution should be faithfully and honestly carried out, and on no subject is this duty more imperative than that of slavery.... The principles asserted by the State courts of Ohio and other free States have at last reached a point at which the tenure of property is rendered fatally insecure, and our equal rights as American citizens utterly disregarded. Our people can no longer remove with their property from one slave State to another, or navigate our great Western rivers, the common property of all, without being exposed to insult and injury, and deprivation of property under the sanction of the law.... [I]t is generally understood by the people of Kentucky, that the cost of recovering a slave under the Fugitive Slave Law, usually exceeds the value of the slave.[87]

The group ended with a strong statement of their opposition to "nullification, come from what quarter it may."[88] In other words, these wealthy border-state community leaders stood firmly against not only what they termed northern "radicalism," but against southern "radicalism" of the South Carolina variety as well. Eventually, this sense of the border states and upper south having different interests from those of the southern interior would define the fault lines along which the nation would fracture in 1861, with the border-states, including Kentucky, rejecting secession and seeking both to remain in the Union and to maintain slavery.

Frustrated in his attempts to regain Rosetta Anderson, Dennison sued to recover his monetary loss and was counter-sued for "malicious prosecution and false imprisonment, in behalf of the girl" for ten thousand dollars in damages. The case was continued through over the next few months with mounting fears of an unfavorable outcome. As one Louisville editorial writer commented:

> There is but little doubt of that cases will be tried before Abolition juries, and with such people justice is a mockery. We may safely anticipate that they will give a verdict for every cent of the damages laid in the declarations. I humbly think that the people of Kentucky, and more particularly the people of Louisville and of Jefferson county owe it to themselves, to take some steps to relieve Mr. Dennison from this difficulty. Most of us are slave owners. These abolition societies are constantly stealing our negroes, and no one of us can tell how soon we may be placed in Mr. D's present position.[89]

The flow of fugitive slaves and Underground Railroad activity in the borderland were at their respective (and related) peaks in the mid–1850s—and several precedent setting slave rescues had been undertaken already in Ohio and other free states. Although Rosetta Anderson became a political symbol, she must also be remembered as a young black woman from Kentucky who, by chance, was afforded an opportunity to be free—and who, by choice, seized that opportunity.

Fugitive: Margaret Garner

Of all the African Americans who escaped from slavery in Kentucky, by far the most tragic and haunting figure was a young woman called "Peggy" by her owner, who is better known as Margaret Garner. For a few months in the winter of 1856, she stood at the center of a series of events that riveted the attention of the nation. Margaret Garner also personified, in the extreme, the types of impossible choices often forced upon African Americans by an institution as unnatural as American slavery.

The facts of Margaret Garner's life and escape are not, in their particulars, atypical. Margaret Garner was born enslaved on June 4, 1833, at the Maplewood plantation in Boone County. She and Maplewood were the property of John P. Gaines, a comparatively prosperous farmer and hog-producer. In 1840, Margaret accompanied Gaines to Cincinnati (only eighteen miles away) as a nurse for his child, a fact that would become unexpectedly important in later years.[90]

In 1849, sixteen year-old Margaret "married abroad" to fifteen year-old Robert Garner, the property of James Marshall who owned a neighboring farm. By autumn 1849, Margaret was pregnant. At roughly the same time, John Gaines was offered the post of Governor of the Oregon Territory by President Zachary Taylor under whom Gaines had served during the Mexican War. Ironically, Gaines was offered this position after Taylor's "first choice, Illinois Whig Congressman Abraham Lincoln, turned it down" and "immediately accepted and almost as quickly arranged a sale of Maplewood and its slaves to his brother, Archibald, still a plantation owner in Arkansas."[91]

With this change in ownership, Margaret's life became considerably more difficult and uncertain. Her oldest child, Thomas, was born in 1850. Another, Samuel, was born in 1852, then Mary in 1854, then Priscilla (or Cilla) in 1855 and, by early 1856, Margaret was again pregnant. How Margaret, Robert and the children were described in subsequent records raises troubling questions regarding Margaret's "role" at Maplewood under its "new management" — and suggests why she was moved to escape. Specifically, census and newspaper accounts describe Margaret Garner as "mulatto," Robert as "black," Thomas as "black," Samuel as "mulatto," Mary as "nearly white" and Cilla as a "bright mulatto." Although no conclusive evidence exists, it is possible that Robert Garner, who was hired out miles away through most of their "marriage," was not the biological father of Samuel and probable that he was not the biological father of Mary and Cilla. Further, if he was not the biological father of the younger children, it is quite possible that he was not the father of the child with whom Margaret was pregnant when the family escaped. If so, as Weisenburger speculates and as the evidence suggests, Margaret was the victim of the type of prolonged sexual exploitation that was perfectly legal, although morally reprehensible, under American slavery. Her later actions and her scars indicated that, if she was a victim, she was neither a willing nor a submissive one.[92]

The winter of 1856 was one of the coldest ever recorded in Kentucky and, as noted, a season during which numerous large-scale slave escapes (or "stampedes") occurred along the length of the frozen Ohio River. On Sunday night, January 27, 1856, the Garner family, including Robert's parents, and several other fugitives escaped in a stolen sleigh and fled along the Lexington-Covington Turnpike. They reached Covington at roughly 3:00 A.M. and then crossed the ice-bound river to Cincinnati. Their initial destination was the home of Elijah Kite, a free person of color living in Cincinnati who happened to be Margaret's cousin. Apparently, Robert had visited Cincinnati (on his owner's business) some weeks before and had contacted Kite who was expected to make contact with the Underground Railroad on the Garner's behalf.[93]

The party reached Kite's house at roughly 6:00 A.M. Kite then departed for Levi Coffin's house three miles away, where Coffin advised him to move the Garners immediately. Unfortunately, Kite delayed (causing Robert Garner to suspect him of betrayal) and, before the fugitives could be moved to a safer location, Gaines,

Marshall and several deputy marshalls descended on Kite's cabin. Hundreds of neighboring whites and free people of color surrounded the posse. Robert Garner, who was armed, fired on Gaines and the others, wounding one man. In response, the posse "used chunks of firewood to smash the door and shuttered window" and soon overpowered and subdued Garner. However, when Gaines and the others burst into the interior of the cabin, they were greeted by the following sight, as described in the initial report of the case:

> In one corner of the room was a negro child bleeding to death.... Scarcely was this fact noticed when a scream issuing from an adjoining room threw their attention thither. A glance into the apartment revealed a negro woman holding in her hand a knife literally dripping with gore over the heads of two little negro children.... The negress avowed herself the mother of the children, and said that she had killed one and would like to kill the three others rather than see them again reduced to slavery.[94]

The stark image of Margaret Garner's tragic moment of determined madness would be immortalized in antebellum poetry and prose, and in Thomas S. Noble's 1867 painting, "The Modern Medea" (alluding to the mythical Carthaginian queen who murdered her children after being abandoned by Jason of the famed Argonauts) and more than a century later in Toni Morrison's prize-winning novel, *Beloved*.[95] Margaret Garner was not the first enslaved African American to prefer death, her own or that or family, to bondage. For example, an enslaved black family was being transported from Louisville to Memphis in 1853. When the husband learned that he was to be separated by sale from his wife and children, he committed suicide by drowning himself.[96] However, the bloody scene in Cincinnati marked a crossroads from the intersection of which

history branched in one direction and popular legend in another.

Margaret and Robert Garner were taken into custody and jailed. Gaines and Marshall pressed for the return of their human property. However, John Joliffe, already mentioned as a member of the anti-slavery movement in Cincinnati, stepped forward as the Garner's attorney — and both the free black and anti-slavery white communities rallied around the fugitives throughout the ensuing trial. As noted in a Kentucky newspaper, "There is considerable excitement, and the Abolitionists, Know-Nothings and free negroes, are very impertinent, and have more than once attempted or meditated a rescue."[97] As the case went to court, the issues were simple but compelling: "Could federal law force Ohio to give up alleged felons because Kentucky law said they were also property? Even when Ohio law expressly prohibited property in human beings?[98]

On Wednesday, January 31, 1856, the most protracted fugitive slave trial in American history began. The prosecution concentrated on proving the legality of Gaines' (and Marshall's) claim to ownership of the fugitives under Kentucky law. Joliffe, for the defense, built his case on the contention that Gaines' claim was invalidated by the fact that Margaret had been taken briefly into free territory in 1840 and that Margaret Garner should be treated as a free woman and, consequently, should be tried for murder. As Margaret Garner stated in her affidavit:

> Margaret Garner, duly sworn, saith that when she, the said Margaret Garner, was a girl, she was brought from Kentucky into the city of Cincinnati ... by John Gaines and Ellen Gaines, his wife ... that she was brought to Cincinnati to nurse Mary Gaines, daughter of said John Gaines, who now lives with her uncle, Archibald Gaines ... that she came here in the morning and went back in the evening.[99]

Testimony continued until February 13 and, incidentally, there was never any indication that either Robert Garner or his parents disapproved of Margaret's actions. Then, on February 26, Commissioner John L. Pendery rejected Joliffe's argument and ordered "...that the parties named ... be delivered into the custody and possession of the claimant, Archibald K. Gaines."[100] On March 2, Margaret Garner and family were remanded to the custody of their owner, conveyed across the Ohio River, and greeted by "a large crowd ... which expressed its pleasure at the termination of the long proceedings ... with triumphant shouts." After the fugitives were safe in jail, "the crowd moved off to the Magnolia Hotel, where several toasts were given."[101]

Although Kentuckians celebrated the return of the Garners to their owners, several pending issues remained. For example, the Governor of Ohio, Salmon P. Chase, could "requisition" Margaret to stand trial for murder and the Governor of Kentucky would be forced to comply. Another possibility was that someone might raise the funds necessary to purchase Margaret, or the entire family, or at least the remaining children. However, Gaines himself, still smarting from the cost of the trial and the public humiliation following allegations of his sexual impropriety, had other plans and proved himself capable of considerable duplicity in bringing them to fruition.

Even before returning to Kentucky with the Garners, he had contacted his brother, Benjamin — a plantation owner in Arkansas — and arranged for the legal transfer of ownership of the family.[102] After returning briefly to Maplewood, Gaines moved the Garner family to Louisville by train and, on March 7, they departed for Arkansas on the steamboat Henry Lewis. However, in the vicinity of Owensboro, the Henry Lewis collided with another steamboat, the Edward Howard. The Garners, chained in steerage, were freed as the steamer broke apart and began to sink. Then, as Weisenburger recounts:

> What happens next is unclear. Cradling Cilla in her arms a now unshackled Margaret Garner was standing at the gunnel with a white woman who traveled with them in steerage.... Then, either the "Edward Howard" gave the "Lewis's" aft section a sudden push, throwing the white woman and Margaret Garner and Cilla into the icy river. Or, seeing that she "had an opportunity," Margaret threw her child into the river and jumped after it.... Witnesses did describe to newsmen how "a black man, the cook on the "Lewis," sprang into the water and saved Margaret.... Apparently, when rescuers brought Margaret aboard the "Edward Howard," she "displayed frantic joy when told that her child was drowned, and said that she would never reach alive Gaines Landing in Arkansas...."[103]

Cilla's body was never recovered and, thus, this steamboat accident afforded Garner an opportunity to "save" another of her children from a life of slavery.[104] The party was soon placed aboard another southbound steamboat, the Hungarian, and reached Gaine's Landing on March 10, 1858. Because of political complications in Kentucky, Gaines was forced to bring Margaret back to Covington on March 31— placing her, technically, within the reach of Ohio authorities should they wish to requisition her for trial. However, Gaines was careful to suppress virtually all knowledge of her return to Kentucky. On April 11, she was transported again to Louisville, barely avoiding a requisition from Governor Chase that "was just in time to be too late," and then returned to Arkansas.[105]

At that point, Margaret Garner was swallowed whole by the anonymity of American slavery. All that is known of her fate was disclosed in an 1870 interview with her husband, Robert — who restored her briefly to personhood. He related that Margaret contracted typhoid fever and died in Arkansas, probably in the autumn of 1858. He also reported that her last words were for him to "…never marry again in slavery, but to live in hope of freedom…."[106] Thus, there were no happy or redemptive endings in store. Margaret Garner would not live to become a haunted middle-aged woman on the outskirts of Cincinnati nor would she ever be visited by the ghost of her dead daughter.

The Margaret Garner case was the most widely publicized fugitive slave case of the antebellum period—the meaning and significance of which many Americans would prefer to, but cannot, forget. In the end, Margaret Garner's story became the property of others as surely as she had been and whatever her life and actions meant to her was lost. As a woman driven by her own experience to believe that death was preferable to slavery, one cannot escape the suspicion that her only regret, when death drew near, was that, failing to achieve freedom, she had then failed to "save" more of her children from slavery.

Fugitive: Rachael

Of the hundreds of cases involving fugitive slaves in the 1850s, several involved interracial relationships that facilitated escapes. One of the best documented was a love affair with an unusual "twist."

On August 27, 1857, "George Cope, a grocer, on the corner of Chestnut and Preston streets" in Louisville "was taken into custody on a charge of assisting a mulatto slave of Mr. Wetherly to escape to Canada." The "mulatto slave," Rachael, escaped in November 1856 and, after "receiving information" concerning her whereabouts, Weatherly "followed her to Chatham, Canada West" in August 1857. Because Rachael was no longer in the United States, the Fugitive Slave Law did not apply and Weatherly could not reclaim his "lost property." He did obtain, however, two letters

and a Bible sent by Cope to Rachael—and Weatherly obtained these incriminating items from Rachael herself.

One letter was addressed to a Mr. Gilchrist of Canada West and read, in part, "from the relationship existing between Rachael and myself, I feel afraid that some unfair means will be adopted against me to cause a separation, and then she will lose the only and best friend she ever had or ever will have again." The nature of this relationship, at least from Cope's perspective, was clarified in a postscript to the effect that "I am on the rack of excitement about that dear girl…. She is my wife before High heaven and our sacred vows are registered there before God." The second letter was addressed to Rachael herself:

> My Own Dear Rachael:—It afforded me a great deal of pleasure to hear that you have arrived safe and in good health at Chatham, and God grant that it may prove a pleasant and happy home for you and me both, when I come out, and hope that the time will be short so I can see my dear wife Rachael, as I am so very lonely without you….

Cope hastened to sell his business, arrange his affairs and then remove to Canada, but the discovery of these letters brought his plans to naught. In the end, he was charged with "assisting a slave to escape" and jailed pending trial. As a further complication, Weatherly, who could not recover Rachael, sued to recover her value from Cope which resulted in the attachment of Cope's property.[107] In a follow-up article, the Mr. Gilchrist to whom Cope addressed his first letter was identified as "a free negro or mulatto, well known here as a sort of steward on the river" believed to have a record of aiding fugitive slaves.[108] Gilchrist had arranged the escape and possibly escorted Rachael to Canada. Still, because he too was living in Canada West, he was also beyond the reach of American law.

The final resolution of this case revealed several unusual facts and answered a few missing questions. Cope was not tried until January 1859 for this affair that "occurred a year or more since, and was attended" by "some romantic correspondence between Cope and the dusky enslaver of his susceptible heart."[109] On Tuesday, January 18, 1859, in Jefferson County Circuit Court, John Weatherly testified that he knew Cope, that Rachael had in fact given him the letters and that the handwriting was recognizably that of Cope. He then added that he

> ... had seen Cope about his premises several times. She washed for Cope some length of time, and was in the habit of visiting him at his store to take the clothes.... Cope had been at his house several times; witness didn't think it was proper for Cope to be talking to the slave in the rear of his premises.... Had been offered $1200 in cash by Dr. Ewing. She was a handsome mulatto; knew Wm. Gilchrist; he removed from here to Chatham.

Several other witnesses testified as the prosecution labored to prove that the handwriting in the letters belonged, conclusively, to Cope. However, W. R. Taylor testified further to the relationship between Cope and Rachael and stated that he

> Knew the slave Rachel; seen her frequently at Cope's store; she was very likely, and worth perhaps $1,200; was perhaps 20 years old; observed conduct between them, which made witness suspect an intimacy; on one occasion Cope and the girl left the store room and went up stairs together ... they were gone some length of time; full long enough to transact any business they might have to do.... [S]hortly after the slave escaped Cope talked with me about selling out his property, and said he was going to St. Louis.... I thought him as clever a man as I ever saw until this thing occurred.

Additional detail was provided by Alonzo Weatherly, who accompanied his father to Canada in August 1857 and who was present at his father's meeting with Rachael. The younger Weatherly stated that he "...saw Rachel give him two letters and a red morocco bible; she was living with some man who was said to be her husband."

The defense called a number of witnesses who vouched for Cope's character as an "honest man, upright, and honorable in his conduct and business transactions." The defense also challenged, rather effectively, that the letters on which the case against Cope rested were actually written by Cope.[110] The jury returned January 20, hopelessly divided: seven for conviction; five for acquittal. As a result, Judge P. B. Muir discharged both the jury and Cope. In a final article, the Louisville Courier stated simply that "The jury did not agree in the case of Cope, charged with conniving at the escape of the slave Rachael, who it seems abandoned him.... 'Ingratitude, thy name is Rachael.'"[111] In the end, Cope lost everything—including, it seemed, his "Dear Rachael."

While the secrets of Rachael's heart cannot be known, the facts of this case suggest strongly that, after she reached Canada, Cope had served his purpose as far as she was concerned. To prevent Cope from following her, she gave Weatherly the evidence that would cost Cope his freedom. What Cope thought or felt when forced to confront the fact of her duplicity also cannot be known. What seems probable is that Rachael mastered the effective use of yet another escape strategy: escape by seduction or, perhaps, by allowing oneself to be seduced.

Friends of the Fugitive: Charles Bell and Oswell Wright

On September 25, 1857, an enslaved African American named Charles escaped from his owner, Henry A. Ditto of Brandenburg. Charles received assistance from several men: David Bell, who owned and operated the Brandenburg ferry; Charlie Bell, his son and assistant; and Oswell Wright, a free person of color living in Corydon. The Bell family migrated to Indiana in 1829 and moved from New Albany to Harrison County in 1839. The elder Bell "was suspected of being an abolitionist," but never made any public declaration of such sentiments. Oswell Wright moved to Indiana from Maryland, probably in the 1820s as well, and found work in Corydon as a laborer.

Virtually nothing is known about Charles, but, when he decided to escape, he knew whom to contact, suggesting that the Bell family and Wright were known, at least in privileged circles, to assist fugitives. Once arrangements were finalized, the Bells ferried Charles across the Ohio and, presumably, delivered him to Wright — who then conveyed Charles to Brownstown where other anti-slavery sympathizers spirited him farther north. Charles vanishes from the formal history at this point.[112] However, as with Delia Webster and Calvin Fairbank in the 1844 Hayden family escape, the aftermath of Charles' successful flight was far more dramatic than the escape itself and demonstrated both the degree to which aiding fugitives had become politicized by the late 1850s and the risks inherent in rendering such aid.

Ditto and his slaveholding neighbors suspected that David and Charlie Bell had contrived to aid Charles. Their suspicions were strengthened by the testimony of C. E. Johnson who claimed that he met Wright in Brownstown, befriended him and gained his confidence, and that Wright admitted his role in Charles' escape. Johnson then claimed to have insinuated himself into the company of the Bell family by posing as someone wishing to arrange for the escape of Charles' wife. Johnson later stated in court that

... he went to the house of the Bells, and after laying around for several days, drinking whisky and telling tales about running off Negroes, until he gained the confidence of the old man Bell, that he (Bell) confessed that he had assisted the boy Charles in getting off.... He said he communicated these facts to Mr. Ditto, whereupon a posse of Kentuckians crossed the river and kidnapped and carried the two Bells across the river, together with the Negro Oswell, and lodged them in the Brandenburg jail.[113]

The events were the same, but the "tone" was slightly different in reports published in southern Indiana and reprinted in Louisville.[114]

The Bells and Wright were indicted subsequently for the crime of "assisting slaves to escape." Wright was charged specifically with "furnishing a forged pass to a slave" although, since Charles could not be found, neither the testimony of the fugitive himself nor the "forged pass" were ever introduced as evidence. All three languished in jail well into 1858 as the case was continued repeatedly.[115] In the meantime, Bell's other sons, Horace and John, were called home from California to rescue their father and brother. The other Bells were well-equipped for such a task, particularly Horace — a colorful and adventuresome figure who had already survived William Walker's ill-fated attempt to seize Nicaraugua in 1857 and who would later rise to the rank of major in the Union Army. In May 1858, Horace and John Bell executed a classic "jail-break":

... on a day when many of the citizens of Brandenburg were away attending a picnic, they went to Brandenburg where they forced the jailor to open the doors and liberated their father and brother. The four ran quickly to their skiff and started to cross the river, but were soon discovered and pursued. Horace stood up in the boat with a revolver in each hand and by keeping up a rapid fire held the pursuers at bay until they reached the Indiana shore.[116]

Oswell Wright was not rescued. Ultimately, he was tried, convicted and sentenced to five years in the Kentucky State Penitentiary. Interestingly, Wright was defended by Judge William A. Porter (1800–1884), one of the most prominent men in southern Indiana and a man also suspected of having aided an occasional fugitive. Wright survived his prison term and returned to Corydon, where he died — a local legend — in 1875.[117]

As a postscript, Iris Cook of the Federal Writers' Project interviewed Mrs. Mattie Brown Smith in the mid–1930s, then a resident of New Albany. Smith's parents had been enslaved in Kentucky and the fugitive slave, Charles, in the Bell-Wright affair, was her fraternal uncle, Charles Woodruff. From her knowledge of family and community oral traditions, Smith added crucial details to the published accounts that are remarkably consistent with those accounts (of which she was unaware). For example, she recounted that her uncle was a blacksmith hired out in Brandenburg who used contacts established through his work to arrange his escape. A white man "found out Uncle wanted to go across" and

> ... got in touch with a certain man who ferried slaves across the river ... an old white man named Charles Bell living in Harrison county, just below Corydon... Mr. Bell had a skiff which he used to carry the slaves over ... and one dark night Uncle Charles got a few things together and he sneaked around and told his wife and children goodbye, and they went down to the Ohio River.... Bell took Uncle Charles across the river in a skiff, and on back through the woods on a mule to his house where he hid him a few weeks and then took him on up thru Corydon ... and he went up to Canada and got out to California.[118]

When the Civil War began, Smith indicated that Woodruff returned from California and joined the Union Army.[119] Interestingly, she mentions the return of Bell's sons from California and their rescue of their father, but is silent where Oswell Wright is concerned. How ironic it would be if Wright was falsely accused and that the only person in the Bell-Wright affair who was innocent — was the only person to serve time in prison.

Friends of the Fugitive: Elijah Anderson and Chapman Harris

Two African Americans stand out as the most important leaders of the Underground Railroad in the Madison area — and among the most important figures in the borderland. One was Elijah Anderson, who was born in Fluvanna County, Virginia and settled in Madison in 1837. Anderson was considered a "superintendent" of the Underground Railroad. As such, he established a key fugitive slave crossing at Carrollton in the 1840s at the mouth of the Kentucky River and made numerous forays into Kentucky to organize and lead slave escapes — venturing as far south as Frankfort. After becoming a hunted man, Anderson moved for a time to Lawrenceburg, Indiana and worked closely with the Ohio Underground Railroad network.[120]

In 1857, Anderson was arrested in Carrollton, was tried and acquitted, initially, as there was insufficient evidence to convict him of any crime related to fugitive slaves. However, he was soon arrested again and conveyed to Bedford in Trimble County. This time, "his carpet bag was found to be filled with incendiary documents, proving that he had been engaged in running-off slaves in the neighborhood of Carrollton. The papers ... also implicated many distinguished northerners."[121] Anderson was convicted and sent to the Kentucky penitentiary at Frankfort. There, he died tragically — probably a victim of murder — in his cell on the day he was scheduled for release.[122] His brother, William, founder of the African Methodist Episcopal Church in Madison, continued his work.[123]

Chapman Harris (1802–1890) was probably the most colorful and heroic figure in the Madison area — perhaps along the entire Ohio River border. Born in Virginia in ca. 1802, he arrived in Madison in 1837 and, in 1841, married twenty year old Patsy Ann, formerly enslaved in Shelby County, Kentucky. As a major Underground Railroad operative, Harris was a prime target of the white mob violence that drove DeBaptiste and Lott from Madison in the late 1840s. However, Harris remained and, in 1849, organized the Second Baptist Church (later St. Paul's Baptist Church). While preaching the Gospel, he and his sons assumed the major responsibility in his region for transporting fugitive slaves across the Ohio River.[124]

Along with being a minister, Harris was also a skilled blacksmith and applied his trade to fashion the unique and memorable signaling system mentioned in the introduction to Chapter VI of the study.[125] He and his associates were deadly serious about their work. As one example, crossing Harris was a nearly fatal mistake for John Simmons, an African American who divulged crucial and incriminating information regarding the Underground Railroad operations in the area. Harris "led a group of men who nearly whipped Simmons to death. Apparently, the only thing that saved the informant's life was that he bit part of Harris' lip off." Harris was arrested, tried, convicted and fined for this beating.[126]

He was arrested again in Louisville, largely by chance, in November 1856. The records of his brief day in court provide both a description and an indication of how dangerous both he and the Madison area were perceived in Louisville. Harris was bound for Charleston, but when strong winds blew his steamboat to the Louisville shore

> Chapman Harris, a huge free Negro, black as the ace of spades, was found in this city — by Officer Ray.... He arrested him, and, on searching him, he was found to be armed with a deadly bowie knife, a pistol, Lucifer matches and powder and ball in abundance. The fellow is a preacher from some where back of Madison, Ind., where he is said to be an active member of the Freedom Party.

Although setting foot in Louisville was no crime, he was nonetheless "held to bail in the amount of $200" and ordered to leave the state.[127]

One of the most tantalizing — although insufficiently corroborated — associations in Harris' long career involved the militant white Abolitionist, John Brown. In 1891, Freeman Anderson, as noted in Chapter VI, mentioned a secret meeting with Brown in the summer of 1859. Presumably, this meeting was held behind Harris' cabin between Brown and more than a dozen African Americans from the Trimble County area. At this meeting, the African Americans present shared with Brown their plans for an insurrection in Trimble and the surrounding area. Such a plan was not as outlandish and implausible as it might seem — given the repeated rumors of large-scale conspiracies that swept the South in the 1850s[128] and the nearby "Henry County Negro Plot" of 1854 (a conspiracy of several enslaved African Americans to murder the Herndon family and possibly others).[129] Brown persuaded them to postpone their uprising until the larger revolt — that Brown would attempt to initiate at Harper's Ferry in October of that same year — began. Whether this meeting ever occurred is problematic. However, documents captured after the Harper's Ferry raid were sufficiently alarming to prompt federal authorities to issue a warning to the Governor of Kentucky.[130]

Friends of the Fugitive: John Parker and the Rev. John Rankin

The Maysville, Kentucky, and Ripley, Ohio, crossing witnessed the passage of thousands of fugitive slaves. Central to the operations of the Underground Railroad in this region was the collaboration between two extraordinary individuals—one white, the Rev. John Rankin (1793–1886), and one black, John P. Parker (1827–1900).[147] Parker was the one of the few African American Underground Railroad leaders in the Kentucky borderland to leave any record of his exploits in his own words. Because of this, his autobiography, dictated to Frank M. Gregg in the 1890s and edited by Stuart Sprague in 1996, is an invaluable source.

Parker was born enslaved in Norfolk, Virginia in 1827. As a child, he was sold and forced to march south to Mobile, Alabama. After failing in an escape attempt in about 1843, Parker, to prevent being sold farther south, convinced a local widow to purchase him for $1800. Having already developed skills as a foundry worker, Parker repaid his benefactor and gained his freedom, legally, in 1845.[132] Parker migrated to Jeffersonville, Indiana, and found work as a molder. He soon moved to New Albany, then to Cincinnati and, eventually, to Ripley, Ohio. Ripley offered a unique combination of opportunities that appealed strongly to Parker—the opportunity to practice his trade in a foundry and the opportunity to aid fugitive slaves.[133]

Parker became principally responsible for conveying fugitives across the Ohio River, working in what he termed "the Borderland" between slave and free territory. He estimated that he rowed an average of roughly one fugitive per week across the river and delivered another 300 or more to the Union Army during the Civil War. Working at night and with confederates living in or near Maysville, Parker transported his charges to the Ohio shore and delivered them into the hands of men such as Rankin, who then arranged for the fugitives to be spirited northward. Parker indicated that he maintained "an accurate list of the names, dates, and original homes of his passengers" until after the passage of the Compromise of 1850 when he, like many of his far-flung comrades, destroyed all potentially incriminating evidence.[134]

His long residence at Ripley and his extensive and varied experiences with runaways provided invaluable insights regarding the land, the character of fugitives and their benefactors, and how fugitives moved through Kentucky and across the Ohio River. In his own words, quoted below at length, he corroborated much of the primary and secondary source evidence cited in this study and added crucial insights of his own:

> When I first began my work among the slaves, all northern Kentucky was still covered with virgin forest … with many trails and few roads. But the prime bluegrass regions were thickly settled and rich with money and slaves. As the settlers began to build their cabins and make their clearings, the forest gradually disappeared. The increased population made it more difficult for the fugitive to pass through the country successfully…. Another disadvantage was the gradual reduction in the number of slaves in the Borderland. This was due to two causes: so many slaves ran away, their owners, fearful of loss, sold the slaves down the river. As the fugitive depended entirely on his own race for assistance, this removal of his own people increased his difficulties…. But these obstacles did not deter those slaves who were intelligent and determined to break away from their bondage. The early fall was the time most of them selected to strike out for themselves…. Frequently, they told me that they would wait weeks, after they had decided to run away, waiting for the corn to ripen…. Men and women whom I helped on their way came from Tennessee, requiring weeks to make the journey, sleeping under trees in the daytime and slowly

picking their dangerous way at night.... As a matter of fact, they became backwoodsmen, following the north star, or even mountains, to reach their destination. These long-distance travelers were usually people strong physically, as well as people of character, and were resourceful when confronted with trouble.... The riff-raff runaways came from the Borderland, where it was comparatively easy to get away and they were not tested by repeated risks....[135]

Parker's comments regarding fugitives from the far interior of Kentucky or states in the deeper south are particularly intriguing. While the Kentucky Fugitive Slave Data Base identified a substantial minority (roughly 20 percent) of fugitives from the southern interior, runaways with such origins may have been even more common than advertisements and articles in extant Kentucky newspapers would suggest. By his own testimony, Parker rowed many fugitives across the Ohio River who escaped through the Appalachians—from western Virginia, eastern Tennessee, northern Georgia and even the upland Carolinas—and emerged in eastern Kentucky or eastern Ohio. Clearly, even a generation later, Parker considered the fugitives, not those who helped them — including himself — as the true heroes. As the evidence suggests, this perspective reflected more than the humility of a truly heroic man, but an honest appraisal from someone who understood and respected fugitive slaves as people.

After the Civil War, Parker opened his own foundry and became "one of only fifty-five African Americans to receive patents before 1901" when he invented his own unique tobacco press. Parker prospered for a time, but his business eventually failed. Still, despite the ebb and flow of his economic fortunes, Parker's family thrived and, at the time of his death in 1900, his three daughters and two sons were all educated and solidly "middle-class."[136]

John Rankin, a Presbyterian minister and abolitionist, migrated to Kentucky in 1821 and served as pastor of the Presbyterian church in Ripley from 1822 to 1866. In 1828, Rankin and his family moved from their first home near the Ohio River to a new brick house on what came to be called "Liberty Hill" overlooking Ripley. This house served as a beacon with its windows ablaze with light and as a haven for fugitives—and Rankin and his associates were chiefly responsible for conveying runaways delivered to them by men such as Parker from southern into central Ohio. One of Rankin's sons, when interviewed by Siebert in the 1890s, stated that his family "lodged and forwarded not less than 2,000 slaves ... not losing one."[137]

A significant body of evidence attests to Rankin's steadfastness and commitment over more than three decades. For example, William Lloyd Garrison, the great New England abolitionist, described himself as Rankin's "disciple and humble co-worker in the cause of emancipation." After Rankin's death in 1886, Siebert declared that "John Rankin did more to propagate practical abolition in Ohio than any other citizen of the State. No other house along Ohio's riverfront was so well situated, or so admirably staffed, to be both magnet and beacon for liberty-loving slaves."[138]

As another indication of Rankin's stature, he and his family were on friendly terms with the Beecher family. Both belonged to the same religious denomination and shared the same commitment to abolition. Through this relationship, Harriet Beecher Stowe became acquainted with most of the real-life characters that formed the basis for *Uncle Tom's Cabin*.[139]

Once again, these sketches offer deeper insights into the lives and experiences of several fugitives and friends of the fugitive who belong to the history of the Kentucky borderland. The degree to which these individuals were ordinary or extraordinary can be gauged in relation to the larger patterns established in the preceding sections of the study.

CHAPTER VIII

Conclusion: The Desperate and the Brave

What is a rebel? A man who says no, but whose refusal does not imply a renunciation. He is also a man who says yes, from the moment he makes his first gesture of rebellion. A slave who has taken orders all his life suddenly decides he cannot obey some new command.... Rebellion cannot exist without the feeling that, somewhere and somehow, one is right.[1]

Assessment of the Evidence: Fugitive Slaves

The division of the United States into free and slave zones in the generation following the American Revolution created a border within the country. For six hundred miles, the Ohio River defined this border in the trans–Appalachian west between Kentucky to the south and Illinois, Indiana and Ohio to the north. The political and economic developments that transformed Kentucky from a western into a border state between the 1770s and 1820 gave its geographic location a new meaning in two specific respects. First, Kentucky was too far north, climatically, to produce cotton and other plantation crops, thus leading to the pivotal role of domestic slave trade in the state's economy. Second, and most important for this study, Kentucky was one of the northern tier of slave states and its proximity to free territory made slave escape at least a "break-even" proposition for enslaved African Americans who were both daring and fortunate.

Not surprisingly, slave escapes were most frequent in those sections of the state nearest the Ohio River and those sections with the heaviest concentrations of enslaved African Americans. Furthermore, the unusual triangular shape of the state meant that the distance from central or western Tennessee to Illinois or Indiana was no greater than the distance from south central and southeastern Kentucky to Ohio. Thus, roughly 20 percent of the fugitives examined in this study originated in Tennessee or points south. As a rule, fugitives from Tennessee and Alabama traveled overland or by minor rivers, while those from Mississippi and Louisiana sought more often to escape by steamboat. In addition, proximity to free territory made the type of temporary escapes to the woods or swamps, so common in the southern interior, relatively rare in Kentucky. In other words, when African Americans escaped from slavery in Kentucky, they seldom had any intention of returning. Likewise, fugitives from Alabama or Tennessee would not endure the risks and privations needed to reach Kentucky if they planned to return to their "old masters."

Fugitive slaves escaping from or through Kentucky were predominantly young and male, and more likely to be racially mixed than the overall African American population. They escaped alone or in small groups, with women and children more likely to escape in the 1850s than before. Slave escapes occurred when opportunity beckoned, but were more frequent on the weekends in the cooler months of the year. In planning their journeys, fugitive slaves depended on information gleaned from travel or travelers, from the "slave grapevine" and occasionally from friends of the fugitive operating in secrecy in the South. In preparation for flight, they hoarded or stole clothes, food, money and, if possible, weapons. In more elaborate escapes, fugitives often concocted deceptions and employed various disguises. Then they proceeded toward the Ohio River — many avoiding settled areas, but, definitely by the 1840s, many more converging on towns and urban centers with significant black populations such as Evansville, Louisville, Madison and Cincinnati. Based on available records, the vast majority escaped without assistance.

It is important to remember that escaping from slavery, even before slave escapes assumed political significance in the 1840s and 1850s, was no summer stroll. The risks were great. Slaveholders and their agents became increasingly vigilant in the 1840s and 1850s. Patrols became more commonplace. The temptations created by sizable rewards spawned a shadowy host of informants, black and white, and slave-catchers. Beyond that, Kentucky was a slave state and, as such, hostile territory — and the southern sections of Illinois, Indiana and Ohio afforded few safe havens. Even if fugitives reached the North or Canada, they faced the same problems of poverty and discrimination faced by free people of color already resident there. Fugitives who were apprehended faced gruesome punishments and the virtual certainty of being "sold down the river" where the probability of escaping successfully was believed to be much lower. Thus, runaways had much to gain but also much to lose, and many enslaved African Americans, weighing the risks — particularly separation from family — chose to bear the yoke of slavery. Others, perhaps, had too little vision and/or too much fear.

The primary source documents reviewed in this study reveal other interesting facts regarding those African Americans who chose or felt compelled to escape. For example, efforts to understand slave escapes and recapture fugitive slaves forced whites to recognize that many enslaved African Americans, rather than being crippled by slavery, possessed intellectual powers and character traits — such as courage, determination, love of family, loyalty, a sense of self-sacrifice, self-respect and personal dignity — that often compelled them to flee bondage and enabled them to outwit their pursuers. While these troublesome facts could not be ignored, they could be misrepresented. In a society in which slavery was considered good and efforts to gain freedom were deemed criminal or psychotic, perhaps it was inevitable that African American courage and intelligence would be viewed more often as a signs of bad character than as evidence of genuine mental ability and strength.

Still, these sources suggest strongly that runaway slaves were exceptional, a conclusion reached by other historians: For example, Wade stated that "the slave-holders' fear of fugitives was understandable ... the traffic usually involved many of the best bondsmen — those with the highest skills, the most literate, the most energetic. Some were also the most obstreperous and ungovernable."[2] Gara concluded that fugitive slaves were often atypical individuals, noting that "it was the gifted and highly intelligent slave who enjoyed the semi-freedom of a hired laborer, and having greater sophistication and more freedom of movement, was better qualified than most bondsmen to conceive and put into action a plan of escape."[3] George Washington Williams, the true "father of African American history," added another important dimension and speculated that slave escapes were "a safety valve to the institution of slavery. As soon as leaders arose among the slaves, who refused to endure the yoke, they would go North. Had they remained, there must have been enacted at the South the direful scenes of San Domingo."[4] Siebert concurred, and suggested that slaveholders might not have bemoaned slave escapes excessively in some cases:

> Yet considering the question broadly from the standpoint of their own interests, the work of the underground system was a relief to the master and to the South. The possibility of a servile insurrection was a dreadful thing for Southern minds to contemplate.... The Underground Railroad ... furnished the means of escape for persons well-qualified for leadership among the slaves and thereby lessened the danger of an uprising of the blacks against their masters.[5]

The institution of slavery, as noted repeatedly throughout this study, was designed to transform people into "slaves." Physical brutality, compulsory ignorance, a constant flood of insidious messages and symbols of black inferiority and forced dependence took a heavy toll — but, as in any large human population, individual African Americans were affected by and responded to the conditions of slavery in different ways. The research literature suggests that the most intelligent, best educated, most widely experienced and most psychologically "whole" African Americans found slavery to be most burdensome. Such human property was, at once, most valuable and most dangerous. Ironically, the "quality" of fugitive slaves was often cited by the defenders of slavery as proof of the benefits of the institution. As Frederick Douglass commented, "We give slavery too much credit, judging it by the fugitive slaves whom we see."[6]

The fugitive slave advertisements and other documents reviewed in this study indicate that Kentucky fugitives were often such exceptional individuals. Still, it is important to note that, while their escapes may have relieved racial tensions in Kentucky, many became leaders in the political struggle against slavery from their new homes in the North and Canada — fugitives such as Josiah Henson, Henry Bibb, Lewis Hayden, Lucie and Thornton Blackburn, and others. In other words, they may have run away from slavery, but they did not run away from the larger struggle of their people — or the larger struggle for human rights.

Of course, more fundamentally, fugitive slaves were not exceptional at all. The frequency of slave escapes from Kentucky and elsewhere meant simply that African Americans did not relish being slaves. Undoubtedly, the lives of African Americans (enslaved and free) were circumscribed by the powerful and paradoxical role of race in antebellum America. However, African Americans responded to captivity as human beings — not as pets or farm animals that could be domesticated and, if fed regularly and treated well, might become reconciled to their lot and "love" their masters. Some African Americans found it expedient to pretend to be the stereotypical slave. Given the physical and psychological violence of slavery, the personalities of others were sometimes warped to conform to this stereotype. But these slaves were made, not born. Most African Americans wore the "mask," in Paul Lawrence Dunbar's memorable words, made the best of a bad situation, and awaited the "right time" and opportunity.

Assessment of the Evidence: The Underground Railroad

One might debate whether slave escapes were a trickle, a stream or a flood — but slave escapes were an undeniable fact of the colonial and antebellum periods. However, the Underground Railroad raises a related, but different, set of questions. To elaborate, scholarly and popular accounts concerning the Underground Railroad have swung from one extreme interpretation to another over the past century. For example, early studies by Coffin (1876), Still (1871) and Siebert (1898) were consistent with antebellum perceptions of an elaborate, organized and far flung "conspiracy" to assist fugitive slaves — based and operating primarily in the North. Later scholars such as Gara (1961), to some extent Blockson (1984), and Franklin and Schweninger (1999) argued that such a conspiracy, if it existed at all, was loosely organized — and that the courage and initiative of fugitive slaves themselves, the dedication of free people of color and, lastly, the involvement of a relatively small number of anti-slavery whites were its constitutive elements. The more recent studies advance a different argument, one that places

African Americans at center stage and restores them fully to the status of actors, rather than objects, in their own history — but one that also, oddly enough, questions or rejects the validity of much postbellum testimony from blacks and whites alike.

Such differences in scholarly interpretation are possible largely because — and legitimate as long as — there is no consensus regarding how to answer two fundamental questions. First, what was the "Underground Railroad?" Second, if the Underground Railroad existed, at what point in time and under what circumstances did the totality of efforts of blacks and whites to assist fugitive slaves become something that could be termed an "Underground Railroad?" Although seldom acknowledged, by not defining the criteria that must be satisfied for there to "be" an Underground Railroad, it has been possible for historians to advance virtually any argument they wished. Under the most liberal interpretation, any assistance rendered to fugitive slaves, however random and even passive, constituted the "Underground Railroad." Under the most conservative, nothing short of a far-flung formal organization — with a board of directors, officers, a budget, a building, a shingle and stationary would suffice.

Based on this research, the criterion that best fits the historical evidence is decidedly simple: the Underground Road or Railroad emerged when significant local and regional coordination of the efforts of friends of the fugitive was achieved. Deepening divisions over slavery in the late 1840s and through the 1850s were the catalyst that wove isolated local efforts into such a larger network in the Kentucky borderland. In other words, crossing this critical threshold transformed friends of the fugitive, collectively, into a more organized social movement. However, becoming better organized was not synonymous with becoming an organization and this movement spawned more formal organizations only in a few sites such as Cincinnati. Perhaps the best analogy is the Civil Rights Movement of the 1960s— the Movement was simply larger than the totality all Civil Rights groups and, of course, one could participate in the Movement and have no organizational affiliation at all.

Slave escapes were sufficiently numerous to sustain both an extensive Underground Railroad network in the Kentucky borderland and to allow for numerous escapes that by-passed friends of the fugitive altogether. But was there an Underground Railroad south of the borderland? Levi Coffin's perception was interesting, as he stated

> I have always contended that the Underground Railroad, so called, was a Southern institution; that it had its origin in the slave States. It was, however, conducted on quite a different principle south of Mason and Dixon's line.... South of the line, money, in most cases, was the motive; north, we generally worked on principle. For the sake of money, people in the South would help slaves to escape and convey them across the line.[7]

Coffin actually had little idea how the fugitives who reached his Indiana farm or his Cincinnati store found their way to the Ohio River. In fact, neither Coffin nor Cockrum — nor any other Underground Railroad activists in the borderland — ever spoke of Underground Railroad contacts in the interior of Kentucky or any other southern state, even years after the Civil War and Reconstruction. These individuals appeared only in scattered and often fragmentary newspaper and court references. Further, none of the fugitives who described their journeys to freedom indicated any such contacts or the existence of any network in slave territory other than scattered free black communities. All of these sources are reasonably forthcoming in their descriptions of help rendered or received — and by whom — near or across the Ohio River. While a code of secrecy governed them before the Civil War, there was no reason for their reticence after the War in identifying and acknowledging the presence (if not the actual names) of Underground Railroad agents well south of the border. The fact that these most important sources were silent reinforces the conclusion that the vast majority of fugitives were either "on their own" or "in the hands" of other African Americans until they reached the borderland.

In other words, the Underground Railroad did not exist everywhere. However, by the 1850s, when wholly unaided escaped became more difficult, fugitive slaves escaping from or through Kentucky were drawn increasingly toward a network of crossroads and crossing points such as Louisville, Madison, Cincinnati and Maysville. This steady stream of fugitive slaves speaks volumes regarding how African Americans experienced and often responded to slavery in the Commonwealth. The fact that so many fugitives received some form of assistance also speaks volumes in support of the presence of the Underground Railroad in and near the Kentucky borderland — at times as an organization, but always as a network, as a "conspiracy of conscience."

The Question of Numbers

The data and documents reviewed in this study date slave escapes from and through Kentucky to the earliest years of settlement. However, while these source materials establish the fact(s) of slave escapes, the raw quantity of such evidence is a fact as well — a fact that argues strongly that the number of slave escapes in the Kentucky borderland was far greater than otherwise supposed. How much greater remains an open question, but one to which a provisional answer is now possible.

The number of enslaved African Americans who escaped from or through

Kentucky could not be calculated precisely in the antebellum period and can only be estimated now. Not every fugitive slave was advertised and many of the newspapers in which advertisements were placed have long-since disappeared. Fugitive slaves who reached free territory and lived as free men and women had rather obvious reasons for not identifying themselves as fugitives—and most African Americans who actually escaped from slavery left no personal testimony and had no biographers.

According to Census records, 96 African Americans in 1850 and 119 in 1860 were listed as fugitives from Kentucky, exceedingly small fractions of the more than 200,000 enslaved African Americans in the state in both Census years. However, the trustworthiness of these data cannot be assumed. It is important to remember that, in these Census years, the executive branch of the federal government was controlled by those sympathetic to slavery and that, by 1850, there was already a history of distorting Census data to "prove" political points related to race. The most glaring example of this practice was the exaggerated count of free people of color listed as insane in the 1840 Census—which was said to prove that freedom literally drove African Americans crazy and, since African Americans were ill-suited for freedom, slavery was their natural condition.[8]

Of course, slaveholders and local Census enumerators were the source of the fugitive slave data that seemed, not coincidentally, to confirm several other useful stereotypes. As noted, according to American racial mythology, the few enslaved African Americans who yearned for freedom were misfits of some sort. Some were misguided or manipulated by evil outsiders, but most were quickly captured by an effective system of patrols and a vigilant citizenry. Still, the question of numbers was a political question that had two distinctly different answers depending on the intended audience. For example, downplaying the number of slave escapes was reassuring to Southerners since too many runaways were as unsettling and as intractable a public relations problem as too many mulattoes. Interestingly, Southerners were not the only sources of such reassurance. The belief that hordes of fugitive slaves were harbored in free black communities placed all free people of color under suspicion—and heightened their vulnerability to kidnapping and police harassment in the 1850s. Thus, for their own political reasons, few leaders of the antislavery movement questioned the 1850 and 1860 Census numbers—since the relatively small numbers of fugitives reported "lost" corresponded favorably to the black population of Canada and its rate of increase. Even leaders such as Frederick Douglass—who, based on his writings and his own work with the Underground Railroad in Rochester, knew (or, at least, believed) the flow of fugitives was much heavier—nonetheless published several accounts contending that the number of fugitives escaping to the North was much lower than the number of African Americans emancipated through legal means who sought residence in the North.[9] In one of the most dramatic examples, Douglass was permitted to "glance over the census returns for two or three hours" in 1851 and stated, on the basis of his cursory review:

> The public impression as to the number of fugitives which may have been at any time or that now remain in the North, is undoubtedly immensely exaggerated. That there are many free in the Northern cities who run at the sound of a Southerner's footstep for fear of being unable to prove their freedom, there cannot be a doubt, and to this circumstance is owing the erroneous impression which has got abroad.[10]

On the other hand, inflating the number of runaways (and thereby magnifying the role of the Underground Railroad) gave southern politicians an effective example of northern meddling in southern affairs and northern lack of respect for southern property rights. Thus, while the likelihood of significant under-counting is considerable, the question remains—by how much?

The problem, of course, with two sets of estimates is that historians in succeeding generations—much as antebellum Northerners and Southerners—could use the set that best suited their interests and needs. Only the weight of additional evidence can tip the interpretive balance in one direction or another. In that respect, data such as those collected by Franklin and Schweninger and presented in this study challenge the validity of 1850 and 1860 Census data on purely empirical grounds. Furthermore, there are other primary sources at least as credible as the 1850 and 1860 Census returns and, of these, the *Congressional Record* is particularly useful. What lends these records some credibility is their consistency over time and the extent to which they agree with other sources. Siebert summarized this evidence in some detail:

> In August 1850, Atchison of Kentucky, informed the Senate that "depredations to the amount of hundreds of thousands of dollars are committed upon the property of people of the border slave states annually." Pratt, of Maryland, said that not less than $80,000 worth of slaves was lost every year…. Mason, of Virginia, declared that the losses to his state … were then in excess of $100,000 per year. Butler, of South Carolina, reckoned the annual loss of the Southern section at $200,000.

These sources estimated that the South lost $30,000,000 in slave property "through the 100,000 slaves abducted from her" between 1810 and 1850.[11] Perhaps, most telling of all, in the debates surrounding efforts to forestall secession in late 1860 and early 1861—when southern representatives had nothing to gain from inflating such statistics—many northern states sought to mollify the South by promising to rescind their personal liberty laws and to make a more serious effort to enforce the Fugitive Slave Law. It was stated in these debates by "Polk, of Missouri," that Kentucky lost $200,000 in slave property annually.[12]

Using this figure and using an average price of $300.00 per enslaved African American (derived from the same sources), 666 fugitive slaves escaped successfully from Kentucky in 1860. Drawing on the Kentucky Fugitive Slave Data Base, one can assume that another 10 to 20 percent above this figure escaped through Kentucky from Tennessee and the deeper South, raising the total to roughly 800 per year. Although no figures exist by which a "capture rate" might be calculated, one can assume further from newspapers and other sources that between half and two-thirds of all slave escapes were successful. If that is so, then the total number of slave escapes from or through Kentucky ranged annually between 1,200 and 1,600. Stated somewhat differently, these calculations yield an average of between 100 and 130 slave escapes per month, or between three and four per day.

This figure represents between one-third and one-half of all U.S. slave escapes as depicted in Table VIII-1.

Although this estimate is considerably higher than the Census figures, it still represents only a small fraction of the total Kentucky slave population. As noted in Table II-1, there were 210,981 enslaved African Americans in Kentucky in 1850 and 225,483 in 1860. Consequently, the rate of loss due to escapes can be estimated at roughly 0.5 percent per year. Still, it is important to remember that this loss of human property was not a one-time event, but an average of how many slave escapes occurred each year over the two generations preceding the Civil War. In other words, this loss approaches 2.5 percent per decade. Following this line of reasoning a bit further, and recalling that 75 percent of

Table VIII-1

Rate of Slave Escapes: Kentucky and United States

	East	West Kentucky	Other	Total
N of Slave Escapes **1810–1829**	24,000	10,000	6,000	40,000
Escapes per Year	1,200	500	300	2,000
N of Slave Escapes **1830–1849**	30,000	22,000	8,000	60,000
Escapes per Year	1,500	1,100	400	3,000
N of Slave Escapes **1850–1860**	15,000	12,000	8,000	35,000
Escapes per Year	1,500	1,200	800	3,500
Total (1810–1860)	**65,000**	**44,000**	**26,000**	**135,000**

Note: Figures in the East are based on a reasonably constant flow of fugitives until the overall increase in escapes in the 1850s. Figures for the West reflect the shift of slave population to the Gulf States and the opening of the Texas "market" in the 1830s and 1840s.

all fugitive slaves in the Kentucky Fugitive Slave Data Base were male, one can then assume that the loss of "prime" adult male African Americans was roughly 2.0 percent of the total Kentucky slave population per decade — or about 4 to 5 percent of the male population (which could approach 10 percent or more of the adult male population).

The loss of fugitives — and population losses attributable to death and the transfer of significant slave property to the southern interior through domestic slave trade — were more than offset by natural population increase. Still, it is clear that, while the institution of slavery was in no immediate danger of hemorrhaging to death in Kentucky, it was being weakened steadily by this slow bleeding. Slaveholders in Kentucky and the other border states were well aware that a higher escape rate would not only ruin them financially, but would destabilize the institution of slavery since the slave population would, in essence, simply melt away. Ironically, the fear of such mass flight, along with a "rig-

orous Union sentiment," were crucial factors in blunting efforts toward secession in Kentucky in 1861. As Siebert elaborated:

> The prospect of a stampede of slaves, in case they should join the secession movement, was a consideration that may be supposed to have had some weight in fixing the decision of the border states. Certainly, it was one to which Northern men attached considerable importance at the time in explaining the steadfast position of these states; and the impossibility of recovering even a single fugitive from the free states in case of a disruption of the Union ... was a thing of which Southern members of the national House were duly reminded by their Northern colleagues.[13]

These fears were well-founded. Fugitive slaves escaping from the Confederate states did, in fact, help to undermine the South during the Civil War. Not as well known, the fear of enslaved African Americans quitting the border states, en masse, helped maintain the loyalty of that critical region, including Kentucky. In other words, the Census figures may be true, but none of the key parties in the antebellum period spoke or behaved as though they were.

Directions for Future Research

The purpose of this study, as stated in Chapter I, was to create an historical record of fugitive slaves and the Underground Railroad in Kentucky and to advance and test several hypotheses. The author hopes that future research will broaden and deepen this knowledge base and sharpen or modify the interpretations presented herein.

This study did not exhaust, by any means, Kentucky fugitive slaves or the Underground Railroad as research topics. For example, several lines of future investigation suggested themselves during the course of this project. First, this project did not venture into the domain of biography or biographic history. Biographic sketches were often included, but only as sketches and only for a few individuals. In some cases, larger biographies or autobiographies exist and were used as secondary source materials. However, in most, only fragments of information are currently available — usually pertaining to a particular individual's moment in the historical sun. Consequently, researching the lives of some of the important, but generally unknown, personalities scattered throughout this history could bear much fruit. Such research has already begun in some cases.

Second, based on the available evidence, it is clear that the region of north central Kentucky centering around Louisville was one of the most important fugitive slave harboring and crossing-points in the country. While the role of Madison, Cincinnati and Ripley are well-known, the presence of such a hub or junction in slave territory is not. Continued research will only add to the richness of this history and illuminate the many Underground Railroad "corridors" that led through the state to the city and its environs.

Third, this project focused primarily on crossing points and escape corridors, and was not concerned with Underground Railroad sites or sanctuaries, per se. Some were mentioned and others suggested, but far more is known regarding sites north of the Ohio River than in Kentucky. There is, however, a substratum of community and family legends involving fugitive slaves scattered throughout the state. While following these leads was not necessary to this study, projects devoted to identifying and authenticating such sites will add important depth to the historical record.

Fourth, the points of origin of runaway slaves, often their Ohio River crossing points and sometimes their ultimate destinations are known in most cases. The broad routes and corridors by which fugitives traveled between their origins and crossing points in slave territory can, as this study demonstrates, be determined circumstantially and by inference. However, there is no detailed Underground Railroad "map" or schematic of fugitive slave escape routes of Kentucky or any other southern state. Research focused on documenting these interior routes holds great promise.

One or more of these lines of inquiring may produce some significant findings.

Legend and Legacy

Fugitive slaves and the Underground Railroad belong to the evermore distant American past. Yet, as indicated by Congressional actions and National Park Service initiatives of the 1990s, the Underground Railroad remains a powerful symbol — a legend with an enduring hold on the American imagination. This legend has one dominant image: one or more fugitive slaves being assisted in some way by one or more well-meaning whites, often Quakers such as Levi Coffin. Obviously, there were many such scenes, played out on thousands of occasions.

A history built around this legend is not inaccurate — only incomplete and subtly misleading. There are other scenes with as much, if not more, historical validity. Two are most representative of all: African Americans escaping alone; and African Americans being aided by other African Americans. These scenes embody the struggle for freedom and their legacy is a powerful affirmation of the humanity and strength of African Americans faced with a type and degree of oppression unique in American, if not global, history. This legacy is also a lesson, repeated often in American history, that African Americans and other oppressed people must first help themselves before they can expect any help from others — that constructive changes in racial conditions and race relations never occur until those "who suffer the wrong" act in their own interests. It is perfectly fitting that the biological and ideological children, grandchildren and great-grandchildren of fugitive slaves and those who assisted them would become the leaders of black America.

Still, the more familiar image is a powerful affirmation of another equally important principle: the ideal of a multiracial democracy. From the time of the American Revolution, the ideals of the Declaration of Independence and the Preamble to the U.S. Constitution have competed with the raw reality of a political economy dominated by one racial (and one gender and class) group. The practical abolitionists, beyond believing that slavery was wrong or evil, actually helped real — not abstract — African Americans. These white Americans risked much and did so in the service of a higher ideal. Their grandchildren, biological or ideological, would press for racial reform in the Progressive era and join with Dr. W. E. B. DuBois to

create the National Association for the Advancement of Colored People in 1909. Their great-great-grandchildren would join with Dr. Martin Luther King, Jr., in the Civil Rights Movement of the 1960s. This ideal of multi-racial democracy remains the stated, but still unrealized, promise that the United States will become a nation in which racial, ethnic, gender and class differences "make no difference." The legacy of the white Underground Railroad workers is the concrete expression of this ideal in action and their willingness to make common cause with others unlike themselves and thereby make themselves outcasts among their own people.

As this study demonstrates, Kentucky is central both to the history and the legend. However, many Kentuckians have been and remain reluctant to claim their rightful share of the legend and its legacy since both contradict the romanticized view of antebellum Kentucky and Kentucky slavery. In simple terms, it is rather difficult for a former slave state to embrace as heroes African Americans and whites who fought against slavery. Still, as each succeeding generation constructs a new vision of the past in seeking to construct its own vision of the present, most myths collapse, ultimately, under the sheer intellectual and moral weight of the "stubborn facts" of history. And, ultimately, the need to know the truth of the past outweighs the need to deny the evils of slavery.

In the end, fugitive slaves and the blacks and whites involved in the "conspiracy of conscience" known as the Underground Railroad were, in the haunting words of Albert Camus, rebels in the finest sense. For African Americans, the flight from slavery embodied a willingness to strive for freedom — even if the meaning of freedom was unknowable at first and even if the reality of freedom proved disappointing in the end. That freedom was circumscribed by racial hostility in the regions "north of slavery" did not prompt

African Americans to yearn for their old masters. Rather, the difficulties of life in the free states and even in Canada simply crystallized for fugitives a fundamental truth of which free African Americans were already aware: that ending slavery was only the half-way point in the long struggle for truly equal citizenship.

In the decades before the Civil War, the Underground Railroad brought African Americans struggling for freedom together with white Americans opposed to slavery. As a symbol of the best of the American past, it brings black and white Americans together still.

APPENDIX I

The Kentucky Borderland

The Ohio River: Its Towns and Tributaries

City/Town	Elevation	Miles below Pittsburgh	Major Regional Tributaries
Ashland, KY	480	325	
Greenup, KY	470	340	
Portsmouth, OH	460	360	Scioto River
Maysville, KY	445	410	Sleepy Hollow Creek
			Lime Stone Creek
			Little Beasley Creek
Cincinnati, OH	430	470	Little Miami River
			Licking River
			Great Miami River
Madison, IN	400	560	Kentucky River
Louisville, KY	375	600	Harrods Creek
			Beargrass Creek
			Falling Run Creek
			Salt River
Owensboro, KY	340	760	Green River
Henderson, KY	325	790	Big Pigeon Creek
Paducah, KY	280	935	Wabash River
			Cumberland River
			Tennessee River
Cairo, IL	250	981	

1850 Kentucky Free Black Population: Counties with 100 or More Free Persons of Color (FPCs)

County	# of FPCs	% Black Population	% County Population	Major Towns or Cities (# FPCs)
Adair	108	6.0	1.1	
Barren	113	2.4	2.4	Glasgow (20)
Bath	116	4.4	1.0	
Bourbon	245	3.4	1.7	Paris (46)
Boyle	317	8.5	3.5	
Bracken	114	11.9	1.3	Augusta (40)
Caldwell	139	4.3	1.0	
Christian	150	1.8	0.8	
Clark	134	2.7	1.1	
Clay	172	25.0	3.2	
Fayette	668	5.8	2.9	Lexington
Fleming	158	6.9	1.1	Flemingsburg (26)
Franklin	357	9.6	2.9	Frankfort (213)
Greene	117	4.3	1.3	
Harrison	146	4.4	1.1	
Henderson	123	2.7	1.0	Henderson (17)
Jefferson	1,637	13.0	2.7	Louisville (1,538)
Knox	200	24.6	2.8	
Lincoln	104	3.0	1.0	
Logan	364	6.2	2.2	Russellville (64)
Mason	386	8.3	2.1	Maysville (142)
Mercer	336	9.3	2.4	Harrodsburg (110)
Montgomery	164	5.1	1.7	Mt. Sterling (39)
Nelson	116	2.2	0.1	
Nicholas	166	9.9	1.6	
Scott	219	3.6	0.1	
Shelby	189	2.8	1.1	
Taylor	148	8.3	2.0	Campbellsville (11)
Warren	209	4.6	1.4	
Woodford	169	2.6	1.4	
Kentucky	10,011	4.5	1.0	

Note: There were also small clusters of free persons of color in Covington (36, in Kenton County), Newport (43, in Campbell County), Smithland (48, in Livingston County) and Paducah (17, in McCracken County). FPC population of Lexington was omitted.

Kentucky Counties Bordering the Ohio River (West to East)

Facing Illinois	Facing Indiana	Facing Ohio
Ballard	Henderson	Boone
McCracken	Daviess	Kenton
Livingston	Hancock	Bracken
Crittenden	Breckenridge	Mason
Union	Meade	Lewis
	Hardin	Greenup

Facing Indiana	*Facing Ohio*
Bullitt	Boyd
Jefferson	
Oldham	
Trimble	
Carroll	
Gallatin	
Boone	

Illinois, Indiana and Ohio Counties Bordering Kentucky (West to East)

Illinois	*Indiana*	*Ohio*
Alexander	Posey	Hamilton
Pulaski	Vanderburgh	Clermont
Johnson	Warrick	Brown
Massac	Spencer	Adams
Pope	Perry	Scioto
Hardin	Harrison	Lawrence
Gallatin	Floyd	
	Clark	
	Jefferson	
	Switzerland	
	Ohio	

1850 Illinois Black Population: Counties with 100 or More Free Persons of Color (FPCs)

County	*# of FPCs*	*% County Population*	*Major Towns or Cities*
Adams	139	0.5	
Clinton	137	2.7	
Cook	378	0.9	Chicago
Gallatin	353	6.5	St. Louis
Joe Daviess	218	1.2	
Lawrence	278	4.5	
Madison	449	2.2	
Morgan	125	0.8	
Pope	104	2.6	
Randolph	383	3.5	
St. Clair	581	2.9	St. Louis
White	109	1.2	

1850 Indiana Black Population: Counties with 100 or More Free Persons of Color (FPCs)

County	# of FPCs	% of Total Population	Major Towns or Cities (FPCs)
Allen	102	0.6	Fort Wayne (81)
Clark	586	3.7	Charleston (154) Jeffersonville (358)
Dearborne	147	0.7	Lawrenceburg (40)
Decatur	156	1.0	Fugit (149)
Floyd	574	3.9	New Albany (502)
Franklin	209	1.2	Salt Creek (122)
Gibson	217	2.0	Patoka (171)
Grant	147	1.3	Mill (89)
Hamilton	182	1.4	Jackson (88)
Hancock	104	1.1	
Jefferson	568	2.4	Madison (298)
Marion	650	2.7	Indianapolis (405)
Montgomery	143	0.8	Union (125)
Orange	251	2.3	Paoli (101) Southeast (117)
Owen	156	1.3	Washington (76) Marion (51)
Posey	98	0.8	
Randolph	662	4.5	Greensfork (163) Stony Creek (144)
Ripley	96	0.6	
Rush	427	2.6	Ripley (354)
Tippecanoe	161	0.8	Lafayette (132)
Vanderburgh	227	2.0	Evansville (121)
Vigo	748	4.9	Terre Haute (227) Lost Creek (138)
Washington	252	1.5	Posey (90) Salem (70)
Wayne	1,036	4.1	New Garden (207) Wayne (179)

1850 Ohio Black Population: Counties with 100 or More Free Persons of Color (FPCs)

County	# of FPCs	% of Total Population	Major Towns or Cities (FPCs)
Athens	106	0.6	
Belmont**	778	2.3	Somersett (115) Warren (158)
Brown*	863	3.2	Eagle (214) Scott (100) Union (163) Ripley (135)
Butler	367	1.2	Hamilton (172)

County	# of FPCs	% of Total Population	Major Towns or Cities (FPCs)
Champaign	494	2.5	Urbana (225)
Clark	323	1.5	Springfield (212)
Clermont*	412	1.4	Ohio (256)
Clinton	598	3.2	Wilmington (182)
			Wayne (158)
Columbiana***	182	0.5	
Cuyahoga	359	0.8	Cleveland (224)
Darke	248	1.2	German (192)
Delaware	135	0.6	
Erie	202	1.1	Portland/Sandusky (113)
Fairfield	280	0.9	Lancaster (187)
Fayette	291	2.3	
Franklin	1,607	3.8	Columbus (1,277)
Gallia**	1,198	7.0	Gallipolis (329)
			Green (145)
			Greenfield (216)
			Morgan (105)
			Raccoon (139)
			Springfield (143)
Greene	654	3.0	Xenia (502)
Guernsey	168	0.6	
Hamilton*	3,600	2.3	Cincinnati (3,237)
			Mill Creek (109)
Harrison	287	1.0	
Highland	896	3.5	Fairfield (245)
			Liberty (221)
			Hillsboro (217)
Hocking	117	0.8	
Jackson	391	3.1	Jackson (102)
			Milton (138)
Jefferson**	665	2.3	Mount Pleasant (228)
			Steubenville (137)
Lawrence*	326	2.1	Fayette (155)
Licking	128	0.3	Newark (100)
Logan	536	2.8	Jefferson (173)
			Monroe (105)
Lorain	264	1.0	
Lucas	139	1.1	
Mercer	399	5.2	Marion (273)
Miami	602	2.4	Troy (148)
			Union (123)
Montgomery	249	0.7	Dayton (234)
Muskingam	631	1.4	Meigs (136)
			Zanesville (229)
Pickaway	412	2.0	Circleville (229)
Pike	618	5.6	Jackson (358)
Ross	1,908	5.9	Scioto (209)
			Chillicothe (803)
			Union (370)
Scioto*	211	1.1	Portsmouth (144)
Seneca	151	0.6	
Shelby	407	2.9	Van Buren (265)
Stark	159	0.4	

County	# of FPCs	% of Total Population	Major Towns or Cities (FPCs)
Summit	121	0.4	
Union	128	1.1	
Vinton	107	1.1	
Warren	602	2.4	Lebanon (128)
			Wayne (175)
Washington**	390	1.3	

* = Ohio/Kentucky Border County
** = Ohio/Virginia Border County
*** = Ohio/Pennsylvania Border County

Kentucky Underground Railroad Workers

Name	Race	Location	Years
Shepherd Alexander	Black	Columbus, OH	1850s
Abraham Allen	White	Clinton County, OH	1850s
Elijah Anderson	Black	Madison, IN	1840s, 1850s
Freman Anderson	Black	Trimble County, KY	1850s
Mrs. Annis	Black	Cincinnati, OH	1850s
James Armstrong	White	Louisville, KY	1850s
James Ashley	White	Portsmouth, OH	1840s
Joseph Ashton	White	Pike County, OH	1840s, 1850s
Barrett Family	Black	Pee Pee Settlement, OH	1850s
James Baxter	White	Madison, IN	1840s
Charles Bell	White	Corydon, IN	1850s
David Bell	White	Corydon, IN	1850s
Griffith Booth	Black	Madison, IN	1840s
Boyd	Black	Cincinnati, OH	1850s
James Charles Brown	Black		1830s
Isaac Brown	White	Brown County, OH	1850s
Nathan Brown	Black	Israel Township, OH	1850s
Thomas Brown	White	Henderson, KY	1850s
Richard Buckner	Black	Louisville, KY	1850s
Burgess Family	Black	Cincinnati, OH	1850s
George L. Burroughs	Black	Cairo, IL	1850s
John Cain	Black	Louisville, KY	1850s
Thomas Carneal	White	Covington, KY	1850s
Willard Carpenter	White	Evansville, IN	1850s
John Carr	White	Madison, IN	1840s
Keziah Carter	Black	Louisville, KY	1850s
George Washington Carter	Black	New Albany, IN	1850s
Richard Chancellor	White	Chillicothe, OH	1850s

Name	Race	Location	Years
Robert Chancellor	White	Chillicothe, OH	1850s
Daniel Churchill	Black	Louisville, KY	1850s
William Cockrum	White	Southwestern IN	1850s
Levi Coffin	White	Newport, IN	1830s, 1840s
		Cincinnati, OH	1840s, 1850s
Samuel Cole	White	Louisville, KY	1850s
William A. Conolly	White	Cincinnati, OH	1850s
Coombs Family	White	Lindale, OH	1850s
Rev. Joseph H. Creighton	White	Ironton, OH	1840s, 1850s
James Cunningham	Black	Louisville, KY	1850s
Rev. Norris Day	White	Madison, IN	1850s
George DeBaptiste	Black	Madison, IN	1840s
Jack Dicher	Black	Lawrence County, OH	1840s, 1850s
Dorum Family	Black	Cincinnati, OH	1850s
Jacob Ebersole	White	Clermont County, OH	1840s, 1850s
Ebenezer Elliott	Black	Israel Township, OH	1850s
George Evans	Black	Madison, IN	1830s
Calvin Fairbank	White	Lexington, KY	1840-1850s
Robert E. Fee	White	Moscow, OH	1850s
W. M. Fee	White	Moscow, OH	1850s
Jesse Fiddler	White	Chillicothe, OH	1850s
John Fiddler	White	Chillicothe, OH	1850s
William Finney	White	New Albany, IN	1830s
John R. Forcen	Black	Madison, IN	1850s
John Freeman	Black	Louisville, KY	1850s
William Gilchrist	Black	Louisville, KY	1850s
		Canada West	
Rev. James Gilliland	White	Red Oak, OH	1830s
Zeke Goins	White?	New Albany, IN	1830s
Simon Gray	Black	Madison, IN	1850s
Hall Family	Black	Cincinnati, OH	1850s
John T. Hanover	White	Southwestern IN	1850s
William Harding	Black	New Albany, IN	1850s
Rev. Chapman Harris	Black	Madison, IN	1840s, 1850s
Alexander Hatfield	Black	Louisville, KY	1850s
Laura Haviland	White	Eastern Indiana	1840s, 1850s
Amanda Hedges	White	Louisville, KY	1850
Shadrach Henderson	Black	Louisville, KY	1850s
Josiah Henson	Black		1840s, 1850s
Elisha Hillyer	White	Louisville, KY	1850s
William Hosea	White	New Albany, IN	1850s
Benjamin Hoyt	White	Madison, IN	1840s, 1850s
Charles B. Huber	White	Williamsburg, OH	1850s
John W. Hudson	Black	Sardinia, OH	1830s, 1840s, 1850s
William Jeter	Black	Louisville, KY	1850s
Gabe Johnson	Black	Lawrence County, OH	1850s
D. C. Jones	Black	Louisville, KY	1050s
Charles Lacey	White	New Albany, IN	1830s
John Lancisco	White	Jeffersonville, IN	1850s
Fannie Latapie	Black	Louisville, KY	1850s
Stephen Latapie	Black	Louisville, KY	1850s
Lewis Family	Black	Cincinnati, OH	1850s
John Knight	Black	Louisville, KY	1850s
William Lewis	White	Louisville, KY	1850s

Name	Race	Location	Years
Joseph Logan	Black	Adams County, OH	1840s, 1850s
John C. Long	Black	Louisville, KY	1850s
John Lott	Black	Madison, IN	1840s
Joseph Love	Black	Chillicothe, OH	1850s
Dan Lucas	Black	Chillicothe, OH	1850s
Sarah Lucas	Black	New Albany, IN	1850s
Dr. Mary Lusk	White	Harrison County, IN	1850s
Matthias Marks	White	Harrison County, IN	1850s
Margaret Matthews	White	Louisville, KY	1850
Mary McCarty	White	Louisville, KY	1850s
Henry Measler	White	Louisville, KY	1850s
Shelton Morris	Black	Louisville, KY	1830–1850s
		Cincinnati, OH	
George Moseley	Black	Louisville, KY	1850s
John Parker	Black	Ripley, OH	1840s, 1850s
Dr. L. T. Pease	White	Williamsburg, OH	1850s
John Peters	White	Ironton, OH	1840s, 1850s
Samuel Peterson	White	Willaimsburg, OH	1850s
Henry Porter	White	Louisville, KY	1850s
Edmund Prince	Black	Madison, IN	1850s
Rev. John Rankin	White	Ripley, OH	1830s, 1840s, 1850s
Isaiah Reed	White	Harrison County, IN	1850s
Andrew Redmond	White	Chillicothe, OH	1850s
Hansel Roberts	Black	Dunlap, OH	1850s
Wade Roberts	Black	Dunlap, OH	1850s
Will Ryker	White	Madison, IN	1840s
John Sering	White	Madison, IN	1830s
Mark Sims	Black	Williamsburg, OH	1850s
Charles Smith	Black	Louisville, KY	1850s
Washington Spradling	Black	Louisville, KY	1830–1850s
James Stewart	White	Madison, IN	1840s
Harriet Beecher Stowe	White	Cincinnati, OH	1840s
William Tatus	White	Louisville, KY	1850s
Charles Taylor	Black	Louisville, KY	1850s
Mason Thompson	Black	Madison, IN	1850s
John C. Todd	White	Madison, IN	1840s
"Little Jimmie" Trueblood	White	Harrison County, IN	1840s, 1850s
Jacob Wagner	White	Madison, IN	1840s
James B. Ward	White	Indianapolis, IN	1850s
Lewis Washington	Black	Columbus, OH	1850s
Thomas Washington	Black	Columbus, OH	1850s
Delia Webster	White	Lexington	1840–1850s
		Trimble County	
Whiting	Black	Louisville, KY	1850s
Miles Wilson	Black	Louisville, KY	1850s
Oswell Wright	Black	Corydon, IN	1850s

Notes

I. Introduction

1. Winthrop D. Jordan, *The White Man's Burden: Historical Origins of Racism in the United States* (New York: Oxford University Press, 1974): 37–54; Orlando Patterson, *Slavery and Social Death* (Cambridge: Harvard University Press, 1982).

2. Frederick Douglass, *The Life and Times of Frederick Douglass* (New York: Macmillan, 1962; reprint of 1892 edition): 95–144.

3. David B. Davis, *Slavery and Human Progress* (New York: Oxford University Press, 1984): 51–82.

4. Leonard P. Curry, *The Free Black in Urban America, 1800–1850* (Chicago: University of Chicago Press, 1981); Edward M. Post, "Kentucky Law Concerning Emancipation and Freedom of Slaves," *Filson Club History Quarterly*, 59(1985): 344–367; Juliet E. K. Walker, "The Legal Status of Free Blacks in Early Kentucky, 1792–1825," *Filson Club History Quarterly*, 17(1983): 382–395.

5. J. Blaine Hudson, "The African Diaspora and the 'Black Atlantic': An African American Perspective," *Negro History Bulletin*, 60, 4(1997): 10–12; Herbert Klein, *African Slavery in Latin America and the Caribbean* (New York: Oxford University Press, 1986): 295–297. Eric Williams, *From Columbus to Castro: The History of the Caribbean, 1492–1969* (London: Andre Deutsch, 1970): 135–156.

6. John Hope Franklin, and Alfred A. Moss, Jr., *From Slavery to Freedom: A History of African Americans* (New York: McGraw-Hill, 1994): 57.

7. Ira Berlin, *Many Thousands Gone: The First Two Centuries of Slavery* (Cambridge: Harvard University Press, 1998): 290–324; Franklin and Moss, 1994: 75;

8. National Historic Landmarks Survey, 1998: 15.

9. *The Indianapolis Freeman*, October 31, 1891; Joe W. Trotter, Jr., *River Jordan: African American Urban Life in the Ohio Valley* (Lexington: The University Press of Kentucky, 1998): xiii.

10. Berlin, 1998: 364.

11. Lerone Bennett, Jr., *Before the Mayflower* (New York: Penguin, 1982): 55–139; B. A. Botkin, Ed., *Lay My Burden Down: A Folk History of Slavery* (Athens: The University of Georgia Press, 1945): 137–190; Robert W. Fogel, *Without Consent or Contract: The Rise and Fall of American Slavery* (New York: W. W. Norton, 1989): 17–40; Herbert G. Gutman, *The Black Family in Slavery and Freedom* (New York: Random House, 1976): 3–44; Nathan I. Huggins, *Black Odyssey: The African American Ordeal in Slavery* (New York: Vintage Books, 1990): 25–80; Brenda E. Stevenson, *Life in Black and White: Family and Community in the Slave South* (New York: Oxford University Press, 1996): 159–319; Donald R. Wright, *African Americans in the Colonial Era: From African Origins through the American Revolution* (Arlington Heights, IL: Harlan Davidson, Inc., 1990): 118–148.

12. Reginald Horsman, *Race and Manifest Destiny: The Origins American Racial Anglo-Saxonism* (Cambridge: Harvard University Press, 1981): 79–186; Winthrop D. Jordan, *White over Black: American Attitudes toward the Negro, 1550–1812* (New York: W. W. Norton and Company, 1968): 403–426; Michael Omi and Howard Winant, *Racial Formation in the United States* (New York: Routledge, 1986): 57–88; Larry E. Tise, *Proslavery: A History of the Defense of Slavery in America, 1701–1840* (Athens: The University of Georgia Press, 1987): 183–362; Howard Winant, *Racial Conditions* (Minneapolis: University of Minnesota Press, 1994): 11–156.

13. Richard C. Wade, *Slavery in the Cities: The South, 1820–1860* (New York: Oxford University Press, 1964: 225.

14. Alexander Thomas and Sillen, Samuel, *Racism and Psychiatry* (New York: Citadel Press, 1972): 16–17.

15. Henrietta Buckmaster, *Let My People Go: The Story of the Underground Railroad and the Growth of the Abolition Movement* (Boston: Beacon Press, 1941); Col. William M. Cockrum, *History of the Underground Railroad, As It Was Conducted by the Anti-Slavery League* (New York: Negro Universities Press, 1969; first published in 1915); Levi Coffin, *Reminiscences of Levi Coffin* (New York: Augustus M. Kelley, 1876); Benjamin Drew, *The Refugee: Or the Narratives of Fugitive Slaves in Canada* (Boston: John P. Jewett and Company, 1856); William M. Mitchell, *The Under-Ground Railroad* (London: 1860); Wilbur H. Siebert, *The Underground Railroad from Slavery to Freedom* (New York: Russell and Russell, 1967; first published 1898); R. C. Smedley, *History of the Underground Railroad* (New York: Arno Press, 1969; first published 1883).

16. Larry Gara, *The Liberty Line: The Legend of the Underground Railroad* (Lexington: University Press of Kentucky, 1961): 164–194; William Still, *The Underground Railroad* (Chicago: Johnson Publishing Company, 1970; reprint of 1872 edition): vii.

17. Calvin Fairbank, *Rev. Calvin Fairbank during Slavery Times* (Chicago: Patriotic Publishing Company, 1890); Randolph Runyon, *Delia Webster and the Underground Railroad* (Lexington: the University Press of Kentucky, 1996); Steven Weisenburger, *Modern Medea: A Family Story of Slavery and Child-Murder from the Old South* (New York: Hill and Wang, 1998).

18. Lowell H. Harrison and James C. Klotter, *New History of Kentucky* (Lexington: University Press of Kentucky, 1997): 171; Marion B. Lucas, *A History of Blacks in Kentucky, Volume 1: From Slavery to Segregation, 1760–1891* (Frankfort: Kentucky Historical Society, 1992): 62.

19. Thomas D. Clark, *A History of Kentucky* (Ashland: Jesse Stuart Foundation, 1980; first published in 1937): 208; National Historic Landmarks Survey, 1998: 32.

20. Charles Blockson, *Hippocrene Guide to the Underground Railroad* (New York: Hippocrene Books, 1994): 287–290; National Historic Landmarks Survey, 1998; Margaret O'Brien, "Slavery in Louisville During the Antebellum Period: 1820–1860," unpublished M. A. thesis, University of Louisville, 1979; Hanford D. Stafford, "Slavery in a Border City: Louisville, 1790–1860," unpublished Ph.D. dissertation, University of Kentucky, 1987.

21. John H. Franklin and Loren Schweninger, *Runaway Slaves: Rebels on the Plantation* (New York: Oxford University Press, 1999).

22. Roland E. Wolsey, *The Black Press, U. S. A.* (Ames: Iowa State Press, 1991): 27–32. African American newspapers were not numerous during the ante-bellum period. Those that were established focused on national rather than local issues and represent extremely valuable sources regarding fugitive slaves and the anti-slavery movement. The first, *Freedom's Journal* began publication in New York City on March 16, 1827 under the joint editorship of John B. Russworm and Samuel E. Cornish. An important but short-lived effort, its last issue appeared on October 9, 1829 after Russworm emigrated to Liberia. Cornish later joined the editorship of *The Weekly Advocate* in January 1837, which became *The Colored American* in March 1837. Martin R. Delany, sometimes considered the first black nationalist, founded and edited the *Mystery* in Pittsburgh from 1843 to 1847. Moreover, as the black population in Canada increased, other black newspapers were established there, most important among them the *Provincial Freeman* by Samuel Ringgold Ward and the *Voice of the Fugitive* by Henry Bibb. Frederick Douglass, the most important black Abolitionist, was also the most important black newspaper editor and publisher. His first publication, *The North Star*, appeared on November 1, 1847 in Rochester, New York — with Martin Delany as co-editor until May 1848. In 1851, *The North Star* merged with the *Liberty Party Paper* and was renamed *Frederick Douglass Paper*.

II. The Borderland

1. Stuart S. Sprague, ed. *His Promised Land: The Autobiography of John P. Parker, Former Slave*

and Conductor on the Underground Railroad (New York: W. W. Norton, 1996): 71.

2. Glenn T. Trewartha, *A Geography of Population: World Patterns* (New York: Wiley, 1969): 139–145.

3. Leland R. Johnson, "Engineering the Ohio," in Robert L. Reid, ed., *Always a River: The Ohio River and the American Experience* (Bloomington: Indiana University Press, 1991): 180–209.

4. Ibid.

5. Ibid.

6. Ellen Eslinger, "The Shape of Slavery on the Kentucky Frontier, 1775–1800," *The Register of the Kentucky Historical Society*, 92(1994): 1–23.

7. G. Glenn Clift, *Second Census of Kentucky, 1800: A privately compiled and published enumeration of tax payers appearing in the 79 manuscript volumes extant of tax lists of the 42 counties of Kentucky in existence in 1800* (Baltimore: Genealogical Publishing Co., 1982): iv-xiii; C. B. Heinenmann, comp., *"First Census" of Kentucky, 1790* (Baltimore: Genealogical Publishing Co., 1981); United States Bureau of the Census, *First Census of the United States, 1790*; United States Bureau of the Census, *Second Census of the United States, 1800* (Washington, D.C., 1801).

8. U. S. Bureau of the Census, *Historical Statistics of the United States: Colonial Times to 1957* (Washington: Government Printing Office, 1960): 8–15.

9. Clift, 1982; iv-xiii.

10. Franklin and Moss, 1994: 114–118; Ullrich B. Phillips, "The Slave Economy of the Old South," in Eugene D. Genovese, ed., *Selected Essays in Economic and Social History* (Baton Rouge: Louisiana State University Press, 1968): 142.

11. Franklin and Moss, 1994: 114–118.

12. Lucas, 1992: 12–13.

13. William D. Postell, *The Health of Slaves on Southern Plantations* (Baton Rouge: Louisiana State University Press, 1951): 85–86.

14. U. S. Bureau of the Census, *Historical Statistics*, 1960): 8–15.

15. Ibid.

16. Paul Wilhelm, Duke of Wurttemburg, *Travels in North America, 1822–1824* (Norman: University of Oklahoma Press, 1973; first published in 1824): 148.

17. Ibid., 150–153.

18. Ibid., 154–158.

19. Ibid., 158.

20. Ibid., 159.

21. Ibid., 162.

22. Ibid., 170–171.

23. Scott Cummings and Michael Price, *Race Relations in Louisville: Southern Racial Traditions and Northern Class Dynamics* (Louisville: University of Louisville College of Urban and Public Affairs, 1990): 1–2.

24. *Lexington: Heart of the Bluegrass* (Lexington: Fayette County Historic Commission, 1982): 72–73.

25. Ibid., 75.

26. *The Colored American*, October 12, 1839.

27. "Views of a Western Man in Kentucky," *The National Era*, June 17, 1847.

28. Ibid., June 24, 1847.

29. Lucas, 1992: 61.

30. Clark, 1992: 1–7; Harrison and Klotter, 1997: 18–79; Lucas, 1992: xv-xviii.

31. Lucas, 1992: xix-xxii; U. S. Census, 1850.

32. J. Blaine Hudson, "Slavery in Early Louisville and Jefferson County, Kentucky," *The Filson Club History Quarterly*, 73(1999): 261.

33. J. Winston Coleman, "Lexington's Slave Dealers and their Southern Trade, *The Filson Club History Quarterly*, 12(1938): 1.

34. Stephen Aron, *How the West Was Lost: The Transformation of Kentucky from Daniel Boone to Henry Clay* (Baltimore: The Johns Hopkins University Press, 1996): 143–149; Berlin, 1999: 95–108, 265; Joan W. Coward, *Kentucky in the New Republic: The Process of Constitution Making* (Lexington: The University Press of Kentucky, 1979): 37–55; Peter Kolchin, *American Slavery: 1619–1877* (New York: Hill and Wang, 1993): 94.

35. Hudson, 1997: 11; *U.S. Census*, 1800, 1810, 1820, 1830.

36. Kevin Phillips, *The Cousins' Wars* (New York: Basic Books, 1999): 317–406.

37. Franklin and Moss, 2000: 170.

38. Jordan, 1968: 348.

39. Emma L. Thornbrough, *The Negro in Indiana before 1900* (Bloomington: Indiana University Press, 1957): 31–91.

40. Curry, 1981: 96–111.

41. Robert R. Dykstra, *Bright Radical Star: Black Freedom and White Supremacy on the Hawkeye Frontier* (Cambridge, MA: Harvard University, 1993): vii-viii, 10–14; U.S. Census, 1860.

42. N. Dwight Harris, "The History of Negro Servitude in Illinois," 1904: 106–107. In the Wilbur H. Siebert Papers, The Underground Railroad in Illinois, Vol. 1, Box 71. The Ohio Historical Society.

43. "Statistics of Illinois," *The Seventh Census of the United States, 1850* (Washington: Robert Armstrong, Public Printer, 1853): 701–702.

44. Harris, 1904: 106–107.

45. Thornbrough, 1957: 6–7.

46. Francis S. Philbrick, ed., *The Laws of Indiana*

Territory, 1801–1809 (Illinois Historical Collections, Vol. 21. Reprinted by the Indiana Historical Society, 1931): 42–43, 136–139.

47. Thornbrough, 1957: 23.

48. Robert L. Reid, ed., *Always a River: The Ohio River and the American Experience* (Bloomington: Indiana University Press, 1991): 76–77.

49. Thornbrough, 1957: 8.

50. U. S. Bureau of the Census, *Negro Population, 1790–1915* (Washington: Government Printing Office, 1915): 44–45.

51. Thornbrough, 1957: 45–46.

52. *Anti-Slavery History of Jefferson County* (Madison, IN: Jefferson County Historical Society, 1998): 1–4; Diane P. Coon, "The Chronicles of Chapman Harris: A Free Black Leader of the Underground Railroad and Pastor of the Second Baptist Church at Madison, Indiana," unpublished manuscript, Department of Pan-African Studies, University of Louisville, 1999: 6–8.

53. Cockrum, 1915.

54. *Cincinnati Commercial*, July 8, 1853.

55. *The National Era*, June 30, 1853.

56. Siebert, 1898.

57. *The Colored American*, November 2, 1839.

58. Ibid., September 25, 1841.

59. *The North Star*, March 10, 1848.

60. *The Colored American*, May 22, 1841.

61. "Statistics of Tennessee," *The Seventh Census of the United States, 1850* (Washington: Robert Armstrong, Public Printer, 1853).

62. Lester C. Lamon, *Blacks in Tennessee, 1791–1970* (Knoxville: The University of Tennessee Press, 1981): 6–10; Chase C. Mooney, *Slavery in Tennessee* (Westport, CT: Universities Press, 1971; first published in 1957): 4–5.

63. Bobby L. Lovett, *The African-American History of Nashville, Tennessee, 1780–1930* (Fayetteville: The University of Arkansas Press, 1999): 4–7.

64. Ibid., 23–24.

65. Curry, 1981; U. S. Census, 1850.

III. Fugitive Slaves

1. Henry Bibb, *Narrative of the Life of Henry Bibb, An American Slave*, 1849, 51–171. In Gilbert Osofsky, Ed., *"Puttin' on Ole Massa: The Slave Narratives of Henry Bibb, William Wells Brown and Solomon Northup* (New York: Harper and Row, 1969): 64.

2. Hudson, 1997: 42.

3. *SPSS Base 9.0* (Chicago: SPSS, Inc., 1999). To avoid needless complexity, the key "numbers" in the statistical tests reported in this section are those related to probability (i.e., the "p"). If a relationship between any two variables could occur by chance less than 5 percent of the time, that relationship would be considered "statistically significant" at the .05 level of confidence — represented by "p < .05." The lower the probability, the stronger the relationship and the less likely it could occur by chance — e.g., "p < .01" represents a stronger relationship than "p < .05," or, a "difference that had a very low probability of occurring by chance."

4. Franklin and Schweninger, 1999: 210.

5. Ibid.

6. Ibid., 211–212.

7. Ibid., 211.

8. Ibid., 214.

9. Ibid., 228–229.

10. Ibid., 231.

11. Ibid., 233.

12. *Kentucky Gazette*, March 15, 1788.

13. *Louisville Public Advertiser*, April 10, 1823.

14. *Louisville Journal*, July 8, 1836.

15. Ibid., June 28, 1841; Kolchin, 1993: 37–56.

16. *Louisville Courier*, August 7, 1848.

17. *Louisville Journal*, July 3, 1852.

18. Ibid., October 12, 1853.

19. *Louisville Courier*, December 24, 1855.

20. *The Kentucky Gazette*, November 8, 1794.

21. *Louisville Public Advertiser*, July 11, 1831.

22. Ibid., November 21, 1831.

23. *Louisville Public Advertiser*, January 10, 1795.

24. Ibid., July 30, 1796.

25. *Louisville Public Advertiser*, February 8, 1826.

26. *Louisville Courier*, March 10, 1854.

27. *Louisville Public Advertiser*, April 14, 1819.

28. Ibid., December 13, 1823.

29. Ibid., October 22, 1825.

30. Ibid. March 11, 1826.

31. Ibid., September 11, 1831.

32. Ibid., November 28, 1832.

33. *Louisville Journal*, June 9, 1836.

34. Ibid., June 30, 1841.

35. Ibid., February 29, 1848.

36. *Louisville Courier*, March 28, 1850.

37. Ibid., August 21, 1851.

38. Ibid., December 23, 1852.

39. Ibid., July 28, 1853.

40. Ibid., December 18, 1855.

41. *Kentucky Gazette*, July 12, 1788.

42. Ibid., December 6, 1803.

43. *Louisville Public Advertiser*, January 16, 1828.

44. Helen T. Catteral, ed., *Judicial Cases concerning American Slavery and the Negro*, Vol. 1 (Washington, D.C.: Carnegie Institution, 1926): 338.

45. *Louisville Public Advertiser*, August 23, 1831.

46. *Louisville Journal*, September 20, 1844.

47. *Louisville Courier*, February 1, 1847.

48. Ibid., July 31, 1847.

49. *Kentucky Gazette*, May 17, 1794.

50. Ibid., April 5, 1799.

51. *Louisville Public Advertiser*, September 29, 1821.

52. Ibid., July 14, 1824.

53. Ibid., October 19, 1822.

54. Ibid., October 5, 1825.

55. Ibid., October 8, 1825.

56. Ibid., January 12, 1830.

57. Ibid., September 28, 1839.

58. *Louisville Journal*, October 27, 1842.

59. *Louisville Courier*, December 24, 1855.

60. Ibid., January 15, 1856.

61. Ibid., February 3, 1859.

62. Ibid., March 17, 1859.

63. *The North Star*, October 12, 1849.

64. Catterall, 1926: 415–416.

65. John Blasingame, *Slave Testimony: Two Centuries of Letters, Speeches, Interviews and Autobiographies* (Baton Rouge: Louisiana State University, 1977); Marion W. Starling, *The Slave Narrative: Its Place in American History* (Washington: Howard University Press, 1988).

66. William W. Freehling, *The Road to Disunion: Secessionists at Bay, 1776–1854* (New York: Oxford University Press, 1990: 502–503).

67. *Louisville Courier*, May 15, 1851.

68. Ibid., August 6, 1852.

69. *Louisville Journal*, September 15, 1852.

70. Ibid., September 25, 1852.

71. "Escape of Slaves," *Louisville Courier*, April 10, 1853.

72. "Stampede of Slaves," *Louisville Journal*, June 16, 1854.

73. *Louisville Journal*, October 25, 1854.

74. Ibid., November 24, 1854.

75. Ibid., December 14, 1854.

76. "Slave Case in Carrolton," *Louisville Courier*, May 29, 1855.

77. *Louisville Courier*, June 5, 1855.

78. Ibid., September 25, 1855.

79. Ibid., October 24, 1855.

80. Ibid., November 8, 1855.

81. Ibid., October 31, 1855.

82. Ibid., December 14, 1855.

83. Ibid., February 20, 1856.

84. Ibid., September 25, 1855.

85. "Underground Railroads," *Louisville Courier*, May 3, 1858.

86. Franklin and Moss, 1994: 198–219.

87. W. E. B. DuBois, W. E. B., *Black Reconstruction in America, 1860–1880* (New York: MacMillian, 1992; first published in 1935): 55–83.

88. Harrison and Klotter, 1997: 210–212; Victor B. Howard, *Black Liberation in Kentucky: Emancipation and Freedom, 1862–1864* (Lexington: University Press of Kentucky, 1983): 5; Lucas, 1992 178–183.

89. *Louisville Democrat*, November 17, 1861.

90. Howard, 1983: 26–29; Robert E. McDowell, *City of Conflict: Louisville in the Civil War, 1861–1865* (Louisville: Civil War Roundtable, 1962): 7–24.

91. *Louisville Journal*, January 20, 1863.

92. Catterall, 1926: 451–452.

93. George P. Rawick, Ed., "Ohio Narratives," in *The American Slave: A Composite Autobiography*, Vol. 16 (Westport, CT: Greenwood, 1972): 21.

94. Ibid., 56–57.

95. George P. Rawick, Ed., "Indiana and Ohio Narratives," in *The American Slave: A Composite Autobiography*, Supplement, Series 1, Vol. 5 (Westport, CT: Greenwood, 1972): 45–47.

96. Amy L. Young, and J. Blaine Hudson, "Slavery at Oxmoor," *The Filson Club History Quarterly*, 74(Summer 2000): 195–199; Harry Smith, *Fifty Years in Slavery in the United States of America* (Grand Rapids: West Michigan Printing Company, 1891). Jefferson County Historic Preservation and Archives.

97. Smith, 1891: 95.

98. Ibid.

99. Quarles, 1969: 147.

100. C. Peter Ripley, et al., Eds., *The Black Abolitionist Papers, Vol. II: Canada, 1830–1865* (Chapel Hill: The University of North Carolina Press, 1986): 3–4; Robin W. Winks, *The Blacks in Canada: A History* (New Haven, CT, 1971): 93–113.

101. William H. Gibson, Sr., *Historical Sketches of the Progress of the Colored Race in Louisville, Kentucky* (Louisville: n. p., 1897): 36.

102. Ibid., 1897: 35.

IV. The Anatomy of Slave Escapes

1. Drew, 1856: 180–181.

2. Franklin and Schweninger, 1999: 17–96; Siebert, 1898: 26.

3. *Kentucky Gazette*, October 25, 1788.

4. Franklin and Moss, 1994: 138–139.

5. *Kentucky Gazette*, April 19, 1803.

6. Ibid., June 14, 1803.

7. Ibid., September 27, 1803.

8. *Louisville Public Advertiser*, June 20, 1821.

9. Ibid., September 11, 1831.

10. *Louisville Journal*, May 24, 1836.

11. *Louisville Courier*, July 28, 1848.

12. Drew, 1856: 180–181.

13. *Louisville Public Advertiser*, October 30, 1822.

14. Speech by Lewis Richardson, Delivered at Union Chapel, Amherstburg, Canada West, 13 March 1846, In C. Peter Ripley, et al., Eds., *The Black Abolitionist Papers, Vol. II: Canada, 1830–1865* (Chapel Hill: The University of North Carolina Press, 1986): 101.

15. Drew, 1856: 358–366.

16. Proceedings of a Meeting of Toronto Blacks, Convened at the Residence of William Osborne, 13 January 1838, in C. Peter Ripley, et al., Eds., *The Black Abolitionist Papers, Vol. II: Canada, 1830–1865* (Chapel Hill: The University of North Carolina Press, 1986): 72.

17. *Louisville Courier*, May 11, 1858.

18. Josiah Henson, *Father Henson's Story of His Own Life* (Boston, 1858): 351–408.

19. Coffin, 1876; Drew, 1856.

20. Elizabeth R. Bethel, *The Roots of African American Identity: Memory and History in Antebellum Free Communities* (New York: St. Martin's Press, 1997): 119–139; Quarles, 1969: 143–167.

21. Franklin and Moss, 1994: 171–182.

22. *The Kentucky Gazette*, November 21, 1799.

23. *Louisville Public Advertiser*, March 11, 1820.

24. Ibid., March 22, 1820.

25. Ibid., September 29, 1821.

26. Ibid., October 2, 1822.

27. Ibid., April 5, 1823.

28. Ibid., October 26, 1825.

29. Ibid., September 27, 1826.

30. Ibid., November 12, 1829.

31. Ibid., January 29, 1830.

32. Ibid.

33. Ibid., July 3, 1830.

34. Ibid., December 16, 1830.

35. Ibid., September 11, 1831.

36. Ibid., November 19, 1839.

37. Ibid., December 27, 1839.

38. Catteral, 1926: 360.

39. *Louisville Journal*, March 30, 1844.

40. Ibid., April 12, 1844.

41. Ibid., October 6, 1845.

42. *Louisville Courier*, July 9, 1853.

43. Ibid., July 14, 1853.

44. Ibid., December 13, 1850.

45. Ibid., November 12, 1852.

46. American Freedmen's Inquiring Commission Interviews, 1863, National Archives Microfilm Publications, Rolls 197–201.

47. *Louisville Courier*, March 14, 1854.

48. Ibid., May 21, 1855.

49. Ibid., June 4, 1856.

50. Ibid., January 8, 1857.

51. Ibid., December 12, 1857.

52. Catterall, 1926: 425–426.

53. Ibid., 1926: 429.

54. *Louisville Courier*, April 14, 1853.

55. Ibid., June 2, 1857.

56. Quarles, 1969: 156.

57. "Fugitive Slave in a Pine Box," *Louisville Courier*, April 2, 1858.

58. "Attempted Escape," *Louisville Courier*, April 23, 1858.

59. *Louisville Courier*, May 11, 1858.

60. Siebert, 1898: 54.

61. J. Blaine Hudson, "References to Slavery in Early Kentucky Newspapers: *The Kentucky Gazette*, 1787–1805," unpublished manuscript. Jefferson County Historic Preservation and Archives, 1997.

62. Siebert, 1898: 59.

63. Coleman, 1940: 208n.

64. *Louisville Courier*, January 30, 1856.

65. Siebert, 1898: 56–57.

66. Jacqueline L. Tobin, and Raymond G. Dobard, *Hidden in Plain View: A Secret Story of Quilts and the Underground Railroad* (New York: Doubleday, 1999): 53–67.

67. Siebert, 1898: 54–77.

68. Ibid., 59.

69. *Louisville Public Advertiser*, August 15, 1821.

70. Ibid., October 9, 1822.

71. Ibid., November 23, 1822.

72. Ibid., November 7, 1829.

73. Ibid., February 4, 1826.

74. Ibid., July 21, 1830.

75. Ibid., September 15, 1835.

76. Ibid., September 19, 1836.

77. Catteral, 1926: 363.

78. Ibid., 338.

79. Ibid., 347.

80. *Louisville Journal*, December 14, 1840.

81. Catteral, 1926: 358.

82. Ibid.

83. *Louisville Journal*, March 27, 1843.

84. *Louisville Courier*, July 6, 1848.

85. Jacob D. Greene, *Narrative of the Life of Jacob Greene* (Huddersfield, England, 1864): 32–35.

86. *The Colored American*, September 4, 1841.

87. *Louisville Courier*, March 28, 1850.

88. Ibid., March 1, 1852.

89. *Louisville Journal*, January 11, 1853.

90. *Louisville Courier*, October 11, 1853.

91. Ibid., March 5, 1855.

92. Ibid., August 30, 1856.

93. "Arrest," *Louisville Journal*, April 7, 1854.

94. Ibid.

95. *Louisville Courier*, December 18, 1854.

96. "Large Haul of Fugitives," *Louisville Courier*, September 28, 1855.

97. *Frederick Douglass Paper*, May 19, 1854.

98. Drew, 1856: 303–304.

99. *The Colored American*, December 16, 1837.

100. *The North Star*, January 12, 1849.

101. "Nine Fugitive Slaves Arrested," *Louisville Journal*, June 16, 1854.

102. "The Cincinnati Fugitive Slave Case," *Louisville Journal*, June 17, 1854.

V: Friends of the Fugitive in the Kentucky Borderland

1. Benjamin Quarles, *Black Abolitionists* (New York: Da Capo, 1969): 167.

2. Douglas R. Egerton, *Gabriel's Rebellion: The Virginia Slave Conspiracies of 1800 and 1802* (Chapel Hill: University of North Carolina Press, 1993): 147–162; Hudson, 1999: 351.

3. David Robertson, *Denmark Vesey* (New York: Alfred A. Knopf, 1999): 117–130.

4. Stephen B. Oates, *The Fires of Jubilee: Nat Tuner's Fierce Rebellion* (New York: Mentor Books, 1975): 147, 163–164.

5. Coffin, 1876: 190; Gara, 1961: 173–174.

6. Siebert, 1898: viii–ix.

7. Paul Wilhelm, 1973/1824: 163.

8. *The Kentucky Gazette*, July 30, 1796.

9. Ibid., May 26, 1796.

10. *Louisville Public Advertiser*, June 20, 1821.

11. Ibid., December 13, 1823.

12. Ibid., September 14, 1829.

13. Ibid., October 8, 1830.

14. *The Kentucky Gazette*, July 30, 1796.

15. *Louisville Public Advertiser*, July 8, 1831.

16. Ibid., February 19, 1834.

17. Ibid., October 29, 1839.

18. Ibid., January 2, 1843.

19. *Louisville Journal*, September 5, 1844.

20. *Louisville Courier*, June 3, 1844.

21. *The North Star*, December 1, 1848.

22. *Louisville Courier*, May 9, 1849.

23. *Louisville Journal*, August 11, 1852.

24. Ibid., February 25, 1853.

25. *Louisville Courier*, August 24, 1854.

26. Ibid., April 24, 1855.

27. Ibid., September 14, 1857.

28. Ibid., September 19, 1857.

29. Ibid., August 6, 1858.

30. Coleman, 1940: 215–216.

31. Alexander M. Ross, *Recollections and Experiences of an Abolitionist; From 1855 to 1865* (Toronto, 1875): 110–113.

32. Catterall, 1926: 441–442; Coleman, 1940: 212–213.

33. *Louisville Public Advertiser*, November 2, 1822.

34. Ibid., February 19, 1823.

35. Ibid., September 25, 1825.

36. Ibid., July 16, 1830.

37. Ibid.

38. Ibid., February 12, 1831.

39. Ibid., March 21, 1831.

40. Ibid., September 28, 1831.

41. Ibid., December 16, 1831.

42. Ibid., June 1, 1832.

43. *Louisville Daily Journal*, February 29, 1844.

44. Ibid., July 12, 1845.

45. *Louisville Democrat*, February 25, 1851.

46. Ibid., October 13, 1851.

47. *Louisville Public Advertiser*, November 30, 1835.

48. Walker, 1983: 382–395.

49. Hudson, 1998.

50. Ordinances of the City of Louisville, In Harrison, J., *Collection of Acts of Virginia and Kentucky Relative to Louisville and Portland* (Louisville: Prentice and Weissinger, 1839).

51. Wade, 1969: 143–179.

52. *Louisville Courier*, February 21, 1856.

53. Ibid.; July 7, 1857; Ibid., July 10, 1857.

54. *Louisville Public Advertiser*, December 28, 1825.

55. Ibid., July 16, 1830.

56. Ibid., January 14, 1832.

57. Ibid., June 1, 1832.

58. *Louisville Journal*, June 8, 1836.

59. Ibid., June 22, 1836.

60. Ibid., June 26, 1842.

61. *Louisville Courier*, July 25, 1846.

62. Ibid., May 9, 1849.

63. Catterall, 1926: 315.

64. Ibid., 426.

65. *The North Star*, August 10, 1849.

66. Franklin and Moss, 1994: 192–197.

67. Freehling, 1990: 453–565.

68. O'Brien, 1972: 130.

69. *Louisville Courier*, November 23, 1852.

70. "Meeting of Slaveholders," *Louisville Courier*, September 5, 1855.

71. "Tampering with Negroes," *Louisville Courier*, January 12, 1856.

72. *Louisville Courier*, March 8, 1856.

73. "The Ohio River to be Patrolled," *Louisville Courier*, March 5, 1856.

74. Ibid.

75. Ibid., March 6, 1856.

76. "Underground Railroads," *Louisville Courier*, May 3, 1858.

77. "Return of a Runaway — Thieving Abolitionists," *Louisville Courier*, October 3, 1850.

78. Ibid.

79. "An Abolitionist at Jackson, Miss.," *Louisville Journal*, October 2, 1854; *Louisville Courier*, October 3, 1850; *Louisville Courier*, August 26, 1856. "More Excitement in Alabama," *Louisville Courier*, September 23, 1856.

80. *Louisville Journal*, June 15, 1854.

81. *The Provincial Freeman*, February 2, 1856.

82. *Louisville Courier*, March 7, 1856.

83. Ibid., June 14, 1857.

84. Ibid.

85. Ibid.

86. Ibid., December 18, 1852.

87. "Arrest," *Louisville Journal*, May 27, 1854.

88. "More Abolitionism in Cincinnati," *Louisville Courier*, March 29, 1855.

89. *Louisville Courier*, February 20, 1856.

90. "Runaway Found," *Louisville Courier*, July 22, 1853.

91. "Arrest of Fugitive Slave," *Louisville Courier*, July 13, 1854.

92. "Negro Stampede: Three Runaways Drowned," *Louisville Courier*, December 19, 1855.

93. *Louisville Courier*, January 1, 1850.

94. "Discharged and Escapes," *Louisville Courier*, February 17, 1854.

95. *Louisville Courier*, February 23, 1854.

96. Ibid., September 26, 1856.

97. Ibid., February 17, 1855.

98. Ibid., 1855.

99. Ibid., March 14, 1855.

100. *Louisville Journal*, April 6, 1855.

101. Ibid.

102. *Louisville Courier*, October 7, 1855.

103. Ibid., October 16, 1855.

104. Ibid., October 5, 1857.

105. Ibid., May 31, 1858.

106. Ibid., October 14, 1858.

107. Coffin, 1876: 398–400; Coleman, 1940: 227.

108. *Louisville Courier*, August 17, 1858.

109. Ibid., August 18, 1858.

110. Ibid., August 20, 1858.

111. Ibid.

112. Ibid., September 15, 1858.

113. Ibid, September 16, 1858.

114. Ibid., January 13, 1859.

115. Ibid., January 21, 1859.

116. James O. Horton, *Free People of Color: Inside the African American Community* (Washington: Smithsonian Institution Press, 1993): 67.

117. Ibid., 55.

118. Ibid., 68–71.

119. Ibid., 61–63.

120. Ibid., 62.)

121. Quarles, 1969: 143–167.

122. Ibid., 143–144.

123. *Louisville Journal*, September 8, 1852.

124. Ibid., February 23, 1853.

125. Smedley, 18.83: 381–387.

126. Cockrum, 1915.

127. Still, 1871.

VI: The Underground Railroad: Escape Routes, Corridors, Crossing Points and Junctions

1. *Louisville Courier*, November 25, 1856; Diane P. Coon, "The Chronicles of Chapman Harris," unpublished manuscript, Department of Pan-African Studies, University of Louisville, 1999: 11–12.

2. Edward O. Purtee, "The Underground Railroad from Southwestern Ohio to Lake Erie," unpublished Ph.D. dissertation, Ohio State University, 1932, in Wilbur H. Siebert Papers, Underground Railroad in Ohio, Vol. XII, Box 112, Ohio Historical Society: 32.

3. J. Winston Coleman, Jr., *Stage-Coach Days in the Blue Grass* (Lexington: The University Press of Kentucky, 1995; first published in 1935): 17–19; Neal O. Hammon, "Pioneer Routes in Central Kentucky," *Filson Club History Quarterly*, 74, 2 (Spring 1978): 124–143.

4. Coleman, 1935: 19–20.

5. Hammon, 1978: 152.

6. Ibid., 152–153.

7. Coleman, 1935: 27.

8. Andrew Jackson, *Narratives and Writings of Andrew Jackson* (Miami, 1969; first published in 1847): 5–23.

9. Coleman, 1935: 196–197.

10. Ibid., 197–198.

11. Catteral, 1926: 356.

12. "Route of Jacob Cummings," Indiana Underground Railroad, Vol., 1, Wilbur H. Siebert Papers, Box 79. Ohio Historical Society: 241.

13. Ibid., 242.

14. Franklin and Schweninger, 1999: 97–123.

15. Ibid., 318–321.

16. *Louisville Public Advertiser*, December 7, 1832.

17. *Paducah American*, February 14, 1855.

18. Ibid., March 28, 1855.

19. Ibid., June 6, 1855.

20. "A Precious Scoundrel," *Louisville Journal*, February 2, 1853.

21. Jacob P. Dunn, "Indiana and Indianans," Indiana Underground Railroad, Vol. 1, Box 79, Wilbur H. Siebert Papers. Ohio Historical Society: 151–152.

22. Ibid., 152–153.

23. Ibid., 154.

24. Cockrum, 1915: 7–20; Siebert, 1898: 134–139; Trotter, 1998: 1–23.

25. Cockrum, 1915: 7–20.

26. Coon, Diane P., "Reconstructing the Underground Railroad Crossings at Madison, Indiana." Unpublished manuscript, 1998.

27. Coffin, 1876; Siebert, 1898: 135–138.

28. Sprague, 1996.

29. Cockrum, 1915: 7–20; Siebert, 1898: 134–139.

30. N. Dwight Harris, "The History of Negro Servitude in Illinois," The Underground Railroad in Illinois, Wilbur H. Siebert Papers, Vol.1, Box 71. Ohio Historical Society: 106–107.

31. Federal Writers' Project, *Illinois: A Descriptive and Historical Guide* (Chicago: McClurg & Co., 1947): 435–437.

32. Wilbert J. Mosimann, "Materials Concerning the Underground Railroad in Illinois," n.d., the Underground Railroad in Illinois, Wilbur H. Siebert Papers, Vol.1., Box 71, Ohio Historical Society: 30–31.

33. Carl L. Spicer, "The Underground Railroad in Southern Illinois," the Underground Railroad in Illinois, Wilbur H. Siebert Papers, Vol.1., Box 71, Ohio Historical Society: 4–6.

34. Spicer, 1925: 8.

35. *Frederick Douglass Paper*, November 18, 1853.

36. Thronbrough, 1985: 39–45.

37. Richard R. Wright, Jr., "Negro Rural Communities in the North," *The Southern Workman*, *37* (1908): 163–165.

38. Thornbrough, 1985: 47.

39. Siebert, 1898: 134.

40. Thornbrough, 1985: 44.

41. Ibid., 40–41; Siebert, 1898: 138.

42. Gail King and Susan Thurman, *Currents: Henderson's River Book* (Henderson, KY: Henderson County Friends of the Public Library, 1991): 21.

43. Ibid., 23.

44. Ibid.; Trotter, 1998.

45. *The National Era*, June 10, 1852.

46. Ross, 1875: 7–12.

47. Ibid., 1875: 33–46.

48. Earl O. Saulman, "Blacks in Harrison County, Indiana," unpublished manuscript, Corydon, Indiana, 1999: 72.

49. Ibid., 2.

50. Probate Records, Harrison County, April 1822.

51. Saulman, 1999: 20.

52. Cockrum, 1915: 21.

53. Cockrum, 1915: 21; Peters, 1998; Thornbrough, 1957: 41–45.

54. *Louisville Public Advertiser*, November 30, 1835.

55. Gibson, 1897: 11–12.

56. Ibid., 12.

57. J. Blaine Hudson, "African American Religion in Antebellum Louisville, Kentucky," *The Griot: Journal of the Southern Conference on African American Studies*, *17, 2*(1998): 43–54.

58. Gibson, 1897: 17–18.

59. *Frederick Douglass Paper*, April 1, 1853.

60. Curry, 1981; Yater, 1987.

61. O'Brien, 1972: 128–129.

62. Beulah Van Metre, "The Underground Railroad Near Charlestown," Federal Writers' Project, unpublished notes, ca. 1936. Presented to the author by Ms. Iris L. Cook's grandniece, 1999: 1–2.

63. Cook, 1936: 1.

64. *Louisville Courier*, May 15, 1855.

65. *Louisville Courier*, October 1, 1855.

66. Ibid., September 14, 1857.

67. Gibson, 1897: 42.

68. Rawick, Vol. 5, 1977: 5.

69. Ibid., 232.

70. Ben Hershberg, "Hoosier is Tracking Underground Railroad," *Louisville Courier-Journal*, March 30, 1998; Pamela R. Peters, *The Underground Railroad in Floyd County, Indiana* (Jefferson, NC: McFarland, 2001): 99.

71. Thornbrough, 1985: 42–43.

72. Cook, 1936: 11–13.

73. Peters, 2001: 94–98.

74. *Louisville Daily Courier*, September 10, 1855.

75. Ibid., September 13, 1855.

76. George P. Rawick, Ed., "Ohio Narratives," in *The American Slave: A Composite Autobiography*, Vol. 16 (Westport, CT: Greenwood, 1972): 57–58.

77. Diane P. Coon, "Reconstructing the Underground Railroad Crossings at Madison, Indiana," unpublished manuscript, Departments of

History and Pan-African Studies, University of Louisville, 1998.

78. Coon, 1998: 8.

79. E. S. Abdy, *Journal of a Residence and Tour in the United States of North America, from April 1833 to October 1834*, Vol. 2 (London: John Murray, 1835).

80. "In the Days of Slavery: How Slaves Escaping from Kentucky Got Through Indiana," *The Indianapolis Freeman*, October 31, 1891.

81. Ibid. 1891.

82. Colonel John Benjamin Horton, *Old War Horse of Kentucky: The Life and Achievements of Albert Ernest Meyzeek* (Louisville: J. Benjamin Horton & Associates, 1986: 1.

83. Ibid, 2–3.

84. Coon, 1998: 12–14; Gwendolyn J. Crenshaw, *Bury Me in a Free Land: The Abolitionist Movement in Indiana, 1816–1865* (Indianapolis: Indiana Historical Bureau, 1993): 31.

85. Crenshaw, 1993: 31.

86. *Anti-Slavery History of Jefferson County* (Madison, IN: Jefferson County Historical Society, 1998): 1–4.

87. *Indianapolis Journal*, January 1880, cited in *Anti-Slavery History of Jefferson County*, 1998: 11.

88. Ibid., 13.

89. Coon, 1998: 9.

90. Ibid., 11.

91. *The Provincial Freeman*, February 9, 1856.

92. Ibid.

93. Wilbur H. Siebert, "Underground Railroad: How Slaves in Early Days were Piloted to Canada," *The Ohio Journal*, November 14, 1894, in the Wilbur Siebert Papers, The Ohio Underground Railroad, Box 105, Ohio Historical Society.

94. Edward O. Purtee, "The Underground Railroad from Southwestern Ohio to Lake Erie," unpublished Ph.D. dissertation, Ohio State University, 1932, in the Wilbur Siebert Papers, The Ohio Underground Railroad, Vol. XII, Box 112, Ohio Historical Society: 71.

95. *The National Era*, June 1, 1848.

96. Purtee, 1932: 36.

97. Wilbur H. Siebert, "The Mysteries of Ohio's Underground Railroad," 1895, draft manuscript, in the Wilbur Siebert Papers, The Ohio Underground Railroad, Box 116, Ohio Historical Society: 1.

98. Elizabeth R. Bethel, *The Roots of African American Identity: Memory and History in Free Antebellum Communities* (New York: St. Martin's Press, 1997): 119–139.

99. Siebert, "Mysteries," II, 1895: 2.

100. H. Lyman to Wilbur H. Siebert, April 1,

1898, in the Wilbur Siebert Papers, The Ohio Underground Railroad, Vol. XII, Box 112, Ohio Historical Society.

101. Siebert, "Mysteries," II.2, 1895: 7–9.

102. Ibid., 3.

103. *The North Star*, May 26, 1848.

104. Ibid.

105. *Frederick Douglass Paper*, August 12, 1853.

106. Ibid., September 16, 1853.

107. Coffin, 1876:

108. Siebert, "Mysteries," II.2, 1895: 6–7.

109. Laura S. Haviland, *A Woman's Life Work* (Cincinnati: Walden and Stowe, 1882): 97.

110. Purtee, 1932: 71.

111. *Frederick Douglass Paper*, December 9, 1853.

112. *Frederick Douglass Paper*, June 10, 1853; Siebert, "Mysteries," II.2, 1895: 6–8.

113. Siebert, "Mysteries," II.2, 1895: 6–8.

114. Ibid.

115. *Frederick Douglass Paper*, February 23, 1853.

116. Letter from M. F. Linton, Wilmington, Ohio, to Wilbur H. Siebert, September 10, 1895, cited in Purtee, 1932: 14.

117. Letter from W. P. Fishback, Indianapolis, Indiana, to Wilbur H. Siebert, May 23, 1882, cited in Purtee, 1932: 14.

118. Siebert, "Mysteries," II.3, 1895: 1–2.

119. Louis H. Everts, *History of Clermont County* (Philadelphia, 1880) in the Wilbur Siebert Papers, The Ohio Underground Railroad, Vol. XII, Box 112, Ohio Historical Society: 441–442.

120. *Louisville Public Advertiser*, June 2, 1836.

121. *Louisville Journal*, January 13, 1837.

122. Lucas, 1992: 77–78.

123. Purtee, 1932: 37.

124. *The North Star*, July 18, 1850.

125. Coffin, 1876: 150.

126. *The Colored American*, October 31, 1840.

127. George P. Rawick, Ed., "Kentucky Narratives," in *The American Slave: A Composite Autobiography, Supplement*, Vol. 16 (Westport, CT: Greenwood, 1972): 71–72.

128. Siebert, "Mysteries," II.4: 8.

129. Siebert, "Mysteries," II.5: 1.

130. Ibid., 2.

131. Siebert, "Mysteries," II.6: 1–2.

132. Ibid., 2–3.

133. Siebert, "Mysteries," II.7: 1.

134. Ibid.

135. *Frederick Douglass Paper*, January 1, 1852.

136. Siebert, "Mysteries," III.1: 2–3.

VII: Individuals and Cases of Note

1. Purtee, 1932: 54.
2. Rawick, Vol. 5, 1977: 245.
3. Ibid., 246.
4. *Louisville Public Advertiser*, July 7, 1831.
5. Karolyn E. Smardz, "There We Were in Darkness, Here We Are in Light: "Kentucky Slaves and the Promised Land," in Craig Thompson Friend, *The Buzzel About Kentucky: Settling the Promised Land* (Lexington: University Press of Kentucky, 1999): 243–248.
6. Ibid., 249–250.
7. Ibid., 250–251.
8. Ibid., 254–255; Karolyn E. Smardz, "From Louisville to the Promised Land: The Story of Thornton and Lucie Blackburn," unpublished paper prepared for the Kentucky African American Heritage Commission, April 2000.
9. Smardz, 1999: 382
10. Henry Bibb, 1849, 51–171.
11. Ibid., 64–66.
12. Ibid., 79–81.
13. Ibid., 83.
14. Ibid., 85–87.
15. Ibid., 89–99.
16. Ibid., 103–106.
17. Ibid., 112–113.
18. Ibid., 119–162.
19. Ibid., 162–163.
20. *The North Star*, April 10, 1851.
21. Ibid., Afua Cooper, "The Fluid Frontier: Blacks and the Detroit River — A Focus on Henry Bigg," *Canadian Review of American Studies, 30, 2* (2000): 136-143.
22. *The National Era*, August 17, 1854.
23. Starling, 1988: 148–149.
24. Bibb, 1849: 150.
25. Fairbank, 1890: 5–7; Runyon, 1996: 1–5.
26. Runyon, 1996: 8–13.
27. Coleman, 1940: 197–198; J. Winston Coleman, "Delia Webster and Calvin Fairbank — Underground Railroad Agents," *Filson Club History Quarterly, 17, 3*(1943): 129–142; *Louisville Courier*, October 3, 1844; Runyon, 1996: 14–15.
28. Coleman, 1943: 134–135.
29. Coleman, 1940: 199–202; Kentucky Penitentiary Records, Register of Prisoners, 1848–1855, Kentucky Department of Libraries and Archives; *Louisville Journal*, January 15, 1845; *Louisville Journal*, January 17, 1845; *Louisville Journal*, January 18, 1845; *Louisville Journal*, February 18, 1845; *Louisville Journal*, February 26, 1845: *The North Star*, October 19, 1849.

30. *The North Star*, December 7, 1849.
31. Coleman, 1943: 138.
32. *Frederick Douglass Paper*, November 20, 1851.
33. Ibid., November 27, 1851.
34. Ibid., February 26, 1852.
35. Ibid., March 25, 1852.
36. Coleman, 1943: 140; Harrison and Klotter, 1997: 171; Kentucky Penitentiary Records, Register of Prisoners, 1855–1861, Kentucky Department of Libraries and Archives; Lucas, 1992: 73.
37. *Louisville Courier*, December 27, 1851.
38. Coleman, 1943: 138–139.
39. *Louisville Courier*, October 22, 1855; *Louisville Courier*, June 25, 1856; *Louisville Courier*, March 14, 1857.
40. (Runyon, 1996: 203–224.)
41. Ibid., 203–224.
42. Joel Strangis, *Lewis Hayden and the War Against Slavery* (North Haven, CT: Linnet Books, 1999): 1–8.
43. Ibid., 9–13.
44. Ibid., 25–26.
45. Stanley J. Robboy, and Anita W. Robboy, "Lewis Hayden: From Fugitive Slave to Statesman," *New England Quarterly, 46*(1973): 591–613.
46. *Frederick Douglass Paper*, August 26, 1853.
47. Ripley, Vol. IV, 1991: 266–268.
48. *Louisville Courier*, August 14, 1848.
49. James M. Pritchard, "Into the Fiery Furnace: Anti-Slavery Prisoners in the Kentucky Staete Penitentiary, 1844–1870," conference paper delivered at the Kentucky Underground Railroad Symposium, June 1999:3.
50. Lucas, 1992: 73.
51. Petition to Governor John J. Crittenden, September 7, 1848, Governor's Office Papers, Folder 15, Kentucky Department of Libraries and Archives.
52. *Louisville Courier*, August 14, 1848.
53. L. R. Bullock to Governor John J. Crittenden, September 8, 1848, Governor's Office Papers, Folder 15, Kentucky Department of Libraries and Archives; John McClung to Governor John J. Crittenden, September 22, 1848, Governor's Office Papers, Folder 15, Kentucky Department of Libraries and Archives.
54. Lucas, 1992: 73.
55. *The North Star*, August 25, 1848.
56. Ibid., September 25, 1848.
57. Petition to Governor John J. Crittenden, September 7, 1848, Governor's Office Papers, Folder 15, Kentucky Department of Libraries and Archives.
58. L. R. Bullock to Governor John J. Crittenden, September 8, 1848, Governor's Office Papers,

Folder 15, Kentucky Department of Libraries and Archives.

59. John McClung to Governor John J. Crittenden, September 22, 1848, Governor's Office Papers, Folder 15, Kentucky Department of Libraries and Archives.

60. Lucas, 1992: 73.

61. Cockrum, 1915: 21; Peters, 1998; Thornbrough, 1957: 41–45.

62. Jefferson County Wills, Book 2: 146 (signed April 2, 1820).

63. Ruth Morris Graham, *The Saga of the Morris Family* (Columbus, GA: Brentwood Christian Communications, 1984): 15–19; Ernestine G. Lucas, *Wider Windows to the Past: African American History from a Family Perspective* (Decorah, IA: The Anundsen Publishing Company, 1995): 88–97.

64. "Testimony of Washington Spradling," American Freedmen's Inquiry Commission, November 26, 1863: 77; Jefferson County Wills, Book 2: 17 (signed September 12, 1814).

65. Jefferson County Marriage Register, Book 2: 18.

66. Gibson, 1897: 28.

67. Ibid., 25–26.

68. Lucas, 1992:112–113; Henry C. Weeden, *Weeden's History of the Colored People of Louisville* (Louisville: H. C. Weeden, 1897): 54; George C. Wright, *Life Behind a Veil: Blacks in Louisville, Kentucky, 1865–1930* (Baton Rouge: Louisiana State University Press, 1985).

69. J. Blaine Hudson, "A Guide to African Americans in the Records of Ante-bellum Louisville and Jefferson County Kentucky: Court Order minutes and Wills, with Special Reference to Slave Emancipations" (Louisville: Jefferson County Historic Preservation and Archives, 1998): 43.

70. Stanley Harold, "Freeing the Weems Family: A New Look at the Underground Railroad." *Civil War-History*, 52, 4(1996): 289–306; Hudson, 1998: 49.

71. Jefferson County Court Order Minutes, Book 17: 129 (November 5, 1835).

72. Jefferson County Court Order Minutes, Book 19: 275 (November 8, 1847).

73. Jefferson County Court Order Minutes, Book 19: 275 (November 8, 1847).

74. Jefferson County Court Order Minutes, Book 19: 551 (May 13, 1850).

75. "Testimony of Washington Spradling," American Freedmen's Inquiry Commission, November 26, 1863: 77.

76. Ibid., 77–79.

77. Lucas, 1996: 94–95; Weeden, 1897: 35.

78. Siebert, 1898: 151.

79. *Louisville Courier*, March 15, 1855.

80. Ibid., March 19, 1855.

81. Ibid., March 31, 1855.

82. Ibid., April 3, 1855.

83. Ibid., April 4, 1855.

84. "The Discharge of Mr. Dennison's Slave," *Louisville Journal*, April 6, 1855.

85. Ibid.

86. Ibid., April 17, 1855.

87. Ibid.

88. *Louisville Courier*, June 28, 1855.

89. Ibid., June 14, 1857.

90. Steven Weisenburger, *Modern Medea: A Family Story of Slavery and Child-Murder in the Old South* (New York: Hill and Wang, 1998): 18–20.

91. Ibid., 34.

92. Ibid., 44–48.

93. Ibid., 54–61; *Cincinnati Gazette*, January 31, 1856; *Cincinnati Gazette*, February 2, 1856.

94. *Louisville Courier*, January 30, 1856.

95. Weisenburger, 1998: 285; Toni Morrison, *Beloved* (New York: Alfred A. Knopf, 1987).

96. *Frederick Douglass Paper*, January 28, 1853.

97. *Louisville Courier*, February 2, 1856.

98. Weisenburger, 1998: 112.

99. *Louisville Democrat*, February 1, 1856.

100. *The Provincial Freeman*, March 15, 1856.

101. *Louisville Courier*, March 3, 1856.

102. Weisenburger, 1998: 208–209.

103. Ibid., 224–225; *Cincinnati Commercial*, March 11, 1856.

104. *The Provincial Freeman*, April 5, 1856.

105. Ibid., April 26, 1856; Weisenburger, 1998: 232–241.

106. Weisenburger, 1998: 278–279.

107. *Louisville Courier*, August 29, 1857.

108. Ibid.

109. Ibid., January 11, 1859; January 18, 1859.

110. Ibid., January 19, 1859.

111. Ibid., January 21, 1859.

112. Saulman, 1999: 72–73.

113. *Louisville Courier*, November 19, 1857.

114. Ibid.

115. Meade County (Kentucky) Court Order Records, Book K: 419, 555, 572.

116. Saulman, 1999: 73.

117. Interview with Fred Griffin, great-grandson of Judge William A. Porter, Corydon, Indiana, May 9, 2000; Saulman, 1999: 77.

118. Iris L. Cook, "Underground Railroad in Southern Indiana," Federal Writers' Project, unpublished notes, ca. 1936. Presented to the author by Ms. Cook's grandniece, 1999: 15–17.

119. Ibid., 17.

120. Coon, 1998: 12.

121. *The Provincial Freeman*, January 3, 1857.

122. Ibid., July 11, 1857.

123. Coon, 1998: 14; Crenshaw, 1993: 31; Kentucky Penitentiary Records, Kentucky Archives and Records.

124. Diane P. Coon, "The Chronicles of Chapman Harris," unpublished manuscript, Department of Pan-African Studies, University of Louisville, 1999: 11–12.

125. Ibid.

126. Crenshaw, 1993: 31.

127. *Louisville Courier*, November 25, 1856.

128. Franklin and Moss, 1999: 192–196.

129. *Louisville Courier*, January 19, 1854; *Louisville Courier*, February 13, 1854; *Louisville Courier*, February 24, 1854.

130. *Indianapolis Freeman*, October 31, 1891; Coon, 1999: 20–21.

131. Purtee, 1932: 37.

132. Sprague, 1996: 8–9, 97–99.

133. Ibid., 25–70.

134. Ibid., 70–98.

135. Ibid., 8–9, 127.

136. Ibid., 137–138.

137. Ibid., 12.

138. Siebert, "Mysteries," II.4: 2–3.

139. Ibid., 8–9.

VIII: Conclusion

1. Albert Camus, *The Rebel: An Essay on Man in Revolt* (New York: Vintage Books, 1956): 13.

2. Wade, 1964: 221–22.

3. Gara, 1996: 42–43.

4. George Washington Williams, *History of the Negro Race in America* (New York: Bergmann, 1968; first published in 1883): 58–59; also cited in Siebert, 1898: 340.

5. Siebert, 1898: 340.

6. *The North Star*, October 20, 1848.

7. Coffin, 1876: 170–171.

8. Thomas and Sillen, 1972: 18.

9. *Frederick Douglass Paper*, October 30, 1851.

10. Ibid., April 3, 1851.

11. Siebert, 1898: 341.

12. Ibid., 351–353.

13. Ibid., 355.

Bibliography

Primary Sources

Newspapers

The Cincinnati Commercial
The Colored American
Frederick Douglass Paper
Louisville Daily Democrat
The Indianapolis Freeman
The Kentucky Gazette
Louisville Courier.
Louisville Journal
Louisville Public Advertiser.
The National Era
The North Star
Paducah American
The Provincial Freeman

Government Documents

American Freedmen's Inquiry Commission Interviews, 1863, National Archives Microfilm Publications. Filson Club, Louisville, Ky.

Collins, Gabriel, *Louisville Directory for the Year 1841* (Louisville: Henkle Logan and Company, 1841).

_____, *Louisville and New Albany Directory and Annual Advertiser for 1848* (Louisville: G. H. Monserrat and Co., 1848).

Kentucky Penitentiary Records, Register of Prisoners, 1848–1855, Kentucky Department of Libraries and Archives;

Kentucky Penitentiary Records, Register of Prisoners, 1855–1861, Kentucky Department of Libraries and Archives;

L. R. Bullock to Governor John J. Crittenden, September 8, 1848, Governor's Office Papers, Folder 15, Kentucky Department of Libraries and Archives.

Jefferson County Court Order Minutes.

Jefferson County Marriage Registers.

Jefferson County Wills. Jefferson County Historic Preservation.

Jegli, John B., Directory for 1845–1846 (Louisville: The Louisville Journal, 1845).

_____, A Directory for 1851–1852 (Louisville: J. F. Brennan, 1851).

John McClung to Governor John J. Crittenden, September 22, 1848, Governor's Office Papers, Folder 15, Kentucky Department of Libraries and Archives.

The Louisville Directory for the Year 1832 (Louisville: Richard W. Otis, 1832).

Meade County (Kentucky) Court Order Records.

Ordinances of the City of Louisville, In Harrison, J., *Collection of Acts of Virginia and Kentucky Relative to Louisville and Portland* (Louisville: Prentice and Weissinger, 1839).

Petition to Governor John J. Crittenden, September 7, 1848, Governor's Office Papers, Folder 15, Kentucky Department of Libraries and Archives.

"Statistics of Tennessee," *The Seventh Census of the United States, 1850* (Washington: Robert Armstrong, Public Printer, 1853).

"Testimony of Washington Spradling," American Freedmen's Inquiry Commission, November 26, 1863.

United States Bureau of the Census, *First Census of the United States*, 1790.

U. S. Bureau of the Census, *Historical Statistics of the United States: Colonial Times to 1957* (Washington: Government Printing Office, 1960).

U. S. Bureau of the Census, *Negro Population, 1790–1915* (Washington: Government Printing Office, 1915).

United States Bureau of the Census, *Second Census of the United States, 1800* (Washington, D.C., 1801).

U. S. Census, 1830, 1840, 1850, 1860.

Theses and Dissertations

O'Brien, Margaret, "Slavery in Louisville During the Antebellum Period: 1820–1860," unpublished M.A. thesis, University of Louisville, 1979.

Stafford, Hanford D., "Slavery in a Border City: Louisville, 1790–1860," unpublished Ph.D. dissertation, University of Kentucky, 1987.

Document Collections

THE SIEBERT PAPERS

Dunn, Jacob P., "Indiana and Indianans," Indiana Underground Railroad, Vol.1, Box 79, Wilbur H. Siebert Papers. Ohio Historical Society.

Everts, Louis H., History of Clermont County (Philadelphia, 1880) in the Wilbur Siebert Papers, The Ohio Underground Railroad, Vol. XII, Box 112, Ohio Historical Society: 441–442.

Harris, N. Dwight, "The History of Negro Servitude in Illinois," 1904: 106–107. In the Wilbur H. Siebert Papers, The Underground Railroad in Illinois, Vol. 1, Box 71. The Ohio Historical Society.

Lyman, H., to Wilbur H. Siebert, April 1, 1898, in the Wilbur Siebert Papers, The Ohio Underground Railroad, Vol. XII, Box 112, Ohio Historical Society.

Mosimann, Wilbert J., "Materials Concerning the Underground Railroad in Illinois," n.d., the Underground Railroad in Illinois, Wilbur H. Siebert Papers, Vol.1, Box 71, Ohio Historical Society.

Purtee, Edward O., "The Underground Railroad from Southwestern Ohio to Lake Erie," unpublished Ph.D. dissertation, Ohio State University, 1932, in Wilbur H. Siebert Papers, Underground Railroad in Ohio, Vol. XII, Box 112, Ohio Historical Society.

"Route of Jacob Cummings," Indiana Underground Railroad, Vol., 1, Wilbur H. Siebert Papers, Box 79. Ohio Historical Society.

Siebert, Wilbur H., "The Mysteries of Ohio's Underground Railroad," 1895, draft manuscript, in the Wilbur Siebert Papers, The Ohio Underground Railroad, Box 116, Ohio Historical Society.

_____, "Underground Railroad: How Slaves in Early Days were Piloted to Canada," The Ohio Journal, November 14, 1894, in the Wilbur Siebert Papers, The Ohio Underground Railroad, Box 105, Ohio Historical Society.

Spicer, Carl L., "The Underground Railroad in Southern Illinois," the Underground Railroad in Illinois, Wilbur H. Siebert Papers, Vol. 1, Box 71, Ohio Historical Society.

Other Document Collections

Interview with Fred Griffin, great-grandson of Judge William A. Porter, Corydon, Indiana, May 9, 2000.

Rawick, George P., Ed., "Indiana and Ohio Narratives," in *The American Slave: A Composite Autobiography*, Supplement, Series 1, Vol. 5 (Westport, CT: Greenwood, 1972).

_____, "Kentucky Narratives," in *The American Slave: A Composite Autobiography*, Supplement, Vol. 16 (Westport, CT: Greenwood, 1972).

_____, "Ohio Narratives," in *The American Slave: A Composite Autobiography*, Vol. 16 (Westport, CT: Greenwood, 1972).

Ripley, C. Peter, et al., Eds., *The Black Abolitionist Papers, Vol. II: Canada, 1830–1865* (Chapel Hill: The University of North Carolina Press, 1986).

_____, *The Black Abolitionist Papers, Vol. IV: The United States, 1847–1858* (Chapel Hill: The University of North Carolina Press, 1991).

Slave Narratives

Bibb, Henry, *Narrative of the Life of Henry Bibb, An American Slave*, 1849, 51–171. In Gilbert Osofsky, Ed., *"Puttin' on Ole Massa: The Slave Narratives of Henry Bibb, William Wells Brown and Solomon Northup* (New York: Harper and Row, 1969).

Clarke, Lewis, and Clarke, Milton, *Narrative of the Sufferings of Lewis and Milton Clarke* (Boston, 1845).

Greene, Jacob D., *Narrative of the Life of Jacob Greene* (Huddersfield, England, 1864):

Henson, Josiah, *Father Henson's Story of His Own Life* (Boston, 1858):

Jackson, Andrew, *Narratives and Writings of Andrew Jackson* (Miami, 1969; first published in 1847).

Smith, Harry, *Fifty Years in Slavery in the United States of America* (Grand Rapids: West Michigan Printing Company, 1891).

Other Unpublished Sources

Cook, Iris L., "Underground Railroad in Southern Indiana," Federal Writers' Project, unpublished notes, ca. 1936. Presented to the author by Ms. Cook's grandniece, 1999.

Coon, Diane P., "The Chronicles of Chapman Harris: A Free Black Leader of the Underground Railroad and Pastor of the Second Baptist Church at Madison, Indiana," unpublished manuscript, Department of Pan-African Studies, University of Louisville, 1999.

_____, "Reconstructing the Underground Railroad Crossings at Madison, Indiana," unpublished manuscript, 1998.

Hudson, J. Blaine, "A Guide to African Americans in the Records of Ante-bellum Louisville and Jefferson County Kentucky: Court Order minutes and Wills, with Special Reference to Slave Emancipations" (Louisville: Jefferson County Historic Preservation and Archives, 1998).

_____, "References to Slavery in Early Kentucky Newspapers: *The Kentucky Gazette*, 1787–1805,*" unpublished manuscript. Jefferson County Historic Preservation and Archives, 1997.

Pritchard, James M., "Into the Fiery Furnace: Anti-Slavery Prisoners in the Kentucky Staete Penitentiary, 1844–1870," conference paper delivered at the Kentucky Underground Railroad Symposium, June 1999: 3.

Saulman, Earl O., "Blacks in Harrison County, Indiana," unpublished manuscript, Corydon, Indiana, 1999.

Smardz, Karolyn E., "From Louisville to the Promised Land: The Story of Thornton and Lucie Blackburn," unpublished paper prepared for the Kentucky African American Heritage Commission, April 2000.

Van Metre, Beulah, "The Underground Railroad Near Charlestown," Federal Writers' Project, unpublished notes, ca. 1936. Presented to the author by Ms. Iris L. Cook's grandniece, 1999.

Secondary Sources

Articles

Coleman, J. Winston, Jr., "Delia Webster and Calvin Fairbank — Underground Railroad Agents," *Filson History Quarterly, 17, 3* (1943): 129–142.

_____, "Lexington's Slave Dealers and their Southern Trade, *The Filson History Quarterly, 12* (1938).

Cooper, Afua, "The Fluid Frontier: Blacks and the Detroit River Region — A Focus on Henry Bibb," *Canadian Review of American Studies, 30, 2* (2000): 129–149.

Eslinger, Ellen, "The Shape of Slavery on the Kentucky Frontier, 1775–1800," *The Register of the Kentucky Historical Society, 92* (1994): 1–23.

Hammon, Neal O., "Pioneer Routes in Central Kentucky," *Filson History Quarterly, 74, 2* (1978): 124–143.

Hudson, J. Blaine, "African Americans in Early Louisville and Jefferson County, Kentucky," *The Filson History Quarterly, 73* (1999).

_____, "African American Religion in Antebellum Louisville, Kentucky," *The Griot: Journal of the Southern Conference on African American Studies, 17, 2* (1998): 43–54.

_____, "The African Diaspora and the 'Black Atlantic': An African American Perspective," *Negro History Bulletin, 60, 4* (1997): 7–14.

_____, "References to Slavery in Early Kentucky Newspapers: *The Kentucky Gazette*, 1787–1805," unpublished manuscript. Jefferson County Historic Preservation and Archives, 1997.

_____, "References to Slavery in the Public Records of Early Louisville and Jefferson County, 1780–1812," *The Filson History Quarterly, 73, 4* (1999): 325–354.

_____, "Slavery in Early Louisville and Jefferson County, 1780–1812," *The Filson History Quarterly*, 73, 3 (1997): 249– 283.

Post, Edward M., "Kentucky Law Concerning Emancipation and Freedom of Slaves," *Filson Club History Quarterly*, 59 (1985): 344–367.

Robboy, Stanley J., and Robboy, Anita W., "Lewis Hayden: From Fugitive Slave to Statesman," *New England Quarterly*, 46 (1973): 591–613.

Walker, Juliet E. K., "The Legal Status of Free Blacks in Early Kentucky, 1792–1825," *Filson History Quarterly*, 17 (1983): 382–395.

Wright, Richard R., Jr., "Negro Rural Communities in the North," *The Southern Workman*, 37 (1908).

Young, Amy L., and Hudson, J. Blaine, "Slavery at Oxmoor," *The Filson History Quarterly*, 74 (Summer 2000): 195–199.

Books

Abdy, E. S., *Journal of a Residence and Tour in the United States of North America, from April 1833 to October 1834*, Vol. 2 (London: John Murray, 1835).

Anti-Slavery History of Jefferson County (Madison, IN: Jefferson County Historical Society, 1998).

Aron, Stephen, *How the West was Lost: The Transformation of Kentucky from Daniel Boone to Henry Clay* (Baltimore: The Johns Hopkins University Press, 1996)

Bennett, Lerone, Jr., *Before the Mayflower* (New York: Penguin, 1982).

Berlin, Ira, *Many Thousands Gone: The First Two Centuries of Slavery in North America* (Cambridge, MA: Harvard University Press, 1998).

Bethel, Elizabeth R., *The Roots of African American Identity: Memory and History in Antebellum Free Communities* (New York: St. Martin's Press, 1997).

Blasingame, John, *Slave Testimony: Two Centuries of Letters, Speeches, Interviews and Autobiographies* (Baton Rouge: Louisiana State University, 1977).

Blockson, Charles, *Hippocrene Guide to the Underground Railroad* (New York: Hippocrene Books, 1994).

Bolster, W. Jeffrey, *Black Jacks: African American Seamen in the Age of Sail* (Cambridge: Harvard University Press, 1997):

Botkin, B. A., Ed., *Lay My Burden Down: A Folk History of Slavery* (Athens: The University of Georgia Press, 1945).

Buckmaster, Henrietta, *Let My People Go: The Story of the Underground Railroad and the Growth of the Abolition Movement* (Boston: Beacon Press, 1941).

Camus, Albert, *The Rebel: An Essay on Man in Revolt* (New York: Vintage Books, 1956): 13.

Catteral, Helen T., ed., *Judicial Cases Concerning American Slavery and the Negro*, Vol. 1 (Washington, D.C.: Carnegie Institution, 1926).

Clark, Thomas D., *A History of Kentucky* (Ashland: Jesse Stuart Foundation, 1980; first published in 1937).

Clift, G. Glenn, *Second Census of Kentucky, 1800: A privately compiled and published enumeration of tax payers appearing in the 79 manuscript volumes extant of tax lists of the 42 counties of Kentucky in existence in 1800* (Baltimore: Genealogical Publishing Co., 1982).

Cockrum, Col. William M., *History of the Underground Railroad, As It Was Conducted by the Anti-Slavery League* (New York: Negro Universities Press, 1969; first published in 1915).

Coffin, Levi, *Reminiscences of Levi Coffin* (New York: Augustus M. Kelley, 1876).

Coleman, J. Winston, Jr., *Slavery Times in Kentucky* (Chapel Hill: The University of North Carolina Press, 1940).

_____, *Stage-Coach Days in the Blue Grass* (Lexington: The University Press of Kentucky, 1995; first published in 1935).

Coward, Joan W., *Kentucky in the New Republic: The Process of Constitution Making* (Lexington: The University Press of Kentucky, 1979).

Crenshaw, Gwendolyn J., *Bury Me in a Free Land: The Abolitionist Movement in Indiana, 1816–1865* (Indianapolis: Indiana Historical Bureau, 1993)

Cummings, Scott, and Price, Michael, *Race Relations in Louisville: Southern Racial Traditions and Northern Class Dynamics* (Louisville: University of Louisville College of Urban and Public Affairs, 1990).

Curry, Leonard P., *The Free Black in Urban America, 1800–1850* (Chicago: University of Chicago Press, 1981).

Davis, David B., *Slavery and Human Progress* (New York: Oxford University Press, 1984).

Douglass, Frederick, The *Life and Times of Frederick Douglass* (New York: MacMillan, 1962; reprint of 1892 edition).

Drew, Benjamin, *The Refugee: Or the Narratives*

of Fugitive Slaves in Canada (Boston: John P. Jewett and Company, 1856).

DuBois, W. E. B., *Black Reconstruction in America, 1860–1880* (New York: MacMillian, 1992; first published in 1935).

Dykstra, Robert R., *Bright Radical Star: Black Freedom and White Supremacy on the Hawkeye Frontier* (Cambridge, MA: Harvard University, 1993).

Egerton, Douglas R., *Gabriel's Rebellion: The Virginia Slave Conspiracies of 1800 and 1802* (Chapel Hill: University of North Carolina Press, 1993): 147–162.

Fairbank, Calvin, *Rev. Calvin Fairbank during Slavery Times* (Chicago: Patriotic Publishing Company, 1890).

Federal Writers' Project, *Illinois: A Descriptive and Historical Guide* (Chicago: McClurg & Co., 1947).

Fogel, Robert W., *Without Consent or Contract: The Rise and Fall of American Slavery* (New York: W. W. Norton, 1989).

Franklin, John Hope, and Moss, Alfred A., Jr., *From Slavery to Freedom: A History of African Americans*, 8th ed. (New York: McGraw-Hill, 2000).

Franklin, John H. and Schweninger, Loren. *Runaway Slaves: Rebels on the Plantation*

Gara, Larry, *The Liberty Line: The Legend of the Underground Railroad* (Lexington: University Press of Kentucky, 1961).

Freehling, William W., *The Road to Disunion: Secessionists at Bay, 1776–1854* (New York: Oxford University Press, 1990).

Gara, Larry, *The Liberty Line: The Legend of the Underground Railroad* (Lexington: University Press of Kentucky, 1961).

Gibson, William H., Sr., *Historical Sketches of the Progress of the Colored Race in Louisville, Kentucky* (Louisville: n. p., 1897).

Graham, Ruth Morris, *The Saga of the Morris Family* (Columbus, GA: Brentwood Christian Communications, 1984).

Gutman, Herbert G., *The Black Family in Slavery and Freedom* (New York: Random House, 1976).

Harrison, Lowell H., and Klotter, James C., *New History of Kentucky* (Lexington: University Press of Kentucky, 1997).

Haviland, Laura S., *A Woman's Life Work* (Cincinnati: Walden and Stowe, 1882).

Heinenmann, C. B., comp., *"First Census" of Kentucky, 1790* (Baltimore: Genealogical Publishing Co., 1981)

Horsman, Reginald, *Race and Manifest Destiny: The Origins of American Racial Anglo-Sax-*

onism (Cambridge: Harvard University Press, 1981).

Horton, James O., *Free People of Color: Inside the African American Community* (Washington: Smithsonian Institution Press, 1993).

Howard, Victor B., *Black Liberation in Kentucky: Emancipation and Freedom, 1862–1864* (Lexington: University Press of Kentucky, 1983).

Huggins, Nathan I., *Black Odyssey: The African American Ordeal in Slavery* (New York: Vintage Books, 1990).

Johnson, Leland R., "Engineering the Ohio," in Robert L. Reid, ed., *Always a River: The Ohio River and the American Experience* (Bloomington: Indiana University Press, 1991): 180–209.

Jordan, Winthrop D., *The White Man's Burden: Historical Origins of Racism in the United States* (New York: Oxford University Press, 1974).

_____, *White over Black: American Attitudes toward the Negro, 1550–1812* (New York: W. W. Norton, 1968).

King, Gail, and Thurman, Susan, *Currents: Henderson's River Book* (Henderson, KY: Henderson County Friends of the Public Library, 1991).

Klein, Herbert, *African Slavery in Latin America and the Caribbean* (New York: Oxford University Press, 1986).

Kolchin, Peter, *American Slavery: 1619 — 1877* (New York: Hill and Wang, 1993).

Lamon, Lester C., *Blacks in Tennessee, 1791–1970* (Knoxville: The University of Tennessee Press, 1981).

Lexington: Heart of the Bluegrass (Lexington: Fayette County Historic Commission, 1982).

Lovett, Bobby L., *The African-American History of Nashville, Tennessee, 1780–1930* (Fayetteville: The University of Arkansas Press, 1999)

Lucas, Ernestine G., *Wider Windows to the Past: African American History from a Family Perspective* (Decorah, IA: The Anundsen Publishing Company, 1995).

Lucas, Marion B., *A History of Blacks in Kentucky, Volume 1: From Slavery to Segregation, 1760–1891* (Frankfort: Kentucky Historical Society, 1992).

McDowell, Robert E., *City of Conflict: Louisville in the Civil War, 1861–1865* (Louisville: Civil War Roundtable, 1962).

Mitchell, William M., *The Under-Ground Railroad* (London: 1860).

Mooney, Chase C., *Slavery in Tennessee* (Westport, CT: Universities Press, 1971; first published in 1957).

Muro-Leighton, Judy; Andrews, Nathalie: and Munro-Leighton, Bill, *Changes at the Falls: Witnesses and Workers, Louisville and Portland, 1830–1860* (Louisville: Portland Museum, 1982).

National Historic Landmarks Survey, *Underground Railroad Resources in the United States* (Washington: U. S. Department of the Interior, 1998).

Oates, Stephen B., *The Fires of Jubilee: Nat Tuner's Fierce Rebellion* (New York: Mentor Books, 1975).

Omi, Michael. and Winant, Howard, *Racial Formation in the United States* (New York: Routledge, 1986):

Patterson, Orlando, *Slavery and Social Death* (Cambridge: Harvard University Press, 1982).

Peters, Pamela R. *The Underground Railroad in Floyd County, Indiana* (Jefferson, NC: Mc-Farland, 2001).

Philbrik, Francis S., ed., *The Laws of Indiana Territory, 1801–1809* (Illinois Historical Collections, Vol. 21. Reprinted by the Indiana Historical Society, 1931).

Phillips, Kevin, *The Cousins' Wars* (New York: Basic Books, 1999).

Phillips, Ullrich B., "The Slave Economy of the Old South," in Eugene D. Genovese, ed., *Selected Essays in Economic and Social History* (Baton Rouge: Louisiana State University Press, 1968).

Postell, William D., *The Health of Slaves on Southern Plantations* (Baton Rouge: Louisiana State University Press, 1951).

Quarles, Benjamin, *Black Abolitionists* (New York: Oxford University Press, 1969).

Reid, Robert L., ed., *Always a River: The Ohio River and the American Experience* (Bloomington: Indiana University Press, 1991).

Robertson, David, *Denmark Vesey* (New York: Alfred A. Knopf, 1999).

Ross, Alexander M., *Recollections and Experiences of an Abolitionist; From 1855 to 1865* (Toronto, 1875).

Runyon, Randolph, *Delia Webster and the Underground Railroad* (Lexington: The University Press of Kentucky, 1996).

Siebert, Wilbur H., *The Underground Railroad from Slavery to Freedom* (New York: Russell and Russell, 1967; first published 1898).

Smardz, Karolyn E., "There We Were in Darkness, Here We Are in Light: "Kentucky Slaves and the Promised Land," in Craig Thompson Friend, *The Buzzel About Ken-*

tucky: Settling the Promised Land (Lexington: University Press of Kentucky, 1999): 243–248.

Smedley, R. C., *History of the Underground Railroad* (New York: Arno Press, 1969; first published 1883).

Sprague, Stuart S., Ed., *His Promised Land: The Autobiography of John P. Parker, former Slave and Conductor on the Underground Railroad* (New York: W. W. Norton, 1996).

SPSS Base 9.0 (Chicago: SPSS, Inc., 1999).

Starling, Marion W., *The Slave Narrative: Its Place in American History* (Washington: Howard University Press, 1988).

Stevenson, Brenda E., *Life in Black and White: Family and Community in the Slave South* (New York: Oxford University Press, 1996).

Still, William, *The Underground Railroad* (Chicago: Johnson Publishing Company, 1970; reprint of 1872 edition).

Strangis, Joel, *Lewis Hayden and the War Against Slavery* (North Haven, CT: Linnet Books, 1999).

Thomas, Alexander and Sillen, Samuel, *Racism and Psychiatry* (New York: Citadel Press, 1972).

Thornbrough, Emma L., *The Negro in Indiana before 1900* (Bloomington: Indiana University Press, 1957).

Tise, Larry E., *Proslavery: A History of the Defense of Slavery in America, 1701–1840* (Athens: The University of Georgia Press, 1987).

Tobin, Jacqueline L., and Dobard, Raymond G., *Hidden in Plain View: A Secret Story of Quilts and the Underground Railroad* (New York: Doubleday, 1999).

Trewartha, Glenn T., *A Geography of Population: World Patterns* (New York: Wiley, 1969): 139–145.

Trotter, Joe W., Jr., *River Jordan: African American Urban Life in the Ohio Valley* (Lexington: The University Press of Kentucky, 1998).

Wade, Richard C., *Slavery in the Cities: The South, 1820–1860* (New York: Oxford University Press, 1969).

Weeden, Henry C., *Weeden's History of the Colored People of Louisville* (Louisville: H. C. Weeden, 1897.

Weisenburger, Steven, *Modern Medea: A Family Story of Slavery and Child-Murder from the Old South* (New York: Hill and Wang, 1998).

Wilhelm, Paul, Duke of Wurttemburg, *Travels in North America, 1822–1824* (Norman: University of Oklahoma, 1973; first published in 1824).

Williams, Eric, *From Columbus to Castro: The History of the Caribbean, 1492–1969* (London: Andre Deutsch, 1970).

Williams, George Washington, *History of the Negro Race in America* (New York: Bergmann, 1968; first published in 1883).

Winant, Howard, *Racial Conditions* (Minneapolis: University of Minnesota Press, 1994).

Winks, Robin W. *Blacks in Canada: A History* (New Haven, CT: 1971).

Wolseley, Roland E., *The Black Press, U. S. A.* (Ames: Iowa State Press, 1991).

Wright, Donald R., *African Americans in the Colonial Era: From African Origins through the American Revolution* (Arlington Heights, IL: Harlan Davidson, Inc., 1990).

Wright, George C., *Life Behind a Veil: Blacks in Louisville, Kentucky, 1865–1930* (Baton Rouge: Louisiana State University Press, 1985).

Yater, George H., *Two Hundred Years at the Falls of the Ohio: A History of Louisville and Jefferson County* (Louisville: The Filson Club, 1987).

Index

Most slave escapes have been indexed by their point of origin rather than by the name of the fugitive or the name of the owner.